The End of Hawaii's Independence
An Autobiographical History by Hawaii's Last Monarch

by Liliuokalani, Queen of Hawaii

Red and Black Publishers, St Petersburg, Florida

Originally published as *Hawaii's Story*, in Boston, Lee and Shepard, 1898.

Library of Congress Cataloging-in-Publication Data

Liliuokalani, Queen of Hawaii, 1838-1917.
 [Hawaii's story]
 The end of Hawaii's independence : an autobiographical history by Hawaii's last monarch / by Liliuokalani.
   p. cm.
 "Originally published as Hawaii's Story, in Boston, Lee and Shepard, 1898"--T.p. verso.
 ISBN 978-1-61001-005-4
 1. Hawaii--History--19th century. 2. Hawaii--Annexation to the United States. 3. Liliuokalani, Queen of Hawaii, 1838-1917. 4. Queens--Hawaii--Biography. I. Title.
 DU627.2.L72 2011
 996.9'027092--dc22
 [B]
                                         2011000014

Red and Black Publishers, PO Box 7542, St Petersburg, Florida, 33734
 Contact us at: info@RedandBlackPublishers.com
   Printed and manufactured in the United States of America

Contents

I. A Sketch Of My Childhood   5
II. Some Incidents Of My Youth   13
III. Kamehameha IV   19
IV. My Married Life   25
V. Hawaiian Music, And A Ducal Guest   31
VI. Kamehameha V   37
VII. Queen Emma   43
VIII. King Kalakaua   51
IX. Heir Apparent   55
X. My First Visit To The United States   59
XI. Mauna Loa   65
XII. Kalakaua's Tour Of The World   71
XIII. My Regency   75
XIV. A Serious Accident   81
XV. Kalakaua's Return   87
XVI. Coronation Ceremonies   93
XVII. Princess Ruth And Mrs. Bernice Pauahi Bishop   99
XVIII. Benevolent Societies   103
XIX. Queen Kapiolani's Journey   107
XX. Washington—The White House—Mount Vernon   111
XXI. Boston And New York—En Route To England   117
XXII. Arrival—Liverpool—Some English Towns   123
XXIII. Sovereign Of England And India   129
XXIV. The Reception At The Foreign Office   133
XXV. The Jubilee—At The Abbey—At The Palace   137
XXVI. The Prince Of Wales, "Grand Master" Mason   145
XXVII. England's Homes And Hospitality   149
XXVIII. Ill News From Hawaii—Our Return   155
XXIX. "The Bayonet Constitution"   161

XXX. Invited To Conspire Against The King   177
XXXI. The King Threatened And Oppressed   183
XXXII. Attempted Revolution   189
XXXIII. The King's Departure — Again Regent   193
XXXIV. The King's Return — My Accession   199
XXXV. The Last Sleep — Lying In State   203
XXXVI. My Cabinet — Princess Kaiulani   207
XXXVII. My Husband Made Prince Consort — His Death   211
XXXVIII. Hawaiians Plead For A New Constitution   217
XXXIX. The "Crimes I Am Charged Withal"   225
XL. Overthrow Of The Monarchy   231
XLI. Some Important Inquiries   239
XLII. Attempt To Restore The Monarchy   247
XLIII. I Am Placed Under Arrest   251
XLIV. Imprisonment — Forced Abdication   257
XLV. Brought To Trial   261
XLVI. Sentenced — My Prison Life   271
XLVII. Released On Parole   277
XLVIII. Mr. Joseph Kahooluhi Nawahi   281
XLIX. A Change Of Scene To Forget Sorrow   285
L. A New England Winter   291
LI. Washington — Pseudo-Hawaiians   299
LII. President And Mrs. Cleveland   309
LIII. Inauguration Of President Mckinley   315
LIV. My Literary Occupation   321
LV. My Official Protest To The Treaty   325
LVI. The Treaty Analyzed   329
LVII. Hawaiian Autonomy   337

Chapter I. A Sketch Of My Childhood

The extinct crater or mountain which forms the background to the city of Honolulu is known as the Punch-Bowl; at its base is situated the Queen's Hospital, so named because of the great interest taken in its erection by Emma, the queen of Kamehameha IV. Funds for the cause were solicited by the reigning sovereigns in person, and the hospital building was completed in 1860. Very near to its site, on Sept. 2, 1838, I was born. My father's name was Kapaakea, and my mother was Keohokalole; the latter was one of the fifteen counsellors of the king, Kamehameha III., who in 1840 gave the first written constitution to the Hawaiian people. My great-grandfather, Keawe-a-Heulu, the founder of the dynasty of the Kamehamehas, the Keoua, father of Kamehameha I., were our cousins (he was also brother of Mrs. Bishop's ancestress, Hakau), and my great-grandaunt was the celebrated Queen Kapiolani, one of the first converts to Christianity. She plucked the sacred berries from the borders of the volcano, descended to the boiling lava, and there, while singing Christian hymns, threw them into the lake of fire. This was the act which broke forever the power of Pele, the fire-goddess, over the hearts of rested in genealogies are referred to the is volume, which show the descent of our st chiefs of ancient days. It has often y of nations that the most eminent men d then, instead of ascending the throne, tive office in the hands of another. deed, the founder of Hawaiian unity, ame of the Great; but it is truthfully recorded in the early histories of the Islands—those written by such men as Mr. Pogue, Mr. Dibble, and others—that he owed his selection for the monarchy to the chiefs from whom the latest reigning family, my own, is descended. This indebtedness was fully recognized during the life of that monarch.

Naihe, the husband of Kapiolani, was the great orator of the king's reign; his father, Keawe-a-Heulu, was chief counsellor to Kamehameha I.; while had it not been for the aid of the two chiefs, Keeaumoku and Kameeiamoku, cousins of the chief counsellor, the Hawaiian Islands must have remained for a long time, if not until this day, in a state of anarchy. My grandfather, Aikanaka, had charge of the guns of the fort on Punch-Bowl Hill, which had been brought from the larger island of Hawaii; as the chiefs, their families, and followers had settled here from the time of the final battle, when all the forces contending against Kamehameha I. were driven over the Pali.

For the purpose of enhancing the value of their own mission, it has been at times asserted by foreigners that the abundance of the chief was procured by the poverty of his followers. To any person at all familiar, either by experience or from trustworthy tradition, with the daily life of the Hawaiian people fifty years ago, nothing could be more incorrect than such assumption. The chief whose retainers were in any poverty or want would have felt, not only their sufferings, but, further, his own disgrace. As was then customary with the Hawaiian chiefs, my father was surrounded by hundreds of his own people, all of whom looked to him, and never in vain, for sustenance. He lived in a large grass house surrounded by smaller ones, which were the homes of those the most closely connected with his service. There was food enough and to spare for everyone. And this was equally true of all his people, however distant from his personal care. For the chief always appointed some man of ability as his agent or overseer. This officer apportioned the lands to each Hawaiian, and on these allotments were raised the taro, the potatoes, the pigs, and the chickens which constituted the living of the family; even the forests, which furnished the material from which was made the tapa cloth, were apportioned to the women in like manner. It is true that no one of the common people could mortgage or sell his land, but the wisdom of this limitation is abundantly proved by the homeless condition of the Hawaiians at the present day. Rent, eviction of tenants, as understood in other lands, were unknown; but each retainer of any chief contributed in the productions of his holding to the support of the chief's table.

But I was destined to grow up away from the house of my parents. Immediately after my birth I was wrapped in the finest soft tapa cloth, and taken to the house of another chief, by whom I was adopted. Konia, my foster-mother, was a granddaughter of Kamehameha I., and was married to Paki, also a high chief; their only daughter, Bernice Pauahi, afterwards Mrs. Charles R. Bishop, was therefore my foster-sister. In speaking of our relationship, I have adopted the term customarily used in the English language, but there was no such modification recognized in my native land. I knew no other father or mother than my foster-parents, no other sister than Bernice. I used to climb up on the knees of Paki, put my arms around his neck, kiss him, and he caressed me as a father would his child; while on the contrary, when I met my own parents, it was with perhaps more of interest, yet always with the demeanor I would have shown to any strangers who noticed me. My own father and mother had other children, ten in all, the most of them being adopted into other chiefs' families; and although I knew that these were my own brothers and sisters, yet we met throughout my younger life as though we had not known our common parentage. This was, and indeed is, in accordance with Hawaiian customs. It is not easy to explain its origin to those alien to our national life, but it seems perfectly natural to us. As intelligible a reason as can be given is that this alliance by adoption cemented the ties of friendship between the chiefs. It spread to the common people, and it has doubtless fostered a community of interest and harmony.

At the age of four years I was sent to what was then known as the Royal School, because its pupils were exclusively persons whose claims to the throne were acknowledged. It was founded and conducted by Mr. Amos S. Cooke, who was assisted by his wife. It was a boarding-school, the pupils being allowed to return to their homes during vacation time, as well as for an occasional Sunday during the term. The family life was made agreeable to us, and our instructors were especially particular to teach us the proper use of the English language; but when I recall the instances in which we were sent hungry to bed, it seems to me that they failed to remember that we were growing children. A thick slice of bread covered with molasses was usually the sole article of our supper, and we were sometimes ingenious, if not over honest, in our search for food: if we could beg something of the cook it was the easier way; but if not, anything eatable left within our reach was surely confiscated. As a last resort, we were not above searching the gardens for any esculent root or leaf, which (having inherited the art of igniting a fire from the friction of sticks), we could cook and consume without the knowledge of our preceptors.

I can remember now my emotions on entering this, the first school I ever attended. I can recall that I was carried there on the shoulders of a tall, stout, very large woman, whose name was Kaikai (she was the sister of Governor Kanoa, and they were of a family of chiefs of inferior rank, living under the control and direction of the higher chiefs). As she put me down at the entrance of the schoolhouse, I shrank from its doors, with that immediate and strange dread of the unknown so common to childhood. Crying bitterly, I turned to my faithful attendant, clasping her with my arms and clinging closely to her neck. She tenderly expostulated with me; and as the children, moved by curiosity to meet the new-comer, crowded about me, I was soon attracted by their friendly faces, and was induced to go into the old courtyard with them. Then my fears began to vanish, and comforted and consoled, I soon found myself at home amongst my playmates.

Several of the pupils who were at the school with me have subsequently become known in Hawaiian history. There were four children of Kinau, daughter of Kamehameha I., the highest in rank of any of the women chiefs of her day; these were Moses, Lot (afterwards Kamehameha V.), Liholiho (afterwards Kamehameha IV.), and Victoria, of whom I shall soon speak. Next came Lunalilo, who followed Kamehameha V. as king. Then came Bernice Pauahi, who married Hon. Charles R. Bishop. Our family was represented by Kaliokalani, Kalakaua, and myself, two of the three destined to ascend the throne. Besides these I must mention Emma Rooke, who married one of the Kamehamehas, Peter Kaeo, Jane Loeau, Elizabeth Kaaniau, Abigail Maheha, Mary Paaina, and John Kinau Pitt; although these were all not there at the same time. Queen Emma, I remember, did not come in until after I had been at school some years.

We never failed to go to church in a procession every Sunday in charge of our teachers, Mr. and Mrs. Cooke, and occupied seats in the immediate vicinity of the pew where the king was seated. The custom was for a boy and girl to march side by side; the lead being taken by the eldest scholars. Moses and Jane had this distinction, next Lot and Bernice, then Liholiho with Abigail, followed by Lunalilo and Emma (after the later had joined the school), James and Elizabeth, David and Victoria, and so on, John Kinau and I being the last.

With the Princess Victoria, who died on the 29th of May, 1866, my younger life was connected in the following manner. When I was taken from my own parents and adopted by Paki and Konia, or about two months thereafter, a child was born to Kinau. That little babe was the Princess Victoria, two of whose brothers became sovereigns of the Hawaiian people. While the infant was at its mother's breast, Kinau always preferred to take me into her arms to nurse, and would hand her own child to the woman attendant who was there for that purpose. So she frequently declared in the presence of my adopted mother, Konia, that a bond of the closest friendship must always exist between her own baby girl and myself as aikane or foster-children of the same mother, and that all she had would also appertain to me just as if I had been her own child; and that although in the future I might be her child's rival, yet whatever would belong to Victoria should be mine. This insistence on the part of the mother was never forgotten; it remained in the history of Victoria's girlhood and mine until her death, although Kinau herself never lived to see her prophetic predictions fulfilled. Kinau died on the 4th of April, 1839, not long after the birth of her youngest child, Victoria.

On any occasion where the Princess Victoria was expected to be present I was always included in the invitation, so that whenever Kekauluohi, the sister of Kinau, invited her niece to be with her, I was also summoned to her residence. This aunt lived in a large stone house called Pohukaina, which stood not more than two hundred feet from the Royal School; and for our enjoyment she used to prepare all sorts of sweetmeats and delicacies peculiar to the Hawaiians, such as (to call them by our native names) kulolo, paipaiee, and koele-palau, with which our childish tastes were delighted.

In 1847 Moses left school, and went to reside with his father. In 1848 Jane Loeau married a Mr. Jasper. Abigail Maheha also left about the same time to reside with her aunt, the Princess Kekauonohi, and it was at this date that the epidemic of measles spread through the land; of those who fell victims to it were Moses Kekuaiwa, William Pitt Leleiohoku, who was a cousin of the Princess Kekauonohi and the first husband of the Princess Ruth (when later my younger brother was born, and adopted by Ruth, he took the name of her deceased husband); the third of these deaths in the families of the royal children was that of my little sister Kaiminaauao, who had been adopted by Kamehameha III. and his queen, Kalama.

This sad event made a great impression upon my younger days; for these relatives and companions of my youth died and were buried on the same day, the coffin of the last-named resting on that of the others. They were all buried in the royal mausoleum, which then was located where is now the yard of Iolani Palace. Since the erection of another building up the Nuuanu Valley, their remains have been removed with those of their ancestors.

From the year 1848 the Royal School began to decline in influence; and within two or three years from that time it was discontinued, the Cooke family entering business with the Castles, forming a mercantile establishment still in existence.

Mr. Cooke and Mr. S. N. Castle were both sent to Honolulu by the American Board of Commissioners for Foreign Missions. As soon as they had become accustomed to life in the Hawaiian Islands, they severed all connection with the board, entered secular and mercantile pursuits, founding the firm of Castle & Cooke. This has now become a very wealthy concern; and although the senior partners are dead, it is still conducted under their name by their descendants or associates. The sons of Mr. Castle have also been actively interested in the present (1893-1897) government of the Hawaiian Islands.

From the school of Mr. and Mrs. Cooke I was sent to that of Rev. Mr. Beckwith, also one of the American missionaries. This was a day-school, and with it I was better satisfied than with a boarding-school.

Chapter II. Some Incidents Of My Youth

I was a studious girl; and the acquisition of knowledge has been a passion with me during my whole life, one which has not lost it charm to the present day. In this respect I was quite different from my sister Bernice. She was one of the most beautiful girls I ever saw; the vision of her loveliness at that time can never be effaced from remembrance; like a striking picture once seen, it is stamped upon memory's page forever. She married in her eighteenth year. She was betrothed to Prince Lot, a grandchild of Kamehameha the Great; but when Mr. Charles R. Bishop pressed his suit, my sister smiled on him, and they were married. It was a happy marriage. When Mr. and Mrs. Bishop were first married they established their modest home at the termination of the beautiful Nuuanu Valley, directly opposite the tombs of the Hawaiian monarchs. They then began housekeeping in a small house on Alakea Street, near the site of the present Masonic Temple. At this time I was still living with Paki and Konia, and the house now standing and known as the Arlington Hotel was being erected by the chief for his residence. It was completed in 1851, and occupied by Paki until 1855, when he died. Then my sister and her husband moved to that residence, which still remained my home. It was there that the years of my girlhood were passed, after school-days were over, and the pleasant company we often had in that house will never cease to give interest to the spot.

Mr. Bishop was a popular and hospitable man, and his wife was as good as she was beautiful. The king, Kamehameha IV., Alexander Liholiho, would often appear informally at our doors with some of his friends; the evening would be passed in improvised dances, and the company always grew larger when it became known that we were thus enjoying ourselves; sometimes we would all adjourn to the house of some friend or neighbor from whom we had reason to expect like hospitality, and the night would be half gone ere we noticed the flight of time.

It was now that the young man who subsequently became my husband first became specially interested in me, and I in him, although we had been very near neighbors during our school-days, and we had seen each other more than once. A Mr. and Mrs. Johnston, a married couple of rather advanced age, established a day-school for children of both sexes in the house next to that of Mr. Cooke; their lot was separated from ours by a high fence of adobe, or sun-baked brick. The boys used to climb the fence on their side for the purpose of looking at the royal children, and amongst these curious urchins was John O. Dominis. His father was a sea-captain, who had originally come to Honolulu on Cape Horn voyages, and had been interested in trade both in China and in California. The ancestors of Captain Dominis were from Italy; but Mrs. Dominis was an American, born at Boston, and was a descendant of one of the early English settlers. The house known as Washington Place was built by Captain Dominis for a family residence. As will appear shortly, Mr. Dominis was not my first or only suitor. My social and political importance would, quite apart from any personal qualities, render my alliance a matter of much solicitude to many. This is not, however, a subject on which I shall care to say more than is necessary.

On June 13, 1855, Paki, my adopted father, died. Soon after this the betrothal was announced of Alexander Liholiho and Emma Rooke. Some of those interested in the genealogies of the historic families of the Hawaiian chiefs, on hearing of this intended marriage, went to the king, and begged him to change his mind. "And why should I?" asked Liholiho. "Because, Your Majesty, there is no other chief equal to you in birth and rank but the adopted daughter of Paki." The king took offense at this counsel, and dismissed the objectors from his presence. Emma was descended from a half-brother of Kalaniopuu, the latter being first cousin to Kamehameha the Great. The royal wedding took place on June 19, 1856. The bridesmaids were Princess Victoria, myself, and Mary Pitman; the groomsmen were Prince Lot (afterwards Kamehameha V.), Prince William, and my brother, David Kalakaua. Honolulu was for the time the scene of great festivity. The ceremony filled the great Kawaiahao church; and thereafter there were picnics, parties, luaus, and balls without number. Each of the nations represented on the island, even to the Chinese, gave its own special ball in honor of the wedding.

The king was returning from Moanalua with a large escort, a cavalcade of perhaps two hundred riders of both sexes. Amongst these was General J. O. Dominis, then a young man on the staff of Prince Lot. He was riding by my side when an awkward horseman forced his horse between us, and in the confusion Mr. Dominis was thrown from his horse and his leg broken. He gained the saddle, however, and insisted on accompanying me to my home, where he dismounted, and helped me from my horse. He then rode home; but by the time he had reached his own home his leg had become so swollen and painful that he could not dismount without assistance, and for some time, until the bone had become united, was confined to his house.

In the following November I accompanied Konia, my mother, to Hawaii, where she went for her health. We visited Kona, Kaei, and Kaleakekua Bay, the latter celebrated as the scene of the death of Captain Cook, the discoverer. The Princess

Miriam Likelike (my own sister) was there brought up, and was well contented; but to one accustomed as I was to the bustle of the city and the life of the court, it seemed to be an excessively quiet and dismal place. After some months spent on Hawaii we went to Lahaina; there I received a letter from my brother Kalakaua, telling me that he was engaged to the Princess Victoria, and asking me to come to Honolulu. So, attended by five women, all from the families of high chiefs, I started for that city; but upon my arrival I found that the engagement was broken, for the Princess Victoria had gone to Wailua, and my brother had heard nothing from her for a fortnight; so I made preparations to return to Maui, but receiving an invitation to remain for a ball to be given by Prince Lot, I deferred my journey. At the ball the Princess Victoria appeared with her suite, and it was said was engaged to Prince William. Be that as it may, we all had a very gay time at the ball, which continued until daybreak.

At two o'clock the day following Prince Lot and Mr. Dominis, with the five ladies of noble birth, attended me to the old schooner *Kekauluohi*, by which I was to make the passage across the channel. My retinue was very large, and nearly filled the cabin. Prince William, who ascended the throne in 1874 under the title of Lunalilo, was the owner of the vessel, and was also at this time on board. He came to me, and insisted on my taking his cabin; and when the berth had been emptied of oranges with which I found it filled, his wearing apparel, boots, and other belongings also cleared out, I complied. He than asked me in the presence of my attendants why we shouldn't get married. There was an aged native preacher on board, Pikanele by name, who at once offered to perform the ceremony. But having heard the prince was engaged to his cousin Victoria, I did not consider it right to marry him on the impulse of the moment. When we arrived at Lahaina he escorted me to my home, there repeating his offer; and I took the matter into serious consideration, agreeing to write to him. He joined his father at Kona; and to that place I directed my letter, sending it by the schooner *Kamamalu*, which also was the

Hawaiian name of the princess. It seemed that she declined to be the bearer of messages to her fickle swain, for the schooner was lost at sea. In the meantime Victoria Kamamalu had written to Prince William, reminding him of his obligations to her, and asking him to return to Honolulu, which he did, stopping at Lahaina on the way to tell me that, having received no answer from me, he supposed that I had rejected his proposal; but on my explanation of the matter, he again renewed his offer, and we became engaged. In May of that year my mother returned with me to Honolulu; but her health was not permanently improved, and on July 2, 1857, she died.

The death of Paki and Konia placed me more yet under the charge of Mr. and Mrs. Bishop, but Prince William claimed that our engagement was in full force. Mr. Bishop asked the king if he considered it a good match, to which Alexander replied that if I were his daughter he should not approve of it, but that if each of us were pleased, he should not oppose it, but advise us to marry. But there were certain other incidents which came to the surface ere long which led me to break the engagement. Neither Prince William Lunalilo nor the Princess Victoria was ever married.

Chapter III. Kamehameha IV

Alexander Liholiho, known to history as Kamehameha IV., had all the characteristics of his race; and the strong, passionate nature of the Kamehamehas is shown in his benevolent as in his less commendable acts. To him was due the introduction of the Anglican Mission. He personally translated the English Prayer-Book into our language. He also founded the Queen's Hospital, as has already been noticed; and both the foreign and domestic affairs of his government were ably administered. Hon. R. C. Wylie continued as his Minister of Foreign Affairs throughout his reign.

In 1859, or just prior to my engagement to Mr. Dominis, a pleasant party was made up in Honolulu for an excursion to the other islands, on which I went, being, as indeed I always was at this time, under the special charge of Mrs. Bishop. We visited the volcano on Hawaii, and descended to the city of Hilo, on whose beautiful bay was then lying the United States ship *Levant*. At this place we were joined by the king with his party; and having many most agreeable acquaintances amongst the naval officers, the time sped quickly in social pleasures. We lived in a large grass house, one side of which was occupied by the ladies and the other by the gentlemen, while the centre was a room used for banquet-hall or ballroom, besides answering the purpose of separating the two lateral apartments so widely that no conversation could be heard from one to the other. When any of the royal party had occasion to go from one place to another, we were drawn in carriages of native construction, the people themselves furnishing the power usually supplied by horses. Sometimes we were stuck in some mud-hole or water-course, from which the most determined efforts of our devoted followers could not extricate us; and it was then necessary to have a horse led to the side of the vehicle to take us off on horseback. But we were light-hearted, merry, and happy; the naval officers were perfect gentlemen, and gallant in their attentions. The king enjoyed the pleasures to which his presence and that of others of the royal line gave a great charm. He even mischievously prevented us from taking an affectionate adieu of our friends aboard the *Levant* by suddenly signalling that we were to be at once on board of the *Kilauea*; and that steamer started without as much as a "By your leave, sir," to the naval commander. At Lahaina the whole party left the ship, and at that port was further increased by the accession of the king's friends and retainers.

The next trip (1860) proposed by His Majesty was to the extinct volcano of Healeala, and orders were given that we should all go in boats from Lahaina to Wailuku. It was a beautiful sight; the waters were calm, each boat was ornamented with the Hawaiian flag, the royal standard fluttered from that of the king, and as we coasted along the shores, we could see the people on the land following our course and interested in our progress; there were, I think, twelve boats in all. We arrived without accident, ascended the mountain, and passed a night on the border of the crater. We had our tents, and there was shelter in the caves and crevices for the remainder of the party. All passed off gayly. There was little sleep, however, some of us being afflicted with asthmatic attacks which the excessive rarity of the air at that altitude made very severe. Such was my portion; but as I sat up, not daring to lie down lest I might lose my breath, I could hear the merry sounds of the singing and dancing which from one tent or another was going on around me.

The first halt in our enjoyment was when word was received that the little Prince of Hawaii, then but a little more than a year old, was ill.

The king was deaf to the entreaties of the queen to be allowed to go directly to her child, because he thought it would delay his own departure and arrival at the bedside of his boy. Fortunately the illness passed away without serious consequences; yet it seemed the first break in our festivities, and was followed by an event of a most tragical nature.

We descended the mountain and returned to Lahaina, where I, accompanied by Mrs. Bishop, left them, and went back to Honolulu. The first news we received was that the king in a fit of passion had shot and mortally wounded one of the party, his own secretary, Mr. H. A. Neilson. After the occurrence all that the tenderest of brothers could have done was proffered by the king to the wounded man; but after lingering for some months, Mr. Neilson died. No legal notice of the event was in any way taken; no person would have been foolhardy enough to propose it. It is not my purpose to defend the right of the king to this execution of summary vengeance, especially as it was done in a moment of anger; yet beyond the sadness of the act, it has a certain bearing on this sketch of my life as one of the descendants from the ruling families of Hawaii.

There were causes which were apparent to any of our people for something very like righteous anger on the part of the king. His Majesty was trying to make us each and all happy; yet even during moments of relaxation, undue familiarity, absence of etiquette, rudeness, or any other form which implied or suggested disrespect to royalty in any manner whatsoever, would never be tolerated by any one of the native chiefs of the Hawaiian people. To allow any such breach of good manners to pass unnoticed would be looked upon by his own retainers as belittling to him, and they would be the first to demand the punishment of the offender. It was in this case far too severe. No one realized that more than the king himself, who suffered much distress for his victim, and was with difficulty dissuaded from the abdication of his throne. The temper of the Kamehamehas had descended to the young prince, and was also the cause of his death. For when the child was about four years old, he became dissatisfied with a pair of boots, and burst into an ungovernable fit of passion. His father sought to cool him off by putting the boy under an open faucet of cold, running water. The little one appeared to be unharmed, but later in the day broke down with nervous weeping, and could not be comforted. Then it was discovered that the cold douche and shock had brought on an attack of brain fever. From this he did not recover, but died on the 27th of August, 1862. The king and queen had the sympathy of all parties in their bereavement; but Kamehameha IV. completely lost his interest in public life, living in the utmost possible retirement until his death.

It may be in place here to notice the opening of the reign of Kamehameha IV.'s successor. It has already been seen that the right of life and death was unchallenged; that whatever it may be in other countries, as late as an epoch thirty years in the past it belonged to the highest chief of the Hawaiian people. In like manner it may be said that the whole people owed its national life to the throne. The first constitution was given to the realm in 1840, and was a voluntary act on the part of the king, Kamehameha III. The second succeeded it in 1852. Both of these were doubtless drafted under the supervision and advice of the missionaries, of whom, even at the latter date, the Hawaiian nation was beginning to feel a little justifiable jealousy. So when Prince Lot came to the throne in 1863, under the title of Kamehameha V., his first official act was to refuse to take the oath to maintain the existing constitution. His success as Minister of the Interior under his brother had been remarkable, and his character was said to resemble that of Kamehameha the Great; it is presumable, therefore, that he understood the needs of his people better than those of foreign birth and alien affinities. In the month of May, 1864, the king issued a call for a constitutional convention, subsequently making a tour of the islands to explain his plans to the electors. In July of that year the convention assembled in Honolulu; but its time being given to what Kamehameha considered useless deliberations instead of business, on Aug. 13 he declared the convention dissolved, dismissed the delegates, publicly abrogated the constitution of 1852, and one week after that date he proclaimed a new constitution of his own devising, under which Hawaii was happily ruled for twenty-three years. There will be no disputing the fact that this was a period of increasing prosperity; yet until the late King Kalakaua was constrained by the foreign element to abrogate this constitution (which my brother did much against his own will and better judgment in 1887), all parties had lived together in harmony throughout the kingdom of the Hawaiian Islands, under a constitution devised and promulgated by one man, and he of the race of the Hawaiian chiefs. I hope this fact will be recalled when I come to speak of the history of the reign of my brother Kalakaua, and my own administration of public affairs. Let it be repeated: the promulgation of a new constitution, adapted to the needs of the times and the demands of the people, has been an indisputable prerogative of the Hawaiian monarchy.

Chapter IV. My Married Life

I was engaged to Mr. Dominis for about two years; and it was our intention to be married on the second day of September, 1862. But by reason of the fact that the court was in affliction and mourning, our wedding was delayed at the request of the king, Kamehameha IV., to the sixteenth of that month; Rev. Dr. Damon, father of Mr. S. M. Damon, at present the leading banker of the Islands, being the officiating clergyman. It was celebrated at the residence of Mr. and Mrs. Bishop, in the house which had been erected by my father, Paki, and which, known as the Arlington Hotel, is still one of the most beautiful and central of the mansions in Honolulu. To it came all the high chiefs then living there, also the foreign residents; in fact, all the best society of the city.

My husband took me at once to the estate known as Washington Place, which had been built by his father, and which is still my private residence. It is a large, square, white house, with pillars and porticos on all sides, really a palatial dwelling, as comfortable in its appointments as it is inviting in its aspect; its front is distant from the street far enough to avoid the dust and noise. Trees shade its walls from the heat of noonday; its ample gardens are filled with the choicest flowers and shrubs; it is, in fact, just what it appears, a choice tropical retreat in the midst of the chief city of the Hawaiian Islands. Opposite its doors is the edifice, recently erected, known as the Central Union Church, which is attended by the missionary families, and indeed most of the foreign residents of American birth or sympathies.

Captain Dominis, father of my husband, had but little enjoyment from the homestead he had planned. He last sailed from the port in 1846, just as the house was on the point of completion, and the ship he commanded was never heard of more. His widow expected, hoped, and prayed, but no tidings of his fate were ever received; slowly she was compelled to recognize the truth so many sailors' wives are constantly learning, and to hope long deferred succeeded grief for irreparable loss. For this reason she clung with tenacity to the affection and constant attentions of her son, and no man could be more devoted than was General Dominis to his mother. He was really an only child, although there had been two daughters older; but while he was an infant they both died in the United States, where they had been left to gain their education. Mrs. Dominis was a native of Boston.

As she felt that no one should step between her and her child, naturally I, as her son's wife, was considered an intruder; and I was forced to realize this from the beginning. My husband was extremely kind and considerate to me, yet he would not swerve to the one side or to the other in any matter where there was danger of hurting his mother's feelings. I respected the closeness of the tie between mother and son, and conformed my own ideas, so far as I could, to encourage and assist my husband in his devotion to his mother. Later in life Mrs. Dominis seemed to fully realize that there had been some self-sacrifice, and she became more and more a tender and affectionate mother to me as her days were drawing to a close.

Soon after our marriage, Prince Lot invited my husband and myself, with Mr. and Mrs. Robert Davis, who were married about the same time, to accompany him on a trip to Hawaii, the largest island of the group, from which its name is taken. We accepted, and it became really my bridal tour. Prince Lot's accession to the throne as Kamehameha V. was then very near. Invitations were also extended to Mr. and Mrs. John Sumner, Mr. Haalelea, another member, like my husband, of the staff of His Royal Highness, and a few other friends of the royal party. It was a most enjoyable trip; we were gone many weeks, but the time passed away most delightfully.

As there are no hotels in our islands, a few words as to the entertainment of the chiefs, with such guests as they might have with them, may not be out of place here. I have always said that under our own system in former days there was always plenty for prince or for people. The latter were not paid in money, nor were they taxed in purse. The chief, by the overseer he appointed, took proper care of their needs, and they in turn contributed to the support of his table. It was a repetition of the principle of family life by extending the same over a large number of retainers. So on the estates of the high chiefs who generally resided at Honolulu were built houses which were sacred to their residence, exclusively devoted to such occasions as the present, when they might choose to visit their people.

Prince Lot had his houses and lands in Hawaii and elsewhere. It was to these we went. His people welcomed our presence; and no matter how protracted our stay, Hawaiian hospitality, or love and loyalty, whichever it may please the reader to call it, was never exhausted. It was the same with all the chiefs of the ancient families, with Mrs. Bishop, for example, who would have found a home on any part of her landed estate; nor has the custom altogether passed away by the many changes which have been wrought through the hands of the foreigner in the Hawaiian Islands. Were any person of the blood of the chiefs, myself for example, to visit Hawaii today, scarcely would the knowledge that we had reached the port of Hilo get to the ears of our people when a house would be provided for our occupancy, food would be brought to our doors, and we would be made welcome amongst our people for weeks, months, indeed years, if we chose to continue our residence.

On this visit to Hilo (1862) occurred the first chapter of an interesting history of which the sequel was the nomination of a younger brother of mine to the throne, although he did not live to enter upon his reign. One of the retainers of the Princess Ruth was in our company, and it was near the time of that lady's confinement. As Kalaikuaiwa, one of her people, was about to return to the neighboring island of Oahu, she inquired of Prince Lot what message she could carry back to Honolulu, to be delivered to Princess Ruth in regard to the little stranger about to enter this world. The prince, in reply, told the attendant to charge his sister from him on no account to give the coming child away, to which that messenger responded that it had been already promised to Mrs. Pauahi Bishop, her cousin. The prince repeated his injunction with still more emphasis, saying, "You must go back and tell my sister that on no account is she to give that child to another. I am an adopted child myself, deprived of the love of my mother, and yet I was a stranger in the house of my adoption." He referred to his own and Lunalilo's grandfather, Hoapilikane. The prince made no further explanations, save to impress it upon the messenger that such must be the message delivered; and as we started for our trip around the great island of Hawaii, the attendant left for her mistress's houses and home in Honolulu.

I may anticipate a little in order to continue the thread of this story. When our tour was over, and we returned to Honolulu, the first day of our arrival was a day of rest; but on the succeeding day, possibly a little later, Prince Lot, Queen Emma, Mrs. Bishop, and perhaps some others, were summoned to be present at the birth of the child of the Princess Ruth. The babe was born that afternoon at about three o'clock, in the house called Halaniani, on the veranda of which the prince waited for tidings of the mother and child for hours. Finally, at half-past five, Queen Emma appeared, and addressing the prince, asked him if he had heard from his sister, to which he replied that he had not. She expressed much surprise, and told him that the newly born infant had been taken away as her own by Mrs. Bishop over an hour ago. This intelligence was extremely unpleasant to the prince, and he at once declared that he would never have anything to do with that child. He carried his purpose into immediate execution by insisting within a week from that time that his sister Ruth should legally adopt as her own my brother Leleiohoku, whom she had taken from his parents at birth. He then made out two instruments of adoption for his sister to sign. By one she gave her child to Mrs. Bishop, irrevocably cutting it off from all interest in her property, and by the other she adopted as her child and heir, William Pitt Leleiohoku, the second of that name. All the papers were carefully drawn up by the prince, and everything connected with the adoption was made complete, so that in no event could the legality of my brother's position be doubted. The innocent cause of this disturbance, the child thus adopted by Mrs. Bishop and named Keolaokalani, died in about six months; my brother lived to be named heir apparent, and indeed to fill the office of regent during the absence of Kalakaua.

After making the tour of Hawaii, Prince Lot, accompanied by his guests, returned as far as the island of Maui, where it is possible we might have remained longer had it not been for the illness of his brother, the reigning king. Having been notified that this was approaching a fatal termination, and that his presence was required at the capital, His Royal Highness returned at once to Honolulu, where Alexander, Kamehameha IV., died on Nov. 30, 1863, after a reign of nine years, and being at the time of his death still a young man of twenty-nine. His widow, Queen Emma, although once a candidate for the throne, was never again in public life. She went abroad, however, in 1865, being received in England in a manner becoming her rank. She returned to Honolulu in 1866 on the United States ship *Vanderbilt*, commanded by Admiral Henry Knox Thatcher, only to learn at once of a new affliction in the death of her adopted mother, Mrs. T. C. B. Rooke.

On the accession to the throne of Prince Lot as Kamehameha V., the last of the Hawaiian monarchs to bear that name, my husband was at once appointed his private secretary and confidential adviser, which position he occupied during the entire reign. The king was surrounded by his own people, with whom he was in perfect accord, but showed this mark of royal favor to my husband simply because he preferred to advise with him on matters of public importance. My husband was further made governor of the island on which Honolulu is situated; and although the appointment was nominally for four years, yet it was always renewed, without the least discussion or hesitation, as long as he lived. It was a part of his official duty to make a tour of the whole island at least once a year; this was always rendered a most agreeable excursion, and I invariably accompanied him in the journey. Besides this position he held other offices of importance under the Hawaiian government, being at one time governor of the island of Maui; commissioner of the administration of the crown lands; attached to the suite of my brother, the late King Kalakaua, on his visit to this country in 1874 in the interest of reciprocity; and finally being a member of the Hawaiian embassy which visited this country and Great Britain in 1887, representing our nation at the Queen's Jubilee. But in the fall of 1891, Governor Dominis, who was then lieutenant-general of the kingdom with the rank of His Royal Highness Prince Consort, was in rapidly failing health; and on the 27th of August of that year, seven months after my accession to the throne, he died. His remains were laid in state in the palace; and on Sunday, Sept. 6, he was buried with royal honors.

His death occurred at a time when his long experience in public life, his amiable qualities, and his universal popularity, would have made him an adviser to me for whom no substitute could possibly be found. I have often said that it pleased the Almighty Ruler of nations to take him away from me at precisely the time when I felt that I most needed his counsel and companionship.

Chapter V. Hawaiian Music, And A Ducal Guest

The Hawaiian people have been from time immemorial lovers of poetry and music, and have been apt in improvising historic poems, songs of love, and chants of worship, so that praises of the living or wails over the dead were with them but the natural statement of their feelings. My ancestors were peculiarly gifted in this respect, and yet it is remarkable that there are few if any written compositions of the music of Hawaii excepting those published by me.

In my school-days my facility in reading music at sight was always recognized by my instructors. At the schools I attended, and of which mention has already been made, there was one boy by my side who could read the airs of new tunes which the teachers were anxious to introduce to the pupils. His name, I remember, was Willie Andrews. The untried music was handed to us; and we sang it by note, the rest of the pupils following by ear until the whole assembly were acquainted with the new music. After leaving school, my musical education was continued from time to time as opportunity offered, but I scarcely remember the days when it would not have been possible for me to write either the words or the music for any occasion on which poetry or song was needed. To compose was as natural to me as to breathe; and this gift of nature, never having been suffered to fall into disuse, remains a source of the greatest consolation to this day. I have never yet numbered my compositions, but am sure that they must run well up to the hundreds. Of these not more than a quarter have been printed, but the most popular have been in such demand that several editions have been exhausted. Hours of which it is not yet in place to speak, which I might have found long and lonely, passed quickly and cheerfully by, occupied and soothed by the statement of my thoughts in music; and even when I was denied the aid of any instrument I could transcribe to paper the tones of my voice.

In the early years of the reign of Kamehameha V. he brought to my notice the fact that the Hawaiian people had no national air. Each nation, he said, but ours had its statement of patriotism and love of country in its own music; but we were using for that purpose on state occasions the time-honored British anthem, "God save the Queen." This he desired me to supplant by one of my own composition. In one week's time I notified the king that I had completed my task. The Princess Victoria had been the leader of the choir of the Kawaiahao church; but upon her death, May 29, 1866 I assumed the leadership. It was in this building and by that choir that I first introduced the "Hawaiian National Anthem." The king was present for the purpose of criticising my new composition of both words and music, and was liberal in his commendations to me on my success. He admired not only the beauty of the music, but spoke enthusiastically of the appropriate words, so well adapted to the air and to the purpose for which they were written.

This remained in use as our national anthem for some twenty years or more, when my brother composed the words of the *Hawaii Ponoi*. He was at the time the reigning king, and gave directions to the master of the band to set these to music. He, being a German, found some composition from his own country which he deemed appropriate; and this has been considered of late years our national air.

In the changes of the past few years, the words written by His Majesty Kalakaua have been found no longer adapted to public occasions; so while the music is still played, such sentiments as "Look to the people" have been substituted for the ancient injunction to "Look to the king."

In the year 1869 the Duke of Edinburgh, Prince Alfred of England, arrived in the harbor of Honolulu, being in command of Her Britannic Majesty's ship-of-war *Galatea*. As soon as the king learned of the duke's presence he made special preparations for his reception; and for his better accommodation on shore he assigned for his use the residence of the late Kekuanaoa, who died in November of the preceding year. My own mother having died about three months prior to the arrival of the *Galatea*, I was not taking part in any festivities, being in retirement from society. But this was considered an exceptional occasion, and the king signified his wish to me that I would not fail to do it honor. So at his specific request I gave a grand luau at my Waikiki residence, to which were invited all those connected with the government, indeed, all the first families of the city, whether of native or foreign birth. Major J.H. Wodehouse, so long the ambassador of Great Britain at Honolulu, had just arrived with Mrs. Wodehouse; and they were of the invited guests, the prince specially inviting them to drive out to my house with him. I suppose the feast would be styled a breakfast in other lands, for it was to begin at eleven o'clock in the forenoon. The sailor-prince mounted the driver's box of the carriage, and taking the reins from that official, showed himself an expert in the management of horses. All the members of the royal family of England are, I understand, excellent horsemen; and in doing this the Duke of Edinburgh was only following customs to which he had been trained in his own land. The Queen Dowager Kalama, widow of Kamehameha III., drove out to Waikiki in her own carriage of state, accompanied by her adopted son, Kunuiakea, and my sister, Miriam Likelike; these two being at that time betrothed in marriage, although the latter married Hon. A. S. Cleghorn, and became the mother of the Princess Kaiulani. The drivers of these carriages wore the royal feather shoulder-capes, and the footmen were also clad in like royal fashion. It was considered one of the grandest occasions in the history of those days, and all passed off as becoming the high birth and commanding position of our visitor. The guests were received with every mark of courtesy by my husband and myself, as well as by His Majesty Kamehameha V., who was one of the first arrivals. When the prince entered he was met by two very pretty Hawaiian ladies, who advanced, and, according to the custom of our country, decorated him with leis, or long, pliable wreaths of flowers suspended from the neck.

As Mrs. Bush, considered one of the most beautiful women in the Hawaiian Islands, advanced, and proceeded to tie the flowery garland about the neck of the prince, he seemed perhaps a bit confused at the novel custom; but, submitting with the easy grace of a gentleman, he appeared to be excessively pleased with the flowers and with the expression of friendly welcome conveyed to him by the act. Balls, picnics, and parties followed this day of enjoyment; and the prince gave an entertainment in return at his own house, which was attended by my husband and myself, and by most of the distinquished persons in the city. The day of departure for the *Galatea* arrived; and the prince called on me to express the pleasure he had taken during his visit, and the regrets he felt at leaving us. On this occasion he presented me with an armlet emblematic of his profession; it was of solid gold, a massively wrought chain made after the pattern of a ship's cable, with anchor as a pendant. He also gave me copies of two of his own musical compositions; and to this day I keep and cherish these three souvenirs of the son of England's good queen, and at the same time one of England's noblest sailors. We have met once since those days, at the Queen's Jubilee, during my visit to London in 1887. Our past acquaintance was cordially recognized by the prince, who was then my escort on a state occasion, my nearest neighbor on the other hand being the present Emperor of Germany.

Chapter VI. Kamehameha V

Early in December, 1872, occurred the death of Prince Lot, as he was often called, even after his accession to the throne under the title of Kamehameha V. On the 10th of that month my husband and I were summoned to the palace to attend the dying monarch; one by one other chiefs of the Hawaiian people, with a few of their trusted retainers, also arrived to be present at the final scene; we spent that night watching in silence near the king's bedside. The disease was pronounced by the medical men to be dropsy on the chest.

At nine o'clock on the day following we were drawn up in a little circle about his bed. Among other considerations forced upon us at this solemn moment was that of a successor to the throne, which, respecting the right of nomination, rested with the king. Those present were his half-sister, the Princess Ruth, Mrs. Pauahi Bishop, Mrs. Fanny Young, the mother of Queen Emma, and myself, all eligible candidates in the female line. At the doors of the apartment were Prince William Lunalilo and my brother, David Kalakaua, also heirs presumptive to the throne, while watching at a respectful distance were retainers of these chiefs. The attorney-general, Hon. Stephen H. Phillips,

Hon. P. Nahaolelua, afterwards a member of my brother's cabinet, my husband, General Dominis, Kamakou, and two women in attendance occupied the space between us and the doors. Although nearing the end, the mind of the king was still clear; and his thoughts, like our own, were evidently on the selection of a future ruler for the island kingdom, for, turning to Mrs. Bishop, he asked her to assume the reins of government and become queen at his death. She hesitated a moment, and then quietly inquired why His Majesty did not appoint as his successor his sister, the Princess Ruth Keelikolani, to which question the king replied that the princess would not be capable of undertaking with success the responsibilities of government, to which Mrs. Bishop rejoined, "Oh, but we will all help her to the best of our ability." Having obtained her opinion, he next turned to Nahaolelua, and demanded of him who would be the proper person to be named for the succession. To this the counselor gave a very truthful, yet scarcely fortunate response, saying, "Any one, may it please Your Majesty, of the chiefs now present." The king again hesitated, and in the intervening time, the messenger whom all must obey was gaining entrance to the death-chamber; from the effort to provide for the future rule of the kingdom he relapsed into unconsciousness, and passed away without having named his successor to the throne.

The foremost candidate for the vacancy was undoubtedly the king's first cousin, Prince William Lunalilo; and in the matter of birth nothing could be said adverse to his claim. His mother was Kekauluohi, niece and step-daughter of Kamehameha the Great; he was popular, and of an amiable, easy disposition. But there were grave reasons why the choice was injudicious, and indeed hardly constitutional; for Prince Willliam's personal habits even at this time were such that he was under the guardianship of Mr. Charles R. Bishop, the banker, his property being out of his own control, while he received from his guardian an allowance of only twenty-five dollars a month as spending money. His selection was chiefly due to the influence of the representatives of the single island of Oahu, but having once been announced, was accepted with the usual cheerfulness and good faith displayed by the Hawaiian people, who have always been loyal subjects to any one of their own acknowledged chiefs.

His cousin, Kamehameha V., had such advisers as Mr. R. C. Wylie, Mr. C. C. Harris, Mr. F. W. Hutchinson, Hon. S. H. Phillips, and others, all men of ability, but not associated with what is known as the missionary party. On the ascension of Lunalilo, this latter party showed a determination to control the king, and by subjecting his weakness to their strength, to influence the fate of the Hawaiian people and the destiny of the Islands. They succeeded in securing the following cabinet: Hon. Charles R. Bishop (Foreign Affairs), E. O. Hall (Interior), R. Stirling (Finance), A. F. Judd (Attorney-General); two out of these four were from families who landed upon our shores with the single intention to teach our people the religion of Christ. The policy of the new cabinet was distinctively American, in opposition to that which may properly be called Hawaiian; the latter looking to the prosperity and progress of the nation as an independent sovereignty, the former seeking to render the Islands a mere dependency, either openly or under sufficient disguise, on the government of the United States. Then, as at the present day, the entering wedge was the concession of a harbor of refuge or repair at Pearl River. The proposition created great excitement, and was vehemently opposed by those of native birth; for patriotism, which with us means the love of the very soil on which our ancestors have lived and died, forbade us to view with equanimity the sight of any foreign flag, not excepting the one for which we have always had the greatest respect, floating as a matter of right over any part of our land. There is a gentleman still living at Honolulu whose boast is that he was the father of the project to annex Hawaii to the American Union. It may, therefore, be perfectly permissible to mention here that the Pearl Harbor scheme of 1873 is declared with good reason to have originated with him—Dr. John S. McGrew—and was then openly advocated by him as a preliminary to the obliteration of the native government by the annexation of the whole group to the United States. But in the midst of the discord produced by the agitation, the king's health began to fail rapidly; and at his express wish the project of the missionary party at that time to enter into closer relations with their own country was laid aside until a more convenient season. A change was recommended to Lunalilo; and arrangements were made for a trip to the largest island, Hawaii, noted with us for its high mountains and the favorable influences of its climate on the health.

By the advice of Dr. Trousseau, the king's physician, it was decided to go to Kailua; and thither went the royal party. Besides Dr. Trousseau, the king's chamberlain, Mr. Charles H. Judd accompanied us; then there were Kanaina, the king's father, Queen Emma, Princess Likelike, Mrs. Pauahi Bishop, Kapiolani, afterwards queen by virtue of marriage with my brother Leleiohoku, my younger brother, some others perhaps—and myself. The Hawaiian Band of native musicians also were with us; and every attempt was made to divert the mind of the king from his malady, and insure a favorable change. During our stay we were often visited by emissaries from Honolulu, urging upon the king the appointment of a successor, or praying him to return to the capital for the consideration of the subject, to all of which suggestions he appeared to be at least indifferent, if not absolutely opposed. In fact, he said openly enough that he himself owed his scepter to the people, and he saw no reason why the people should not elect his successor. I suppose it is no secret, but really a matter of history, that the person most ambitious to succeed him in the rule of the Hawaiian nation was Emma, the widow of Alexander Liholiho, Kamehameha IV. She and a number of her retainers were with us during our entire stay, although she had taken advantage of residence there to make some excursions in the neighborhood. Amongst these I especially recall a trip she made to the mountain, Hualalai, to visit the celebrated temple of Ahuaumi. This place once devoted to our ancient worship is a wonderful pile of rock, built by one of the kings of past centuries, and its construction was comparatively a short work, and yet each single stone must have been raised by a multitude of strong hands and muscular arms, passed from one set of laborers to another until it found its location in the structure; and the whole building thus completed was consecrated by Umi to the gods, and used for purposes then deemed most sacred. Visitors usually make this one of the celebrities to be seen if they are near enough to its location; but I regret to say there must have been those in the vicinity who had no respect for sacred antiquities, for a number of these stones, so laboriously erected, have been torn down, and from them a goat-pen has been built.

It was not long, however, that any of our party could indulge in recreation, for the rapid failure of the health of the king rendered it necessary for some one of us to be always watching with him. When it came to be the turn of Queen Emma, she urged him in plain language to nominate her to assume the reins of government at his decease; but his determination appeared to be unchanged to leave the selection to the people. Even when I was by his bedside, doing my duty as one of those chosen by birth to stand near during his dying hours, Queen Emma did not cease from her persistency, but again broached the subject of succession, and spoke to the king of the great importance to his people of naming an heir to the throne. The indelicacy of this persuasion from a Hawaiian point of view will be understood by those who have studied our national customs. He made her no reply, but turned from her as he lay on his bed. It was considered best that he should return to Honolulu, to which reluctantly he consented; so, accompanied by the chiefs and their attendants, we returned with him home. As long as he retained consciousness he insisted that the selection of a successor should be left to the people, and even his ministers were powerless to change his determination; and with a full intention of allowing the succession to be settled by ballot rather than by his constitutional right of appointment, he passed away, apparently without pain. Indeed, so peaceful was his end that the appearance of death began long before its reality, and the marshal of the realm, supposing the king to be dead, undertook the draping of the palace; scarcely had the long festoons of crape been hung upon the outer walls when it was discovered that the king was living. It was not thought best to remove these emblems of mourning, for their use might be appropriate at any moment; so an attempt was made to cover or conceal them and they were really in position about two days before the final scene.

Although Queen Emma was not named by the king as his successor, it was found that he had liberally remembered her in his will. A most important proviso of that instrument was the fund left for the founding of the Lunalilo Home for aged and indigent Hawaiians. This institution admits those of both sexes, the men being in one department and the women in another. It is well managed, and its inmates are happy and contented, so much so, indeed, that they often conduct themselves as if youth and hope were still their portion, and from the sympathy of daily companionship they wish to enter the closer tie of matrimony. This they are permitted to do without severing their connection with the institution, and there is a separate department provided for those who have thus agreed to finish their journey of life together.

Chapter VII. Queen Emma

The contest for the succession which resulted in the elevation of my family—the Keaweaheulu line—to royal honors is of course a matter of history. Since the king had refused to nominate his successor, the election was with the legislature. It must not be forgotten, however, that the unwritten law of Hawaii Nei required that the greatest chief, or the one having the most direct claim to the throne, must rule. The legislature could not choose from the people at large, but was confined to a decision between rival claimants having an equal or nearly equal relation in the chiefhood to the throne.

Queen Emma's claim was not derived through her own family, but as the widow of Liholiho, one of the Kamehamehas. The great-grandfather of Kalakaua (the other claimant), and Kamehameha I. were own cousins; and, as I have already noted, it was to this ancestor and to other chiefs of our family that the late dynasty had owed its succession, and the uniting of the kingdoms of Hawaii under one government.

Now, it is not denied that Queen Emma had a rightful candidacy. It has already been seen that the king hesitated, and finally failed to decide between her rights and those of our family to succession. It was not the duty of the legislature to determine the question.

From the fact that Queen Emma was a resident of Honolulu, the capital, and the immediate scene of the election, has arisen the impression that she was the real choice of the Hawaiian people. She naturally had about her a considerable personal following, scheming for office, and a large body of retainers, all within the city and environs; and hence could there make a formidable showing. She had also, of course, partisans here and there throughout the Islands. Her canvass was, however, limited almost exclusively to intrigue within the city, while Kalakaua and his friends sought the suffrages of the country people and their representatives. Each party was vigorous in its own way, and there was great excitement. It cannot be said that either party felt much assurance as to the result, until the vote was actually declared. But Queen Emma herself seems never to have doubted that she must be the chosen sovereign; and it was policy for her advisers to flatter her expectation, upon which their own fortunes hung. For this she should rather have our sympathy than our reprobation. Her active candidacy was legitimate, and compatible with public spirit. But for her subsequent course there is little justification. Her disappointment assumes too personal a manifestation to be excused in the representative of royal responsibilities. It is therefore because of its political consequence that I deem it proper to record here what will doubtless seem to the public, from any other point of view, a mere detail of feminine pettiness.

It is a fact that Queen Emma ardently desired and hoped to succeed King Lunalilo, and that during the time that he lay unconscious, with life barely perceptible to those of us who stood nearest him, she was busily whispering among her friends the details of her plans. I was presently informed that she purposed to supersede General Dominis by Mr. F. S. Pratt as governor of Oahu, and that various other government positions had been promised. But if our party attended with its eyes to the intrigue, it at least maintained silence until the king died, and his remains were removed to Iolani Palace, and laid in state in the Red Chamber on the royal feather robe of Princess Nahienaena, the sister of Kamehameha III.

The legislature assembled in the old court-house, now the merchandise warerooms of Hackfeld & Co., the shipping merchants. At the first and only ballot it was found that David Kalakaua was elected, receiving thirty-nine votes to the six votes cast for the rival candidate, Queen Emma.

The vote, no doubt a surprise to Honolulu, being declared to the people who surrounded the legislative halls, was received with acclamation, mingled with shouts of disapproval. Naturally, the partisans of Queen Emma, being residents of Honolulu, and some of them inspired with liquor, were easily incited to riotous action. They were re-enforced by her own dependants, who came to their assistance from her residence. This was between three and four o'clock of the afternoon of the 12th of February, 1874.

An attack was made by the mob on the legislature; furniture was demolished; valuable books, papers, and documents which belonged to the court or to the attorney-general's office were scattered abroad or thrown from the windows. Clubs were freely used on such unlucky members of the assembly as could be found within the walls, and some were thrown through the open windows by the maddened crowd. Many men were sent to the hospital for treatment of their broken heads or bruised bodies. But this was not an expression of the Hawaiian people; it was merely the madness of a mob incited by disappointed partisans whom the representatives of the people had rebuked.

In the meantime, the newly elected King Kalakaua, the Princess Likelike, and myself were quietly awaiting returns in the house which had been the residence of Queen Emma while her husband was the reigning monarch. At this date she resided in the house of her mother, Mrs. Fanny Rooke, and we were the only occupants of the mansion of Liholiho. There was complete tranquility also at Iolani Palace, where the late king's remains still lay in state, a few soldiers only being on guard about the chamber in which rested all that was mortal of the deceased monarch.

Presently a lady, Miss Hannah Smithies, came into our presence, and abruptly told my brother that he was the king of the Hawaiian people. He could not believe the matter already settled, and leaving us, walked out a little distance with an idea of meeting someone to confirm or deny the report; he soon returned, closely followed by Mr. Aholo and Mr. C. H. Judd, who not only brought him the same news, but informed him of the disturbances at the court-house, from which they said they had but just escaped with their lives. These two friends were followed by Hon. Charles R. Bishop, Minister of Foreign Affairs under the late king, who warmly congratulated my brother on his ascension to the throne, and confirmed the statement that a most serious riot was in progress in the business part of the city. No dependence could be placed on the police nor on the Hawaiian Guards; these had proved unfaithful to their duties to preserve order, and had in some cases joined the partisans of Queen Emma in their riotous actions. So Mr. Bishop asked the king's advice as to whether it would not be wisest to appeal at once to the foreign vessels of war, of which there were three in the harbor, that they might land their forces and restore tranquility to the city.

In view of the fact that a riot was in progress, that the halls of justice were in possession of a mob rendered irresponsible by the use of liquor, and that night was approaching, when incendiarism might be feared, my brother, the king elect, my husband, the late Governor Dominis, and Hon. Charles R. Bishop, Minister of Foreign Affairs, united in a request to Hon. Henry A. Pierce, the American Minister, that armed men might be landed from the American ships *Tuscarora* and *Portsmouth*, to sustain the government in its determination to preserve order, and protect the lives and property of all residents of the city of Honolulu. A force was also landed from the British man-of-war *Tenedos*, whose commander, Captain Ray, being absent on shore, the responsibility was assumed by his executive officer, Lieutenant Bromley. Commander Belknap and Commander

Skerrett of the United States forces took possession of the square on which the court-house is built; and on seeing this, the mob melted silently and entirely away. The armed marines subsequently, at the request of the Hawaiian authorities, guarded the treasury, arsenal, jail, and station-house. The British marines were marched to the residence of Queen Emma, and, after dispersing the rioters assembled there, they occupied the barracks and guarded the palace itself. There was no permanent damage done by the disturbance. The Hawaiian people are excitable, but not given to bloodshed or malignant destruction of property.

I may here remark that the action of United States Minister Henry A. Pierce has been quoted as furnishing a precendent for that of Minister John J. Stevens. Nothing could be more incorrect. When the town was in danger, and the lives and property of all classes in peril, even then, until written request was made by the king, by the governor of Oahu, and by the Minister of Foreign Affairs, no interference was made by foreign war-ships. When armed forces were landed it was to sustain and protect the constitutional government at a mere momentary emergency from a disloyal mob. The constitutional government of 1893 and the governor of Oahu not only made no request to Minister Stevens, but they absolutely protested against his actions, as an unwarranted interposition of foreign forces in a dispute which had arisen between the queen and a few foreign residents. It was on the request of these latter that Minister Steven's acts were based, at a time when, save for differences of political opinion, the city was perfectly tranquil. Even had there been a disturbance, no one but the government could have authorized the employment of alien troops.

Governor Nahaolelua of Maui, one of her trusted adherents, had left the house early to carry to Queen Emma the news of Kalakaua's election. When she learned the result from the lips of one of her own friends, she could no longer doubt its truth, though it was unexpected and unacceptable. On the day following the riot she set for Mr. Nahaolelua, and demanded of him if it were not possible to ask for another vote in the legislature on the question of the succession. What might have been the result had he consented to this, cannot be told; for while the matter was in discussion at Queen Emma's residence, there broke in upon their deliberations the booming of the salute of twenty-one guns, indicated that my brother Kalakaua had taken the oath of office. This would have made any further opposition nothing less than treason, and the matter was consequently dropped.

Queen Emma never recovered from her great disappointment, nor could she reconcile herself to the fact that our family had been chosen as the royal line to succeed that of the Kamehamehas. All those arrested for disturbing the peace the day of the election were her own retainers. Two days after the trouble she came to the palace, and used her influence with King Kalakaua to have them released. As the king went to the audience chamber to receive her, he spoke to the queen and myself, asking us to be present and assist at the reception with himself; but before we could comply with his wishes she had seen him, made her request, and then withdrew hastily from the rooms without awaiting the entrance of Queen Kapiolani or myself. Why she should cherish such bitterness of spirit against the queen is past my comprehension. Queen Kapiolani had been aunt to Queen Emma, having been the wife of her uncle Namakeha, and had nursed the young prince, the son of Alexander Liholiho, although her rank not only equaled, but was superior to, that of Queen Emma, the child's mother.

The sweet disposition and amiable temper of Queen Kapiolani never allowed her to resent in the least the queen dowager's bitterness, nor would she permit herself to utter one word of reproach against the mother of the child she had herself so dearly loved. In this respect my brother's wife showed her truly Christian character, and there were occasions when the lack of courtesy on the part of the Queen Emma became something very like insult. For instance, it is the custom with the members of the highest families, the chiefs of the Hawaiian people, at such time as it is known that any one of their rank is ill, to go the house of the chief so indisposed, and remain until recovery is assured, or to be present at the deathbed, if such should be the result. On these occasions, if Queen Emma met Queen Kapiolani, who, of course, from this date became, as my brother's wife, the lady of the highest rank in our nation, she would studiously avoid recognizing her. Many and many a time did Kalakaua make the effort to bring about a reconciliation between the two ladies; but although Queen Kapiolani would have assented to anything consistent with the dignity of womanhood, Queen Emma would not make the least concession. Even in the very residence of my brother, visiting the palace at the invitation of the king, if the queen were present she avoided recognizing her, and would at times rise and leave when Queen Kapiolani entered, saluting no one but the king as she retired; although this was an outrageous impertinence to the queen under her own roof, it was through Christian charity ignored by its recipient. Notwithstanding this persistent anger, my brother-in-law Hon. A. S. Cleghorn, prevailed on his wife, the Princess Likelike, to continue the acquaintance. I confess that my own patience with such displays was not equal to a like forbearance; and, as I would not stoop to court her favor, nor could accept, without proper and dignified notice, her overbearing demeanor towards myself, Queen Emma never forgave me my own rank and position in the family which was chosen to reign over the Hawaiian people. It did not trouble me at all, but I simply allowed her to remain in the position in which she chose to place herself.

Kalakaua never forgot to invite Queen Emma to all the entertainments given at the palace, and on state occasions he strove to do her the highest honor. At the opening or closing of the legislature a seat was reserved for her appropriate to her rank as queen dowager, but she never showed the king in any way that she appreciated his courtesy.

Chapter VIII. King Kalakaua

My brother's reign began on Feb. 12, 1874; and on the fourteenth of the same month he appointed, by the consent of the nobles under the twenty-second article of the constitution of 1864, our younger brother, William Pitt Leleiokoku, his successor to the throne. The prince became regent during the first absence of Kalakaua from his kingdom, on a tour abroad of which I shall soon speak. He was a very popular young man, about twenty years of age, having been born on the 10th of January, 1854. But the amiable prince was not to live to ascend the throne, or even for any extended enjoyment of those social pleasures in which he bore so prominent a part. He died on the 10th of April, 1877, having been in the position of heir apparent for about three years. He had the same love of music, the like passion for poetry and song, which have been so great a pleasure to me in my own life, as well as to our brother, King Kalakaua. He had a taste for social pleasures, and enjoyed the gay and festive element of life. During the absence of the king, there were three separate clubs or musical circles engaged in friendly rivalry to outdo each other in poetry and song. These were the friends and associates of the prince regent, those of the

Princess Likelike, and my own friends and admirers. Our poems and musical compositions were repeated from one to another, were sung by our friends in the sweetest rivalry, and their respective merits extolled: but candor compels me to acknowledge that those of Prince Leleiohoku were really in advance of those of his two sisters, although perhaps this was due to the fact that the singing-club of the regent was far superior to any that we could organize; it consisted in a large degree of the very purest and sweetest male voices to be found amongst the native Hawaiians. They were all fine singers, and these songs, in which our musical circles then excelled, are to be heard amongst our people to the present day. And yet it still remains true that no other composer but myself has ever reduced them to writing. This may seem strange to musical people of other nations, because the beauty and harmony of the Hawaiian music in general and of these songs in particular have been so generally recognized. But as soon as a popular air originated, it was passed along from its composer to one of his most intimate friends; he in turn sang it to another, and thus its circulation increased day by day. It was not long before everyone had the same knowledge of the new melody as happens in communities where a new and favorite air is introduced by an opera company. With other nations' music is perpetuated by note and line, with us it is not. The ancient bards of the Hawaiian people thus gave to history their poems or chants; and the custom is no different to this day, and serves to show the great fondness and aptness of our nation to poetry and song.

 I will now return to the date of the departure of my brother, King Kalakaua, to the United States. Yielding to the wishes of those residents of his domains who were from American or missionary stock, my brother had organized the negotiation of a treaty of closer alliance or reciprocity with the United States; and even before leaving home he had commissioned Judge Allen and Minister Carter to submit such a treaty to the American government. To advance the interests of this movement by his personal presence, he accepted passage for himself and his suite on the ship-of-war *Benicia*, and sailed for San Francisco in the autumn of 1874. My husband, the late General J. O. Dominis, and the United States Minister Henry A. Pierce accompanied him on his travels. One of the officers of this steamship was Lieutenant Whiting, who received permission to accompany King Kalakaua to Washington. He is now a commander, and has since married Miss Afong, one of a large family of children, all girls, whose mother is one of our people, but whose father was a rich Chinese resident, now returned to his native land. From the moment of landing my brother made friends, and was treated with the kindest consideration by the American people of all classes. There was a very strong feeling of friendship between the king and the late General U. S. Grant. It amounted almost to recognized fraternity.

The result of this visit is well known. It secured that for which the planters had gained the endorsement of the king; it resulted in the reciprocity treaty of Jan. 30, 1875. So this, one of the first official acts of King Kalakaua, was very satisfactory to the party in power; but even then there were a few who protested against the treaty, as an act which would put in peril the independence of our nation. The impressions of the people are sometimes founded upon truth; and events have since proved that such was the case here—that it was the minority which was right in its judgment of the consequences of the Hawaiian concession of 1875 to the power of the foreigner.

On Oct. 16, 1876, at the house on Emma Street, was born to Princess Miriam Likelike (Mrs. A. S. Cleghorn) the child now known to the world as the Princess Kaiulani. She was at once recognized as the hope of the Hawaiian people, as the only direct heir by birth to the throne.

Kaiulani was only six months old when my brother, Prince William Leleiohoku died; and it was evident that the vacancy must be instantly filled. The Princess Ruth, daughter of Pauahi and Kekuanaoa, who had adopted Leleiohoku, had asked of the king if she herself could not be proclaimed heir apparent; and this suggestion was placed before the king's counselors at a cabinet meeting, but it was objected that, if her petition was granted, then Mrs. Pauahi Bishop would be the next heir to the throne, as they were first cousins. At noon of the tenth day of April, 1877, the booming of the cannon was heard which announced that I was heir apparent to the throne of Hawaii.

Chapter IX. Heir Apparent

From this moment dates my official title of Liliuokalani, that being the name under which I was formally proclaimed princess and heir apparent to the throne of my ancestors. Now that this important matter had been decided by those whom the constitution invests with that prerogative, it became proper and necessary for me to make a tour of the islands to meet the people, that all classes, rich and poor, planter or fisherman, might have an opportunity to become somewhat acquainted with the one who some day should be called to hold the highest executive office. The first journey undertaken was that of encircling the island on which the capital city of Honolulu is situated; we therefore started from our home to make the trip around the coast-line of Oahu, a tour of nearly one hundred and fifty miles, following the roads which wind along on the brink of the ocean. This we proposed to do on horseback; although my carriage, where I could rest if required, accompanied the party. Our cavalcade was a large one; my immediate companions being my husband, General J. O Dominis, governor of the island, and my sister, the Princess Likelike, wife of Hon. A. S. Cleghorn, who was attended by her personal suite. But large numbers are no discouragement to Hawaiian hospitality, especially under the additional inspiration of the love and loyalty to their chiefs; so the people opened their doors with an "*Aloha nui loa*" to us in words and acts, and wherever we went a grand reception awaited us on arrival. Our route was first to the eastward, past Diamond Head, Koko Head to the point of Makapur, then turning to the northward and around to Waimanalo, where we found ourselves the guests of Ah Kua, a very wealthy Chinaman, who owned a large plantation there devoted to the cultivation of rice. Intelligence of our approach must have traveled faster than we had ridden; for as soon as our cavalcade drew near to this estate we were greeted with a discharge of firecrackers and bombs, let off to do honor to the presence of the heir to the throne and her companions. There was no cessation of the salutes during the feast of good things which had been spread by Ah Kau for our refreshment, to which, and to the professions of loyalty on the part of our host, we did ample justice. From thence we proceeded to Maunawili, the beautiful residence of Mr. and Mrs. Edwin Boyd, whose doors were already opened for our reception; and here we spent the night and remained an entire day, enjoying the entertainment prepared for us, which can be described in no better terms than by saying that we received a royal welcome indeed. Our progress continued on the day following through Kaneohe, our noonday rest being at the house of Judge Pii, where a generous lunch awaited us on the moment of our arrival. The people of that entire district had congregated to do us honor, and showed us in every way that there was no doubt or disloyalty in their hearts. Yet, while still at Kaneohe, a letter was received by the Princess Likelike from her husband, in which that gentleman advised his wife to return to Honolulu, and stated it was his opinion that if it was the purpose of my tour to meet the people and cultivate their love, the time spent on the route would be wasted because they were all zealous partisans of Queen Emma. My sister acquainted me with these views of her husband, and asked my advice as to her course. I did not wish to influence her in any way, and therefore left it to her option to continue the journey with me, or to take Mr. Cleghorn's advice. But we had already advanced far enough on our pathway amongst the people to prove that her husband had made a great mistake, for no heir to the throne could have been more royally received by all than I had been. The princess had not failed to notice this, and as we proceeded it was still more apparent; the most zealous of Queen Emma's people, now that the question had been officially decided, hastened to do us honor. So, after due consideration, Princess Likelike decided that she would not return. A decision she had no after occasion to regret, and was one which made me very glad; for she was welcomed and showered with marks of favor by the very adherents of Queen Emma, of whose disappointment she had been warned by her husband. It would be tiresome to others, perhaps, should I go on and describe with minute particulars the steps of our party as they passed around the island. From place to place the reception was the same, cheerful, hearty, and enthusiastic—Kahuku, Waialua, Makahao, Waianae, and so on to our latest stopping-place, which was with Mr. James Campbell and his sweet wife at Honouliuli. He had the advantage of a little more time in his preparations for our reception than was possible to some of our other places of rest, and had spared no pains to give us an ovation in every way worthy of himself and his amiable companion. The result was a manifestation of kind feelings and generous hospitality such as, even at this distant day, cannot, no, nor ever will be, effaced from my memory. From thence we started for Honolulu; and as it was noised abroad that the party would enter the city, there was scarcely space for our cavalcade to pass between the throngs of people which lined our way. From Leleo to Alakea Street it was a mass of moving heads, through which only slowly could our carriages, horses, and outriders pass. It was understood and accepted as a victorious procession; and out of sympathy for the disappointed dowager queen, our people refrained from noisy demonstrations and loud cheering, and instead the men removed their hats, and the women saluted as we passed.

I have been thus careful in reviewing this my first trip as heir to the throne, both because it is a pleasure to recall the memory of that epoch in my life, and further that I may speak with pride of the continued affection, of the unshaken love, of these my people. In some nations the leaders, the chief rulers, have gone forth through districts conquered by the sword and compelled the people to show their subjugation. Our progress from beginning to end was a triumphal march, and might well be described as that awarded to victors; but there were no dying nor wounded mortals in our track. We had vanquished the hearts of the people, they showed to us their love, they welcomed me as Hawaiians always have the ruling chief; and to this day, without the slightest appeal on my part, they have shown that their love and loyalty to our family in general, and to myself in particular, have known no change nor diminution, even under the circumstances, now so different from those of twenty years ago.

Chapter X. My First Visit To The United States

In the early part of the year 1878 I was not in the enjoyment of my usual good health; and my physician Dr. Tisdale of Oakland Cal., advised a trip to that coast, trusting that the change might be of benefit to me. At this date steam communication was not as frequent nor as convenient as has since been established; yet we had very comfortable and pleasant accommodations on the steamer *St. Paul*, on which we departed. I was accompanied by my husband, General Dominis; and amongst the agreeable company on board were Mr. and Mrs. Wm. F. Allen, Mr. Nott, who married Miss Mary Andrews, and Mr. C. O. Berger, who married a daughter of Judge Weideman. Besides these, I recall the names of Mrs. J. I . Dowsett and her son, J. I. Dowsett, both deceased, and Mrs. C. B. Wilson. The trip was made in nine days; and at its termination I obtained my first view of the shores of that great country, the United States, of which land I had heard almost without cessation from earliest childhood. If first impressions be accepted as auspicious, surely I found nothing of which I could complain on this visit; for many prominent citizens of the great city of the Pacific coast came to do us honor, or entertained us during our stay. Amongst these were my husband's old friend and playmate of earlier days, Governor Pacheco; also Mr. Henry Bishop, brother of Mr. Charles R. Bishop, who married my sister Bernice; Mr. H. W. Severance, at that time in the consular service of the Hawaiian government at San Francisco; Mr. R. S. Floyd and wife, the gentleman being connected with the great observatory established through the munificence of the late James Lick; Mr. and Mrs. Toler of Oakland; Mrs. Haalelea and Mrs. Coney (at this time residing at Oakland with the children of Mrs. Coney); and many others, who united to give us a delightful introduction from the islands of the tropics into that land with whose history we have been so intimately connected. The first welcome of strange shores is not often forgotten by the traveler, however numerous may be the subsequent experiences; so these flattering attentions were most sincerely appreciated then, and have never ceased to awaken emotions of gratitude in my heart.

While we did not travel extensively through the State, yet our visit to Sacramento must not be passed by without a word; for many were the visitors who called to welcome us while staying at the Golden Eagle Hotel. Amongst these I recall the name of Mr. H. S. Crocker, a prominent citizen; then there was Mrs. Charles Crocker, whose home we visited. She occupied a most elegant mansion; and in its pleasant surroundings, and the generous hospitality with which we found ourselves entertained, the welcome there was not unlike that I have noticed in my account of our tour around our island home. Where all are so perfect, it seems scarcely possible to distinguish one feature above another; yet her art-gallery made a great impression on me at the time, and I can see again, as I recall the past, the many beautiful paintings by prominent artists with which it was adorned. They were works of genius indeed, so true to nature and so lifelike; but they were far too numerous for me to try at this day to recall them by name. The least detail of her grand and beautiful residence was nothing less than perfection. The floors were paved with artistic designs in tiles of white, of blue, and other colors. There were apartments devoted to several branches of natural history, and the cabinets of stuffed and mounted birds, as well as of quadrupeds and animals in great variety, interested and amused me as if I had been a child taken to a museum of curiosities. The whole collection must have been of great value, and it has given me pleasure to learn that since my visit it has been turned over to the State of California for the delight and information of future generations.

From thence we returned to San Francisco, and after a month's absence prepared for our homeward voyage, which was made on the steamer *Wilmington*, Captain Fuller, now harbor-master by commission of the present rulers of the port of Honolulu. The ocean air, charming company, that cordial welcome of friends which so quickly dispels the sense of loneliness one feels when a stranger in a strange land, all had combined to prove the wisdom of my physician's advice; and I returned in most excellent health and my accustomed good spirits.

During the summer of that year, 1878, my husband and I visited the island of Maui, and while General Dominis was for a brief time recalled to Oahu, my brother, His Majesty Kalakaua, came to Maui especially to have an interview with me. He was always kind enough to seek my opinion on questions of public interest, but this trip was undertaken for the special object of consulting me about some appointments to official positions then under discussion. It was at Wailuku, where my husband had left me at the residence of Hon. H. Kuihalani, that the king arrived with a few attendants. I recognized his great consideration for me in this act, and his deference to my opinion; for had he so wished, these appointments could have been made without the least consultation and the names of his selections would have been known to me only through the regular channels of information to all, and the king would have been spared a trip from his capital to another island. He spoke to me about the appointment of Mr. Charles H. Judd, whom he proposed to nominate to the office of chamberlain, and further to that of special agent for the management of the crown lands. Both of these offices were held by my husband at this time. That of chamberlain was only temporary, but the other had been his official position since the days of Kamehameha V.; and under his administration of the leases and revenues of these lands, both during the reign of that monarch and ever since, all things had been considered very satisfactory. The king's proposition to withdraw both of these appointments from General Dominis in order to confer them upon another caused me much anxiety, and I must confess no little indignation. But I restrained these feelings, and replied to the king with proper meekness, telling him as my sovereign that whatever seemed best to him ought to be done, and that it was clearly his privilege to act upon his own views of what was right in the matter. He then asked me in plainer terms if I had no opinion to offer to him, to which I replied that I had; and then went on to inform him that this Charles H. Judd, whom he was now to bring into favor by public office, and by placing him nearer to his person, had worked against him, and had opposed his nomination to the throne of the sovereigns of the Hawaiian Islands. Mr. Judd had not been content with silent opposition, but had gone over to Koolau and openly canvassed that district in the interest of Queen Emma. When he heard that my brother had received the majority vote of the legislature, he then with soft words returned to try the arts which we call "to malimali," to ingratiate himself into the royal favor. My honest opinion having been demanded of me by the king, it was given in the above terms; and I added, "I see that Mr. Judd has been successful; he schemed for favors at your hands; he has obtained what he coveted, and procured of Your Majesty the displacement of my husband, although General Dominis has been faithful to every trust, a constant and true friend of yours for years, and a loyal follower to this very day of his removal." My husband's absence gave me the right and the courage to speak thus plainly to the king. "Well," he replied, "say that I have made my appointments, what is there remaining that I can do for you, my sister?" To this I answered that I would be pleased if he would appoint Governor Dominis to be governor of Kauai and of Maui in addition to the office he held, the governorship of Oahu. The king most cheerfully consented, and I wrote at once to my husband telling him just what had been said and done; my letter not only met his approval, but he showed it to Hon. C. C. Harris, who commended me in the highest terms for the stand I had taken in the discussion of this delicate and difficult matter.

It was with good reason that I had selected the office of governor of Maui as a token of the king's appreciation of the constant loyalty of my husband. Independent of his fitness for the position by reason of his long experience on the island of Oahu, it was well known that the ruling governor, Moehonua, could not live for any length of time; he was dropsical, and the disease was approaching its final stage; so I could indicate my preferences without feeling that I was asking that any person should be displaced to please me. The very next mail from the island brought the intelligence of the governor's death. He was a most estimable man, far superior to many of a corresponding rank, which was not of the highest; yet he was a good specimen of the Hawaiian race, of noble birth and patriotic sentiments. On the confirmation of the appointment to General Dominis, he appointed Hon. Mr. Aholo as his secretary and lieutenant-governor of the island, to which we immediately proposed to make a visit; for we had heard that the people were extremely contented and even enthusiastically pleased with my husband's appointment. The experience of this visit would seem to most abundantly prove the wisdom of the king's choice of General Dominis. Our people feel that in honoring their chiefs, in respecting those who are legitimately their rulers, they are doing not only a duty, but a pleasure to themselves. It was only needful to let it be known that the governor of their island accompanied by the heir to the throne was to be with them, to give the signal for the opening of every door, and the most cordial greeting by every wayside. Consequently the unremitting attentions shown to us by all classes of the people, the many tokens of kindness received by us on that journey, are still and always will be gratefully cherished in my heart. It may be interesting to some to read the names of those who at that time, nearly twenty years ago, were residents of this island. There were the Hon. and Mrs. Aholo, Mr. and Mrs. Hayselden, Mr. A. Fornander, Mr. and Mrs. Nahaolelua, Hon. Adam Kakau, Mr. and Mrs. Kuihalani, Mr. and Mrs. John Richardson, Mr. and Mrs. Everett, Mr. W. H. Corwell and his family to two generations, Mr. and Mrs. W. H. Daniels, Mr. and Mrs. James Makee, Mr. and Mrs. Henry Turton, Mr. and Mrs. Unna, and representatives of the distinctively missionary families of the Alexanders and the Baileys.

To go over in detail the steps of our tour would be to repeat that which has been written of my trip around the island of Oahu; so I will only say that the above families, and many others not mentioned by name, absolutely vied with each other in making us welcome, and providing a generous hospitality for our entertainment. The mere mention of these names recalls to me with sadly interesting vividness the past in my native land, when those of Hawaiian and of foreign birth were united in a common love of country, and only too eager to compete with each other for the privilege of showing to us their loyalty and love.

Chapter XI. Mauna Loa

In the year 1880 Miss Helen Aldrich of Berkeley, Cal., made me a visit. She was the daughter of Mr. W. A. Aldrich, a banker, who had married a first cousin of my husband, Elizabeth, the child of Mr. R. W. Holt. Shortly after her arrival we took a trip to the largest of our islands, Hawaii, on which is situated that volcano called with truth one of the greatest natural wonders of the modern world. I was attended by my retainers, and after a short and pleasant voyage we arrived at the port and chief city, Hilo. As though to illuminate in honor of my visit, on the night preceding our ascent of the mountain a bright glow was seen on the top of Mokuaweoweo. This was the portent which preceded that great flow of lava which soon commenced from Mauna Loa, and took its course down the sides of that mountain towards the city of Hilo. We were thus witnesses from the very beginning of one of the most extensive and long-continued eruptions which has ever been recorded in history, for it was protracted over a period of eleven months. Early on the morning following we started on horseback on our journey to the crater of Kilauea, where we arrived about five o'clock the same evening. This is not, as some strangers suppose, a mountain by itself, totally distinct from the general volcanic system of Mauna Loa. That word in our language signifies the great long mountain, and the nature of the elevation well deserves the term; for in height, 13,700 feet, it is exceeded by few in the world, while in extent it includes about one-third of our largest island. The eruptions are not usually from the summit, but generally through fissures in its sides. One of these is the crater lake of Kilauea, a region of perpetual fire, of an activity more or less pronounced, yet never entirely extinct, and situated some twenty miles or so east from the summit, at an elevation of about four thousand feet. It is one of the few, if not the only one, of the volcanoes in the world which can be visited at the periods of its greatest displays without the least danger to the observer; because it is always possible to watch its bubbling fires from a higher point than their source. It is not the lava from the burning lake which makes its way down the mountain, but that from other places where the concealed fires of Mauna Loa burst forth.

There is now a modern hotel at a spot commanding a good view of the points of interest; but at the date of this visit we were received and made very comfortable in a large grass house with thatched roof, under which some forty persons could have been accommodated. Here we were most hospitably received, our tired horses were cared for and sheltered near to our resting-place, and we did ample justice to the evening meal which had been provided for our company. After our refreshment, darkness quickly succeeded the setting of the sun (there being no long twilight, as in more northern climates); so we spent the evening in watching the fiery glow in the crater, the brilliance of which seemed to be spreading along the level floor of the pit. From a flooring of light and heat the surface changed at times to billows of actual fire; then jets burst up or fountains played high in air, standing by themselves a moment like burning columns; then steam intervened to stifle the flames. Mist following this, the crater was for a while hidden from our sight, and nature's gorgeous fireworks suspended. At one of these intervals we retired for the night; but at two o'clock we were all awakened by our host to see an exhibition such as has seldom been furnished for the inspection of any of the many tourists who visit that region. This was a most brilliant illumination at the summit of Mauna Loa itself; and far from lessening, its manifestation seemed to render more vivid, the fires of the crater of Kilauea. The mists had cleared away in that direction, and we thus had the good fortune to watch on one and the same occasion the outbursts of light at the summit and the jets of dancing flame in the sides. It was a night never to be forgotten by any of our party, and well worth the time and labor of the journey, were there no more to be enjoyed. That which was nearest to us, the rising, boiling sheet of liquid fire, seemed to show no abatement by reason of the vent at the mountain-top, but in its agitations disclosed each moment sights more and more wonderful to our gaze. The next day was spent by our party in descending the crater to the very limits of its seething fires, but I remained at the hotel. They were all provided with some offerings to Pele, the ancient goddess of fire, reverenced by the Hawaiian people. This custom is almost universal, even to the present day. Those born in foreign lands, tourists who scarcely know our ancient history, generally take with them to the brink of the lake some coin or other trinket which, for good luck, as the saying is, they cast into the lava. Our people, the native Hawaiians, have no money to throw away on such souvenirs of the past; but they carry wreaths of the pandanus flower, leis, made like those seen aboard the steamers at the departure of friends, necklaces, and garlands of nature's ornaments, which are tossed by them into the angry waves of the basin. As I have mentioned this incident, my thoughts have gone back to that paragraph wherein I wrote of the overthrow of the superstitious fears of the fire-goddess through the brave acts of my aunt, Queen Kapiolani, when she defied the power of the elements at this very spot. So, to prevent misunderstanding now, perhaps it would be well to notice that this propitiation of the volcano's wrath is now but a harmless sport, not by any means an act of worship, very much like the custom of hurling old shoes at the bride's carriage, or sending off the newly wedded couple with showers of rice; usages which form a pleasant diversion in the most highly cultivated and educated communities. After a day spent in watching the activity of the crater, the party returned to our hotel, weary, hungry, and ready to enjoy the refreshment and repose of which they were in need. One night more was spent at the volcano house of the olden time, and then we all started on our ride down the mountain for the city of Hilo. The display had not diminished in extent nor in its strange, wild beauty. The lake in the crater was still boiling, and over Mokuaweoweo the location of the opening was easily distinguished by the brilliant glow of light. But turning our backs on these natural wonders, nature was perhaps more lovely in the charms by which she lined our pathway towards the sea; for this road is justly considered to be one of the most beautiful exhibitions of the scenery of the tropics in Hawaii, and our cavalcade passed between lines of verdure or flowers enchanting to the eye and fragrant to the sense; there were the bright blossoms of the lehua, both yellow and red varieties, and other plants or trees shading and pleasing each of us as we advanced. Although we did not arrive at our destination until about five that afternoon, and were quite fatigued with our long ride, yet it had been an excursion of great enjoyment, and I am sure no one of the company was other than satisfied with it.

The great increase in the lava flow which subsequently took place had not at this time threatened the peace of the city; so our return to our friends was made the signal for a round of social pleasures. A grand entertainment in honor of the visit of the heir to the throne was given by Mr. and Mrs. Luther Severance; and it afforded me much satisfaction to show to my California cousin some examples of the generous style of the hospitality of those days, in which those of foreign or of native birth vied with each other in a friendly rivalry of good things. Judge F. S. Lyman was then lieutenant-governor of the island, and with his amiable wife showed us all the attention in his power; then there were Judge Akao and his wife, Mr. and Mrs. Governor

Kipi and their agreeable family. The family of Mr. D. H. Hitchcock, especially his wife and daughters, were also most kind and attentive to me and those who accompanied me. If, in these reminiscences, I should fail to name those who have made such occasions pleasant, it must be accepted simply as an unintentional omission, the names I have given being but examples of that universal kindness received by me from all. Just as we were leaving our kind entertainers, Sir Thomas Hesketh arrived in the port on his own yacht for a visit to the island; he was accompanied by Hon. Samuel Parker, whom he had invited to be his guest during this excursion. The regular steamer of passenger service between Hilo and Honolulu received me and my company for our return to Oahu, where we arrived in safety; and not long after my cousin, Miss Aldrich, took her departure for her home, with, I am sure, some very pleasant memories of the natural beauties and social pleasures of life on the Hawaiian Islands.

Chapter XII. Kalakaua's Tour Of The World

In the early part of the month of January, 1881, a message through the telephone reached me at my private residence at Washington Place, that my presence was required immediately at Iolani Palace. I answered the summons at once; but on my arrival the king was not to be found at the palace, but I eventually discovered him in a long building adjacent thereto, in which were kept some of his favorite boats. He was selecting some oars for the boat named the *Kanoelani*, and while still engaged on this work he communicated to me his wishes and instructions. He notified me that he expected soon to sail on his trip around the world, and that he desired me to assume the control of the government, and the charge of public affairs as regent, during his absence. He then went on to inform me that he had already held a meeting of the cabinet council on this matter, at which it had been proposed by the members that there should be a council of regency, of which I should be the head; but that the action of the council should be required for the full exercise of authority. This is an important page in

Hawaiian history, because it shows how persistently, even at that date, the "missionary party" was at work to undermine at every point the authority of the constitutional rulers of the Hawaiian people. As the king had sent for me with the express purpose of asking my opinion, I gave it in terms too plain to admit of the least misunderstanding between us. I told him that I did not admit either the necessity or the wisdom of any such organization as that of a council of regency. I then proceeded to explain my reasons for this opinion, saying that if there was a council of regency, there would be no need for any regent. In case such a body were to be commissioned to govern the nation, who, then, would be the chief executive? In fact, why was any such individual required at all? To these considerations the king gave careful attention, and appeared to see that my views of the situation were founded upon reason and justice. The result of this informal conference was that before his departure I was appointed sole regent, with the functions of the reigning sovereign of the Hawaiian Islands during his absence. On the 20th of January, 1881, accompanied by Mr. C. H. Judd and by Mr. W. M. Armstrong, both from missionary families, amidst the salutes of the shipping and the booming of cannon, His Majesty Kalakaua took his departure, being the first of the sovereigns of the nation to undertake a tour of the globe.

In nothing has my brother been more grossly misjudged and even slandered by those whose interests he had at heart than in this journey. Probably he did have some love for travel, some sense of pleasure in visiting foreign lands—who amongst us had not felt the desire to see the great and beautiful world which God made, and on which man has built so many magnificent cities and works of art? Why should he not have felt this interest? But the master motive for this enterprise was the good of the people of the Hawaiian Islands over whom he had been called to rule. I have already spoken of his visit to Washington for the purpose of assisting at the ratification of the reciprocity treaty. That negotiation successfully carried through by his commissioners created a new want in his domains. The sugar-fields demanded laborers, and at this time it was a problem to decide from whence these could be obtained. Soon after landing at San Francisco, the king first visited Japan; from there he proceeded to China; with the statesmen of both these nations, including the celebrated Li Hung Chang, my brother conferred upon questions of international interest, but more especially in regard to the emigration of their subjects from their territory to the sugar plantations of our islands. While he was thus working for the prosperity of the residents of his kingdom, and for an immigration which should result in the wealth of those of foreign ancestry or affiliations, they were accusing him of a reckless spending of money, and of the waste of time and revenues in foreign travel. From China the king went on to Siam, where he was most royally entertained by the ruling monarch; then to India, whose climate, resembling ours, caused him to be in favor of initiating an emigration thence to our cane-fields. Nothing, however, resulted from his examination of the chance of employing the coolies of India; but China and Japan have since then sent many laborers to our plantations. We know now what imported or contract labor means. It must be remembered that at this date the experiment was in its infancy, and the question was to find some class of laborers who would not suffer in our tropical climate at field labor. The conclusion cannot be avoided, that if my brother had indeed sought his own pleasure rather than the good of all residents under our flag, his family would be in their hereditary rights to this day. By his liberality to those of American birth he inaugurated the treaty of reciprocity; by his investigations and solution of the problem of labor he gave them the opportunity to raise sugar at an enormous profit; and he thus devoted the earlier part of his reign to the aggrandizement of the very persons who, as soon as they had become rich and powerful, forgot his generosity, and plotted a subversion of his authority, and an overthrow of the constitution under which the kingdom had been happily governed for nearly a quarter of a century. This was accomplished by them in 1887, as will be seen when I reach that date in my recollections. After his studies of the labor question in the East, my brother made a tour of the chief countries of civilized Europe, returning by way of Washington, and in every place receiving from all classes many marks of personal attention or national courtesy. He arrived home on the 29th of October, 1881; and this was naturally followed by my immediate resignation of the office of chief ruler, which I had held for nine months and as many days.

Chapter XIII. My Regency

But there are a few matters of interest during this time of which I must now speak. King Kalakaua had been gone but a few weeks when the startling news was in circulation that the smallpox had broken out in the city. It was supposed to have been introduced from China; but our past experience with the disease had shown us how fatal it might become to the Hawaiian people, and whatever the inconveniences it became necessary at all hazards to prevent its spread. Summoning the cabinet, I had all arrangements perfected to stay the progress of the epidemic. Communication between the different islands of the group was stopped. Vessels were absolutely prohibited from taking passengers. A strict quarantine of all persons infected or under suspicion was maintained; and so scrupulously and energetically were these regulations enforced, that when they were relaxed and quarantine raised, it was found that no case had been reported outside the place of its first appearance. But it was a serious thing to confine its ravages to the city of Honolulu, in which there were some eight hundred cases and about three hundred deaths.

After the privileges of travel were restored to all alike, I had a desire to visit Hilo again; and so, with a large company of retainers, as was fitting to my regency, I started on this excursion. Mrs. Pauahi Bishop, the Princess Ruth, Mrs. Haalelea, and their immediate attendants, had preceded me; and I invited the Royal Hawaiian Band of native musicians to form part of my retinue, not for my own pleasure especially, although music forms to me a great part of the enjoyment of life, but because I wished to bring with me, to my friends and my people on that island, a delight which I knew to them was quite rare, and in which I was quite sure all would find much satisfaction.

It was in the month of August, six months after I had watched the commencement of that lava flow which is now celebrated in the history of that region of wonders. I found Mauna Loa was still alarmingly active, and that three streams of molten fire were creeping down its sides, so that the good people of Hilo were living in daily apprehension that the fiery element would reach their doors, their houses be consumed, and their lives, perhaps, imperiled by the rivers of flame. It was a grand and beautiful sight, in spite of the suggestion of danger, as you rode along the borders of the lava stream, which had chosen the channels of the watercourses or filled the basins where these had formerly spread themselves out into pools of refreshing fluid; their origin, even when rolling along, or falling as a great cascade into some hollow, which was soon filled up with the melted elements of the earth's centre, making one level plain where had been channels or pits in the earth's surface.

In some directions it seemed to be miles in width and of a length up the mountain-side to the summit of which the eye could not reach; while at night the surface of moving fire resembled a plain on which was situated a large city in conflagration. It was a display of fireworks of nature's manufacture such as has been seldom seen in the world, and which never could be seen excepting at the base of Mauna Loa. There was intense excitement at Hilo, for it was not known how soon the on-coming rivers might reach the city; yet there was a fascination in the display, or in the danger, which drew thousands out to watch the streams of moving flame. Some of the spectators were doubtless attracted by motives of curiosity, others were prompted by their fears; but of one thing there could be no manner of doubt, all were vividly, even if painfully, interested. There have always been features peculiar to the flow of lava from this region which can scarcely be explained by natural causes; while this our grand volcano is capable of inspiring fears which cannot be concealed, yet it is no less a fact that it has never been destructive to human life, nor made havoc with property. At this very time, while the people of Hilo were flocking to the sides of the immense river of molten lava, as it steamed down the mountain-sides on its way to the sea, or watching from the banks bordering the seething mass the course of its flow, it would creep up sidewise on the rise of a hill, with no apparent cause for the action; or nearing a stone wall it would surge upward, filling in solidly the topmost crevices at an elevation of perhaps three feet from the soil, instead of running downward and to the lower level, or pouring itself into the hollows and lowest places. The residents of Hilo, who lived in their handsome houses constructed of wood and so easily inflammable, on finding that time did not abate the extent or volume of the flow, lived in terror of losing life and property, dreading at any moment to see the fiery river turn its course towards their dwellings. Consequently the churches were opened, meetings were held, and earnest prayers offered to the Almighty Ruler of the elements that he would spare the people from the great misfortune which threatened to overtake them. To one of these prayer-meetings I received a special invitation, and attended with my suite. In the course of about a week thereafter, there was no doubt in the attitude of the volcano; its flow had been stayed, and the volume of the lava was diminishing, although for another week sparks of light or streaks of flame were here and there to be seen, but the great danger was over. Naturally, devout men remembered the days of fervent prayer, and said that the God to whom they had cried at the moment of peril had listened to the supplications of his people, and delivered them from threatened evil.

On the next arrival of the steamer *Kinau* from Honolulu, my sister, the Princess Likelike, joined me, and by the same steamer we with our entire retinues took departure, intending to visit Kau, where the people, in anticipation of my visit had made great preparations for a reception; but on arrival of the steamer at Kaalualu, Mr. George Beckley, the purser of the steamer, requested me earnestly not to land, assigning as his reason that the stay of the steamer there would be very short, not over a few minutes, and that she could not be longer detained. To my knowledge the people had already arranged for my promised visit with lavish hospitality, so I did not like to disappoint them, as there was to be a grand luau. I therefore requested the Princess Likelike to go ashore and represent me on the occasion, which she kindly did; but the assembled multitudes were excessively disappointed that I could not be present, and expressed to my sister their sentiments of keen and sincere regret. Leaving that landing-place, our steamer proceeded to Hookena, where corresponding tokens of welcome awaited our arrival, and where the people had come together to show to me their friendship. Here I was met with the same objections on the part of the purser, who would have prevented a landing if he had been able to do so; but the crowds on shore were determined not to be disappointed, and as for myself, I shared their intention that the grand preparations made for my entertainment should not be in vain. Besides, there were special causes for my resolution that this district should not be passed by. It was at that time distinctively Hawaiian. The pure native race had maintained its position there better than in most localities. There had been no introduction of the Chinese amongst the people, nor had any other race of foreigners come to live near their homes. The Hawaiian families had married with Hawaiians, settling side by side with those of their own blood. Thus it was that only on Hawaii, and in no other part of the group of islands, could there be found a district so thickly populated, where the population was so strictly of my own people, as this to which I was now a visitor. This made it peculiarly interesting to me; and my reception, and enjoyment of the welcome of the inhabitants, were all that one could have desired. From thence my progress continued, first to Keauhou, then Kailua, and last of all Kawaihae; of these, and in truth of all the districts at which we had touched in our progress from Hilo, it may well be said that each had vied with the other in friendly rivalry, each had striven to outdo its neighbor in the grandeur of its preparations made for my entertainment. It was not the flattery of words; their loyalty and love were expressed by everything which was done to render my stay attractive, each person assisted at the welcome, and the parting was a sorrow to all my faithful friends. Amongst the larger landholders who did all possible to make my stay on Hawaii pleasant was Hon. Samuel Parker, who with his family most cordially received and hospitably entertained us at his seaside residence there. He spared no pains in his efforts to furnish my table with all which the most fastidious taste could desire; there were fish from the sea in great variety and of delicious freshness, many of the other delicacies, such as "opihi" for example, being especially Hawaiian in use or origin. All these were furnished from the vast estates on the island owned by Mr. Parker or subject to his control, and time would fail to speak of the many other attentions or numberless kindnesses shown by him. Mr. Parker became my Minister of Foreign Affairs under the latest cabinet commissioned by the constitutional monarchy of the Hawaiian Islands. After a most delightful journey, and many happy days spent on the island of Hawaii, I returned to Oahu, glad, as most tourists are, to find myself once more at my own home, and to settle down to my domestic life at Honolulu.

Another necessary excursion, however, had already been planned for me; namely, a trip around the island of Oahu, at the very outset of which there arrived news of an event which stirred the world with horror; this was the assassination of President Garfield. The stores were at once draped in mourning, meetings expressive of sympathy for the family of the deceased president, and of regret at his untimely end (which we shared with the American people), were called at once by those of his nation, but were attended by both Hawaiians and foreigners. To one of these, which was to be held in the large Congregational Church on Fort Street, on the evening of the 6th of October, I think, I was especially invited to be present; but, as before the sad intelligence of his death was received all arrangements had been made for my tour, I did not feel that these could well be changed, and I therefore sent a note of regret, expressing to those in charge the assurance of my sympathy with the object for which the meeting had been called.

Chapter XIV. A Serious Accident

Then leaving Honolulu, attended by some few of my retainers, I went first to the residence of Mr. J. A. Cummins, a gentleman who subsequently undertook a diplomatic errand for me to the city of Washington, and who in 1895 was suspected and even punished by the present rulers of Hawaii for participation in the attempt to smuggle arms for possible use by the people desiring a return to the monarchical form of government.

At that time the possibility that the monarchical form of government could be overthrown would have been incredible, and my visit to Waimanalo was simply the occasion of a renewal of that social welcome and hearty entertainment such as had attended me everywhere since my nomination to the Hawaiian throne. In fact, I might claim with reason that the future hopes of the Hawaiian people were with my party. I was accompanied by my sister, the Princess Likelike, who had with her the little child-princess Kaiulani and that infant's governess, Miss Barnes; Mr. J. H. Boyd was of the number of our attendants. After a generous lunch at Waimanalo, on the estate of Mr. Cummins, we left for Maunavili, the country-place of Mr. and Mrs. Boyd, in whose hospitable mansion we passed the night, and left our gentle hostess regretting that our stay had been so short; but events proved that my tour was not to be extended far beyond her residence, for we had proceeded on our way to Kaneohe but a few steps, when a singular accident happened to my carriage. My horses were driven by Mr. Joseph Heleluhe, and in some unaccountable manner the reins of one of the horses became entangled in the bit of another. We were descending the steep side of a hill, and the result was that the driver had no longer control of the animals. Consequently the carriage came down the hill with such velocity that I was thrown violently out, and landed between two rocks; but fortunately there was a bit of marshy ground where I struck. It was a matter of immediate wonder that my life had been spared. Certainly no one could have been nearer to instant death. This had been witnessed from the homestead of our hosts; and Mr. Cummins, arriving on the scene almost immediately, sent for a stretcher, which was sent at once from the residence of Mrs. Boyd. On this I was placed, and the litter raised upon the shoulders of four men; thus was I carried all the way to Waimanalo. Mr. Cummins, having preceded the sad procession, met us at the foot of the hill with a wagon. It was a sorrowful breaking-up of what had promised to be a delightful journey. Messages were immediately sent to all the points on the island I had intended to visit, informing the people of the accident which had befallen me, and notifying them that it would be useless to go on with preparations for my reception, as it was the intention of those who had charge to send me at once to Honolulu. So, under the kind care of Mr. Cummins and Mrs. Kaae, the wagon was driven to the wharf, where the little steamer *Waimanalo*, belonging to Mr. Cummins, awaited me. All that tenderest care and kindest heart could suggest was done to make me comfortable by my kind hosts; and the cavalcade of retainers, with which I had come out so gayly, followed in demure silence. Despatches had also been sent to Honolulu; and my husband, Governor Dominis, and the princess's husband, Hon. A. S. Cleghorn, were acquainted with the particulars of the accident. Mr. Cummins, Mr. Kaae, and Mr. Frank Harvey, assisted by other friends, saw that I was put on board the steamer with as little pain or inconvenience as possible. My sister and little niece were by my side; and all the company were safely accommodated on board the *Waimanalo*, which at about three o'clock that afternoon steamed out to sea. After a smooth and uneventful run we drew near the wharf at the foot of Fort Street, in the port of Honolulu. It was nine o'clock at night when the little craft got alongside the wharf, where crowds of people awaited her arrival. The night was fine and clear; the moon was shining brightly. As the boat was fast, I turned my eyes toward the shore, and saw a line of soldiers drawn up to receive me. When the litter was taken from the deck and placed in a wagon, I discovered that these men were to draw my carriage to the place prepared for my reception. When all had been made ready, the word was given to proceed, and the procession started. To me it was a solemn moment, one which can never be forgotten—the shops and houses of the merchants still draped with crape in memory of the fallen president at Washington, the crowds of native Hawaiian people which lined the way, their respectful silence broken only by their smothered sobs or subdued weeping, and with it all the steady, measured tread of the soldiers who were drawing the wagon on which I had been laid by my devoted friends. Although I had suffered much, was still in pain, and not out of danger, yet in it all there was the sweet assurance for which much can be borne—the blessed consciousness that all this manifestation was because my people loved me. My husband was walking by the side of my wagon, and the tramp of the soldiers was growing shorter as we neared our home, while the throng of sympathetic followers who had attended our march grew less only when we reached our very doorway. My return thus to my people and my family from the very border of death left an impression upon me which is too sacred for any description.

    On arrival I asked to be placed in one of the cottages on our grounds, preferring to occupy this small, one-story house rather than to be carried upstairs to the more commodious apartments of the great house known as Washington Place. My wishes were complied with at once by my kind husband and faithful attendants.

The nature of my injuries was such that a long rest was required. At first it was thought my back was broken by my fall; for when I endeavored to rise after recovering from the first shock, it was impossible to do so, nor could I change in any way my position until assisted by my followers, Mr. Heleluhe being one of the first to offer me aid. Even then, when depending upon their strength of arm as they tried to raise me, the least exertion or motion gave me the greatest pain. My physician, Dr. Webb, arrived at the cottage at Washington Place about the same time as myself, although he had been a long distance in search of his patient. The moment he received news of the accident he had ridden to *Waimanalo*, a distance of twelve miles by the shortest route, and not finding me had at once returned. He made a careful examination of my condition, and was relieved to find that the injuries to my back were no more serious than a very severe wrench and strain. He was a homoeopathist, and left some medicines to be administered, directions to be followed by my nurses; and watches were to be regularly set, and relieved by night and by day. At the end of three weeks I was not yet able to raise myself, or even sit up in my bed; so finally it was the opinion of my medical advisers that I should make a great effort and persevere in spite of the pain, lest I should become bedridden. These instructions were followed out with a result which proved the wisdom of the course recommended; for I was soon able to ride about in my buggy, still weak, but improving slowly.

But the process of recovery was very gradual, and only successful by the most constant care and great patience of my attendants. These were divided into watches of three hours each, and three persons were always at my bedside. To one of these was assigned the duty of waving the kahili, or long-plumed staff of state, the insignia of royalty; to another that of using the fan for my comfort, both of these being women; while to the third, a male attendant, belonged the duty of doing any necessary errands, and of making my female attendants comfortable in whatever way their needs might require. Whenever I was lifted, or even turned, it was done by the strong yet tender hands of six men, three on each side. Had these been nurses trained by years of experience to manage the sick they could not have proceeded with more skill and gentleness; so quietly and gradually was my position changed that I could scarcely perceive the movements, which were such as to give me the least pain. It was the same when it was judged best for me to leave my bed. By the strong arms of my native attendants I was lifted in a sheet, then easily laid on an extended but movable chair, which was raised to an erect posture without the least strain on my muscular system. Even when I began to move about the room my dependence on my faithful retainers did not cease, and with one on each side it was almost impossible for me to fall. From the reclining-chair I was transferred without movement or strain to my carriage, and taken from it in the same manner, thus securing change and fresh air with no exertion to myself. My position was not without its amusing side, even at the most critical moments; for when I was supposed to be asleep or unconscious, conversations or little actions would take place in the sickroom which were perfectly understood by me, but of which I was supposed by my attendants to have no knowledge whatever. When scarcely able to sit up I was consulted about the mottoes with which it was the intention to crown the triumphal arches throughout the city at the approaching return of my brother, the king, from his tour around the world; and it was a great satisfaction to me to receive such marks of deference while I lay a helpless invalid.

All classes of adherents had been represented in the watchers about my bedside. There were Colonel C. P. Iukea, Colonel J. H. Boyd, Major Anton Rosa, Governor John T. Baker, Mr. C. B. Wilson, Captain Leleo, Mr. Joseph Heleluhe, Mr. Isaac Kaiama. These and many others had their watches in the invalid chamber, while Hon. Samuel Parker and Mr. Charles Williams were present from time to time. Most of these gentlemen were accompanied by their wives as assistants in their kind offices.

Princess Ruth and my sister, the Princess Likelike, were daily visitors.

Chapter XV. Kalakaua's Return

It was during this period of convalescence that my regency was brought to a close. With that enthusiasm always shown by the Hawaiian people in doing honor to their sovereigns, the grandest preparations were made throughout the islands to welcome the arrival of the king. In Honolulu the joy was general, and the foreign element was well represented in the festivities. The streets were given up to the people, and were crowned with triumphal arches. Before the day of his expected landing at the wharf, the most elaborate preparations had been made to give him a royal greeting. The mottoes, in the selection of which numberless parties had consulted me, were displayed in every part of the city, and there was an especial arch designed for each district of the island of Oahu.

The long-expected day came; and there was a long cavalcade of horsemen in attendance on the king, who rode ahead, accompanied by the gentlemen of his personal staff. Outriders and aids were seen on every side. A week was devoted to the festivities of the reception. Iolani Palace was not available; for the old building had been pulled down, and the new one was not then completed, although in process of erection. So the king with his queen, Kapiolani, occupied a smaller building which is named Kinauhale. It was in this building that during my brother's absence I had conferred the order of Kalakaua on two persons distinguished in the Roman Catholic Mission, both of them now having passed to their reward—Hermann, the Bishop of Olba, and Father Damien, the leper priest.

When the festivities of my brother's return were over, I moved to my Waikiki residence, accompanied by some of my retainers or attendants, amongst whom I might mention Mrs. Kapena and Miss Sheldon. In the course of a very few weeks, and under the beneficent influences of this change, I had recovered my strength, and was able to walk without assistance. Hamohamo is justly considered to be the most life-giving and healthy district in the whole extent of the island of Oahu; there is something unexplainable and peculiar in the atmosphere at that place, which seldom fails to bring back the glow of health to the patient, no matter from what disease suffering. In order to encourage the people who might be semi-invalids to resort there, I have always left open my estates on that shore, so that the air and the sea-bathing, the latter most essential in our climate, might be enjoyed without any charge by all who choose to avail themselves of the privilege. I have also caused trees to be set out, both those whose fruit might be of value and those of use for shade alone, so that the coast might become attractive to chance visitors. When it is the malolo season, the fishermen living in my neighborhood will go to my beach to launch their canoes, and push off two or three miles into the incoming surf to catch the flying-fish; it is a very exciting sport, and at the same time it is a means of livelihood to them. Nor are they the only people benefited by this free fishing-ground. Most of their catch is taken to the markets of the city. Some part is brought in, and landed on the beach at "The Queen's Retreat," where whole families of visitors are often to be found passing the day in rest or pleasure. These have brought with them an abundance of our national dish, the wholesome poi and perhaps have added bread and butter and wine, and stores of other nice things; to these they may now, if they wish, join the sweet and toothsome flying-fish. Oftentimes they make a further purchase of the latter to carry home for the family supper. Political events have brought me leisure, and from the view through the porticos of my pretty seaside cottage, called Kealohilani, I have derived much amusement, as well as pleasure: for as the sun shines on the evil and the good, and the rain falls on the just and the unjust, I have not felt called upon to limit the enjoyment of my beach and shade-trees to any party in politics; and my observation convinces me that those who are most opposed to my system of government have not the least diffidence about passing happy hours on domains which are certainly my private property. To watch the families of the Royalist and the Provisionalist mingling together, sharing each the other's lunch-baskets, and spending the day in social pleasures at the "Queen's Retreat," one would never suspect that racial or political jealousy had any place in the breasts of the participants. While in exile it has ever been a pleasant thought to me that my people, in spite of differences of opinion, are enjoying together the free use of my seashore home.

The king having resumed the executive office, affairs of state were no longer committed to my charge. But I was in a position to observe that our industries were moving along on the high road to prosperity, and that with a fair degree of harmony between the king and his ministers, our government was administered smoothly, and in a manner conducive to the welfare of all his subjects, whether native or foreign born. But there are a few events of the days of my regency which, ere I pass on to another era, may be worthy of mention.

During the king's absence, and while Mr. H. A. P. Carter was Minister of the Interior, he notified me one day that there was a death-warrant awaiting my signature. This was the first time it had been forcibly brought to my notice that the executive held the power of life and death, and it seemed to me a most terrible thing that I should be obliged to sign an order which should deprive one of my fellow-mortals of life. I simply could not do it, and so said to Mr. Carter. He regarded it as only an official act; but I asked the cabinet if they could not devise some other method of punishing the culprit in order to spare me the pain of signing the death-warrant. Minister Carter tried as best he could to convince me that in no event would I be held responsible, that any mistake or culpability would rest on the shoulders of the cabinet, and I need not feel in the least degree responsible. But he failed to convince me. I told him that I would take the matter into consideration, and notify him if, after thinking it over, I could conform to his views. Two weeks, perhaps three, went by, and I had never felt that I would in this case attend to my official duty. Finally Minister Carter again pressed the subject upon my attention; reminding me of the fact that the matter had been considered and judged, that the cause of justice was delayed, the sentence unexecuted, and that it was absolutely my duty to sign the warrant, which I finally did, but with the greatest reluctance.

In the month of July, while the king was absent, Chief Justice C.C. Harris, a man who in many ways had been prominent, died; there were some elements of peculiar sadness in the death of Judge Harris. His wife, a daughter of a former chief justice, Allen, was at the time under restraint in another room of the same house, being hopelessly insane. His death made it necessary for me to appoint some person in his place. The first associate was at that time Mr. Albert F. Judd, and the second Mr. L. McCully. At one of the public functions in the government building at which I was expected to preside, there occurred an incident which will suggest the eagerness for distinction and precedence manifested at the time by prominent representatives of the "Reform" party. At such state occasions there were seats assigned to the ladies of the cabinet at the right of the king's dais. The wives of ministers had the front row of seats. (In times of more ancient date the first seats of honor were always taken by the native Hawaiian chieftesses; but by "Reform" regulations, especially in the reign of King Kalakaua, his family were the only natives of rank present, so it became a very easy matter to provide for them.) Directly behind the seats of the cabinet ladies were placed those intended for the ladies of the justices of the supreme court. On this occasion, I being the regent, my sister Likelike stood at my right, my husband (who had a right to the title of prince although he never assumed it, but preferred to be called governor or general), accompanied by Hon. A. S. Cleghorn, father of the little Princess Kaiulani, were at my left.

As yet no appointment had been made by me to the vacant place on the bench of the supreme court, because I had consulted my brother, the absent king, and was awaiting a reply. But Mr. A. F. Judd had instructed his wife that she should occupy a seat with the cabinet ladies, and even to take the first seat, thus assuming precedence over all. It was a surprise to Minister Carter on entering to find the seat which belonged to his wife occupied by another person. After a little discussion betwixt them, the question was referred to me for decision. I immediately said that the seat belonged to Minister Carter's wife, and suggested that Mrs. Judd resume the place which belonged to her with the other ladies of the associate judges of the court, adding that she was no more at present than the lady of the first associate justice. "But," expostulated her husband, "I am as good as chief justice already, as I am to be appointed to that office;" and then he proceeded to demand of me if I had not already received notice of his appointment. I replied that I had not, and that my decision of the question of precedence was announced. Then, as the assembly was in readiness to proceed with its duties, although Mrs. Judd obstinately refused to yield the place which belonged to the wife of Minister Carter, I turned my attention to other and more important matters.

While I was a prisoner in Iolani Palace, now called Executive Building, it seems that the little comedy of precedence was re-enacted under the "Republic" in the rooms beneath mine, at the assembling of the legislature. Minister Cooper arrived with his wife; and to his astonishment and anger, there was Mrs. Judd again, seated in the place which should have been reserved for Mrs. Cooper. In order to secure the coveted precedence, Mrs. Judd had arrived very early, secured for herself the seat of honor, and, as before, absolutely refused to leave it. Words passed between the chief justice and the minister. Mr. Judd claimed that he was the highest officer in the islands. To which Minister Cooper retorted that he held no cabinet position, and was certainly out of place among cabinet ministers; while he, Cooper, as the minister of foreign affairs, should be entitled to the first place in the government after that held by the president himself. The disputants did not on this occasion send to me for an opinion on this perplexing question. Had they done so I should have decided without a moment's hesitation that the position of Mr. Cooper was the correct one, according to the usages of nations, whatever may be the relative rank in republics as between the executive and judicial departments. But it would seem from this second occurrence that the passion for dignity and place is not confined to courts of royalty or to those who sustain them.

Chapter XVI. Coronation Ceremonies

In the early part of the year 1883, preparations were made to formally ratify the accession of the new dynasty to the Hawaiian throne by investing both His Majesty Kalakaua, and his queen, Kapiolani, with the crown and other insignia of royalty. To this end all needful articles had been ordered from Europe, excepting such as could be readily obtained in the nearer port of San Francisco, Cal. This was very properly intended by the king to be a jubilee year with his people, and at the grand celebration nothing was to be left undone which could contribute to the general enjoyment. All the people, high or low, rich or poor, from Hawaii to Kauai, were to be made welcome at Honolulu; and elaborate preparations were made for their reception. The two crowns were made in England, and were of gold studded with precious stones; from the same country came also the dresses of the queen and those of her sisters, the Princess Poomaikalani and the Princess Kekaulike. My toilets were furnished from Paris dressmaking establishments, and consisted of two complete costumes. The gown to be worn during the day at the coronation ceremony was of gold and white brocaded silk; that intended for the soirée and the royal ball was of crimson satin; each costume was perfect in itself, the lesser details being in harmony with the dress; both were heavily embroidered, and were generally considered to have been the most elegant productions of Parisian art ever seen in Hawaii on this or any other state occasion. My sister, the Princess Likelike, had sent to San Francisco for her wardrobe, which, like mine, consisted of two complete costumes, one of which was of white silk of figured brocade handsomely trimmed with pearls; her full evening dress was of silk, in color or shade styled at that time "moonlight-on-the-lake," and, with head-dress to match, it was very effective.

Even in the early part of January, from all parts of the islands, crowds began to flock to Honolulu, impatient for the promised ceremony; and from thence to the 12th day of February, 1883, the number of those visiting our capital city was daily increasing. It was an unusually rainy winter, and our streets were very muddy; but the good-natured multitude waded through the rain or mud to see what was going on, or to make their purchases at the stores, without complaint. Money was spent lavishly by the visitors; all the stores were thronged from morning to night by eager and easily satisfied purchasers. The principal establishments benefited by the money of the people were those of John Thomas Waterhouse, who had two places of business, B. F. Ehlers & Co., H. Hackfeld & Co., and T. H. Davies & Co. Besides these there were the jewelry shops, notably that of the Wenners; even the Chinese merchants came in for their share in the circulation of the money of the people.

The day to which all had been looking with eager anticipation arrived. Iolani Palace, the new building of that name, had been completed the previous year, and a large pavilion had been erected immediately in front of it for the celebration of the coronation. This was exclusively for the accommodation of the royal family; but there was adjacent thereto a sort of amphitheatre, capable of holding ten thousand persons, intended for the occupation of the people. In this building there were assigned proper stations to all the principal officers of the government, besides which the members of the diplomatic or consular bodies had their appropriate places; then there were the nobles and the delegates to the legislative assembly, the chief justice, his associates, and other officers of the court, while on the veranda of the palace on the one side were seated the officers of the vessels of war in the port, and on the other persons of rank or position who had not been otherwise assigned to stations.

Promptly at the appointed time His Majesty Kalakaua, King of the Hawaiian Islands, accompanied by Her Majesty, Kapiolani, his queen, made their appearance. I give the order of the procession to the royal pavilion. Princess Kekaulike, bearing the royal feather cloak, and with her the Princess Poomaikalani; then the Princess Likelike, with the child-princess Kaiulani, and her father, Hon. A. S. Cleghorn; Governor Dominis, and myself; we were all attended by our kahili bearers, and those ancient staffs of royalty were held aloft at our sides. Then followed Prince Kaiwananakoa, bearing one of the crowns, and Prince Kalaniaanole bearing the other crown, succeeded by two others of noble birth and lineage bearing insignia of royalty of either native or traditional usage, the tabu sticks, the sceptre, and ring. Then came Their Majesties the King and Queen, attended by their kahili bearers, who stationed themselves just inside the pavilion. As the royal party entered, the queen was immediately attended by her ladies in waiting, eight in number, all attired in black velvet trimmed with white satin. The long and handsome train of Her Majesty's robe was carried by two ladies high rank and of noble lineage, Keano and Kekaulike.

The Ceremonies were opened with prayer by Rev. Mr. Mackintosh; and then followed one of those coincidences which are so striking on any such occasion, and was certainly noticed as one of the most beautiful incidents of the day. In the very act of prayer, just as he put forth his hand to lift the crown, before placing it on the brow of the king; a mist, or cloud, such as may gather very quickly in our tropical climate, was seen to pass over the sun, obscuring its light for a few minutes; then at the moment when the king was crowned there appeared, shining so brilliantly as to attract general attention, a single star. It was noticed by the entire multitude assembled to witness the pageant, and a murmur of wonder and admiration passed over the throng. The ceremonies proceeded with due solemnity, and the whole scene was very impressive and not to be forgotten. At its close the company retired to the palace in the same order as that in which it had come forth; and the day ceremonies being over the crowd dispersed, retiring to rest from the fatigues and excitements of the day, so as to be able to enter with zest into the festivities of the evening, as a grand ball was to be given at the palace. Indeed, the entire grounds were given up to pleasure such as can only be fully imagined by those who have actually mingled with a happy people in the festivities of a tropical night.

Throughout the week one diversion followed another; until, with citizens and visitors almost surfeited with merrymaking, it came to an end, and Honolulu once more settled down to its everyday quiet and routine. Certainly the coronation celebration had been a great success. The people from the country and from the other islands went back to their homes with a renewed sense of the dignity and honor involved in their nationality, and an added interest in the administration of their government. Honolulu had been benefited in the mean time financially, the merchants and traders of every degree reaping a bountiful harvest from the free expenditure of money by every class. The king has, however, been blamed for expending the public revenues for such a purpose, and this festival is still cited as an instance of his "reckless extravagance." A considerable contingent of the people of New England objected, if I have read correctly, to the building of the Bunker Hill Monument. In my own view the expenditure in either case was quite justified by the end sought. The Saviour himself was once accused of extravagance, or at least of permitting it, not, however, by a truly loyal disciple. The men who "carry the bag" are not always the best judges of royal obligations. It was necessary to confirm the new family "Stirps" — to use the words of our constitution — by a celebration of unusual impressiveness. There was a serious purpose of national importance; the direct line of the "Kamahamehas" having become extinct, it was succeeded by the "Keawe-a-Heulu" line, its founder having been first cousin to the father of Kamahameha I. It was wise and patriotic to spend money to awaken in the people a national pride. Naturally, those among us who did not desire to have Hawaii remain a nation would look on an expenditure of this kind as worse than wasted.

Chapter XVII. Princess Ruth And Mrs. Bernice Pauahi Bishop

In the Spring of 1884 the Princess Ruth completed a handsome residence on Emma Street, and gave a grand luau to celebrate the event. This was followed by a splendid ball in the evening, which was attended by all the best society of Honolulu, whether of native or foreign birth. But after this festivity the princess was taken suddenly ill, and left for Kailua on Hawaii in hopes that the journey would restore her health. She was accompanied by Mrs. Bernice Pauahi Bishop, her own cousin, and also by Mrs. Haalelea. She received every attention, but notwithstanding this, did not recover; and on the twenty-forth day of May her remains were brought back to Honolulu, and laid in state in the handsome new house, Keouahale, which she had just erected. Keouahale has recently been purchased for school purposes by the present government of Hawaii. While lying there in state, the usual native ceremonies attending the death and obsequies of a high chief were accorded to her remains. There were the daily attendance of watchers, the waving of kahilis, and singing of the chants of the departed. To explain the latter I might add that whenever a child was born into one of the families of the high chiefs, it was customary to compose a chant, not only in honor of the event, but further rehearsing the genealogy of the infant, the deeds of its ancestors, and any daring acts of wonderful valor and prowess in which they had participated. These chants were committed to memory, and passed along from mouth to mouth amongst the retainers of that chief. At the death, as at the birth, they were intoned in honor of the one for whom they were composed. I have my own chant, which has been sacred to me all my lifetime. Any child of noble birth who has no such record, were it possible to suppose such a case, would be judged unworthy its rank. It was a further custom observed amongst us for all chiefs of rank parallel to that of the deceased to remain at the house which contained the remains whilst the body was lying in state. So on this occasion Queen Emma, Mrs. Bishop, the Princess Likelike, and myself, all took up our residence at the mansion so recently occupied by Princess Ruth. The celebration of the last rites of interment did not take place until three weeks after her death. When all the honors which her royal rank required had been accorded to her remains, and these had been laid in the mausoleum, it was found that her sole heir was Mrs. Bishop, her nearest living relative, who not only inherited the beautiful residence, but further, all the property of her cousin. Not long after these events it was found that Mrs. Bishop was in failing health; and on consultation with Dr. Trousseau, she was told that the nature of her malady was so grave that she should lose no time in taking advice from the best physicians in San Francisco, to which city he counseled she should go at the earliest opportunity. She accordingly went. On her arrival, she was informed by Dr. Lane that her disease was of the nature of cancer, and that immediate surgical treatment was the best course. She submitted to an operation, and on her recovery from this, returned to the islands. My sister, the Princess Likelike, was in San Francisco at the same time, and returned to Honolulu with her towards the end of that summer. Mrs. Bishop went to her Waikiki residence; and when I called to see if there was anything I could do for her, she besought me to come and stay with her, which I did until the day of her death. It was here that I first noticed the great change which had come over the mind of Queen Emma, and which was more plainly noticed at or just after Mrs. Bishop's decease. About two weeks before the close of her life, it was thought best to remove Mrs. Bishop to Keouahale; but she failed rapidly from the day of the change until the 16th of October, 1884, when she was released from her painful experience. Then there followed a repetition of those rites and ceremonies customary on the death and burial of the high chiefs, such as that house had but just witnessed in the case of Princess Ruth. It was at this time more especially that Queen Emma showed plainly by her peculiar actions that she was suffering from some malady. As time passed away the progress of physical disorder seemed to go on; she grew nothing better, but rather worse, and in the month of April, 1885, she died. Then followed a queer proceeding on the part of her agent. At first the remains were laid in state at her own house; but Mr. Cartwright and a few of his friends took it into their heads to have the casket removed to Kawaiahao church, the apology being that her house was not large enough to accommodate such a gathering as would come together on the day of the funeral. This was accordingly done, much to the wonder and displeasure of those who had charge of the church, and of the friends of the departed queen. Queen Emma was not an attendant there. On the contrary, she had been chiefly instrumental in the founding of the Anglican Mission, and was an Episcopalian. Why, then, supposing it had been at all necessary to select a church for her funeral, did they not select the Episcopal church? That was her own church, and she should have been buried therefrom; for while living she had shown strong attachment to it, and an equally strong feeling of opposition to other denominations. The persons selected by her agent to guard her remains showed no regard for the sacredness of the place. They smoked, feasted, and sang songs while awaiting the last solemn rites due to the dead. However, when the day of the burial came, Bishop Willis of the English Church adapted himself to the circumstances, and officiated from the

Congregational pulpit with the ritual of his own church; after which, with all the pomp and splendor due to her state as a queen amongst the sovereigns of the Hawaiian people, she was borne up the Nuuanu Valley, and laid by the side of her husband, Alexander Liholiho, or Kamehameha IV.

When the will of Mrs. Bernice Pauahi Bishop was read, in which she disposed of her own estate, I did not happen to be present; but her husband, Hon. Charles R. Bishop, informed me that I had been duly remembered, that his wife had bequeathed me the lands of Kahala, island of Oahu, Lumahai on Kauai, Kealia in Kona, Hawaii; besides which he sent me a pair of diamond wristlets, a diamond pin with crown which had once belonged to the Princess Ruth, and a necklace of pearls beautifully chased and set in tigers' claws. But nevertheless I must own to one great disappointment. The estate which had been so dear to us both in my childhood, the house built by my father, Paki, where I had lived as a girl, which was connected with many happy memories of my early life, from whence I had been married to Governor Dominis, when he took me to Washington Place, I could not help feeling ought to have been left to me. The estate was called Haleakala, or House of the Sun, and the residence received the name of Aikupika; but both these are forgotten now in that of the Arlington Hotel. This wish of my heart was not gratified, and at the present day strangers stroll through the grounds or lounge on the piazzas of that home once so dear to me. Yet memories of my adopted parents still cling to that homestead, and rise before me not only when I pass its walls, but as I recall in a foreign land the days of my youth.

Chapter XVIII. Benevolent Societies

Another provision of the will of Mrs. Bishop may be noticed here. It was found that she had made ample provision for the education of the people of her race; and an educational and industrial institute was to be erected, specially limited in its mission to young Hawaiians. The privileges of this commendable charity were likewise restricted by the benefactor to those of the Protestant faith. The Presbyterian churches in Hawaii may profit by this devise; but those of the English Catholic or Roman Catholic Missions are excluded because of their religion, which scarcely makes the institution a national benefit.

In the early part of the year 1886 His Majesty Kalakaua designed and established an organization for benevolent work amongst his people; it was called the Hooululahui. The first meeting of the society having been appointed at Kawaiahao Church, there was a good attendance of the first ladies of the city, not only those of Hawaiian families, but also of foreign birth. It was my brother's intention that the society should have as its head Her Majesty Kapiolani, his queen; but to make it more efficient and systematic in its work, the society was divided into three departments. Of these, the first embraced the central part of the city of Honolulu, and this was under the presidency of the queen. Next came the lower part of Honolulu, Kaumakapili, extending as far as Maemae, and embracing all the district beyond Palama, which was assigned to my management and presidency. In like manner the third division, Kawaiahao, extending through Waikiki and Manoa, Pauoa, and a certain portion of the city, was assigned to my sister, the Princess Likelike. All denominations, including the Roman Catholics, were invited to co-operate in the good work. The Princesses Poomaikalani and Kekaulike, neither of whom is now living, gave their aid to the queen. The former was made governess of Hawaii, and the latter governess of Kauai. These two ladies did all in their power to assist Queen Kapiolani in her work of charity, and my sister and myself were equally interested to attend the needs of our departments; but the responsibility for the general management was really upon the King, who not only had to assume the financial burden, but gave to the work the weight of his official influence, and always responded cheerfully to our calls upon him for advice, giving to us with liberality the advantage of his own good judgment. The people responded with good-will from other parts of the islands, and the work has gone on for over ten years since it was first established by my brother. Of those then interested, Queen Kapiolani and myself are the only two of the managers now living. As Princess Likelike and the other two princesses died, their departments came more under the personal management of the queen. Like many other enterprises of charity, the original intentions of the founders have been improved upon; and the society is merged in other good works, or its purposes diverted to slightly different ends. The organization is now consolidated in the Maternity Home; the charitable funds which used to be distributed amongst the poor, the amounts contributed by the people everywhere to carry out the designs of the king, are still doing good through this institution, of which the Dowager Queen Kapiolani is the president, assisted by a board of managers consisting of notable Hawaiian ladies, and by others of foreign descent.

In the year 1886 I organized an educational society, the intention of which was to interest the Hawaiian ladies in the proper training of young girls of their own race whose parents would be unable to give them advantages by which they would be prepared for the duties of life. As no such association had ever existed, although there had been frequent cases of private benevolence, it seemed a good time to interest those who had the means in this important work. Therefore I called a meeting, notifying all whom I thought would be likely to attend. The response was very gratifying, and on the appointed afternoon a goodly number of our best ladies assembled in the Kawaiahao church. The meeting was opened with prayer; after which I arose, made a short address, and explained to the audience my purpose in requesting attention to the moral and intellectual needs of those of our sex who were just beginning life. These remarks seemed to meet the approval of all present; but yet, in looking around, it was evident to me that the society would be more prosperous in two divisions, as there were those in attendance who could not work well together. My sister, the Princess Likelike, was of our number; so I suggested that she should be the head or president of one division, and I would take the other. Names were then taken, those who announced their willingness to work for the subject were enrolled, and the association was called "The Liliuokalani Educational Society." At our second meeting a constitution was drawn, submitted for approval, and adopted. Both branches then began their work, which went on with results that at one time appeared to be most encouraging. But my sister did not live a year after this movement had begun, and on her death circumstances operated to impair the efficiency of the society. However, her branch of it came under my personal direction; and the object for which I had called the meeting was never forgotten, nor was the education of the young girls of Hawaiian birth neglected either by myself or by those I had interested in its importance, until the changed conditions of January, 1893, obliged me to live in retirement.

On the twenty-fourth day of September; 1886, by request from the king, a charter was granted by the privy council to the Hale Naua, or Temple of Science. Probably some of its forms had been taken by my brother from the Masonic ritual, and others may have been taken from the old and harmless ceremonies of the ancient people of the Hawaiian Islands, which were then only known to the priests of the highest orders. Under the work of this organization was embraced matters of science known to historians, and recognized by the priests of our ancient times. The society further held some correspondence with similar scientific associations in foreign lands, to whom it communicated its proceedings. The result was some correspondence with those bodies who officially accepted the theories propounded by the Hale Naua; and in recognition of this acceptance medals were sent from abroad to the members highest in rank in the Hawaiian society. Unworthy and unkind reflections have been made on the purposes of this society by those who knew nothing of it. Persons with mean and little minds can readily assign false motives to actions intended for good, and attribute to lofty ideas a base purpose or unholy intention. That some good has been done by this organization the members themselves could readily certify. It had been the custom before the days of His Majesty Kalakaua (it is the usage even to the present day) for the chiefs to support the destitute and to bury the dead. This society opened to them an organized method of doing this; it cared for the sick, and it provided for the funerals of the dead. Had the king lived, more good would have been done, and the society would have been in a more flourishing condition; yet the money contributed for its purposes while he lived was invested in stocks, and many persons have drawn benefits from the dividends. Although it was small, it was a beginning.

Chapter XIX. Queen Kapiolani's Journey

On the second day of February, 1887, died the Princess Miriam Likelike, wife of Hon. A. S. Cleghorn, leaving one child, an interesting little girl of eleven years of age, to begin the serious business of life without a mother. She is now the Princess Kaiulani, and has been receiving her education abroad since her fifteenth year. I was tenderly attached to my sister, so much so that her decease had an unfavorable effect on my health. It was, therefore, with satisfaction that I received from my brother, the king, a most unexpected proposition. This was that I should accompany the queen to the grand jubilee at London, in honor of the fiftieth year of the reign of the great and good Queen of Great Britain. It was on a Saturday night early in April that I received this invitation, which I at once accepted. As I was at that time living at my Palama residence, early on Sunday morning I sent a despatch to my husband, who was with his mother at Washington Palace, asking him to come to see me immediately, which he did. I then told him of what had transpired between His Majesty and myself, and that it was my wish and intention to accept. He cordially agreed with me, and said that he would like to be of the party, of which I was very glad. But I was still better pleased when, acting under my advice, he consulted the king, and returned as quickly as he could to tell me that it was settled that he should go with us. Only a few days of necessary preparation were left to us; and by the 12th of April we were ready to embark on the steamship *Australia*, by which we had taken passage for San Francisco.

But I could not think of leaving without saying farewell to some little girls, five in number, the charge of whose education I had assumed, and who were at Kawaiahao seminary. So on the day of departure, at about eleven o'clock I stopped at the schoolhouse. At my coming all the pupils were gathered together into the large room, where I made them an impromptu address, telling them of my intention to sail immediately for foreign lands, encouraging them to be faithful to their duty to their teachers, and warning them that it would distress me more than could be expressed should I ever hear that any of them had done other than right during my absence. After these few farewell words I left the institution, I must confess with some fears in my heart, some misgivings as to the future of some of the girls whom I had addressed. But these doubts were set at rest by their letters, and it made me very happy while I was abroad to hear accounts of their progress and continued good behavior.

The next call after my leaving the seminary was upon my mother-in-law, Mrs. Dominis, to whom, at her home in Washington Place, I bade an affectionate adieu. Then, accompanied by my husband, I proceeded directly to the steamer. Queen Kapiolani and her attendants were already on board; the king was awaiting us there to bid the party farewell. When this was over, and His Majesty had gone ashore, the word was given to get under way, and the steamer took her departure in the presence of one of those immense crowds which throng the wharves on such occasions. On the seventh day out we were boarded by the pilot off the Golden Gate; it was early morning, but by nine o'clock of the same day we were steaming toward our berth at the wharf. On the third day at sea my husband was attacked with rheumatism, which rendered him perfectly helpless, so that he had to be carried ashore on a stretcher. Kind friends succeeded in taking him to the Palace Hotel without occasioning him severe pain, for which attentions they earned my gratitude.

We remained in the city of San Francisco about one week, during which the health of General Dominis improved so that we took one of the northern routes for the city of Washington. While at San Francisco the queen improved every moment to see what she could of the city, this being her first visit to any foreign country. In this pleasure I was unable to participate, my husband's illness having rendered me a watcher by his bedside. But I made the acquaintance of two very charming princesses from Tahiti. They were lovely ladies; one was the Princess Moetia, the other the Arii Manihinihi.

From San Francisco our party pursued its journey across the continent. At Sacramento we received some pleasant attentions, and there were peculiarities of nature in scenery and changing seasons which were most interesting to those from a land of perpetual summer. When we arrived at Summit, for example, there were the lofty peaks covered with their snowy mantles. This was similar, but more extensive, to what we could witness on the tops of the highest mountains on Hawaii; but here it was universal, and the valleys were also filled with snowbanks. Then, when we passed through the long snow-sheds the train came to a stop for a few minutes while some members of our party got off to examine the snow, which blew through the cracks or crevices in the boards to the railroad track. Taking it up and rolling it in their hands, they made snowballs, and pelted each other with it, quite ordinary sport for cold climates, but a rare opportunity for those born in the Hawaiian Islands, and to be always remembered as a novel experience. After coming forth from the sheds again into the light of day, we descended gradually until we reached the Great Salt Lake; and at the city of the same name, the capital of Utah, we stopped a few hours, meeting not only many of the prominent elders of the Mormon Church, but quite a number of our own people who were living there. These were naturally much delighted to meet visitors of their nation so far from home. After a short rest we resumed our eastward course.

The next principal place of which I have a vivid recollection is Denver, which was an infant city then, comparatively just springing into being; there were but a few scattered houses, quite distant from the line of the railway, and not very suggestive of such a thriving city as it is now, I hear, on the site of those humble beginnings. But that which had interested us most along our line of travel was the trees without a sign of leaves or blossoms, since with us the verdure is perennial; and the sight of shrubs or bushes, or even lofty trees, standing out bare of foliage or flower, struck us very strangely. We made no stop in Chicago, and the oil regions of Pennsylvania were the next natural wonders to interest us as we passed through them on the train. Here there were signs of the coming of the summer, the tree-tops being covered with opening foliage, and the grass growing greener. There were some few spring flowers to be seen in bud or blossom by the waysides, and Nature welcomed us with a display of her beauties akin to those of which we had taken farewell in our own beautiful islands.

We arrived safely at Washington, and found comfortable quarters at the Arlington Hotel. Our party consisted of the following individuals: Her Majesty Queen Kapiolani, wife of my brother, the reigning king; Lieutenant-General J. O. Dominis, governor of the island of Oahu, and myself; Colonel C. P. Iaukea, Colonel J. H. Boyd; besides which each of us had our attendants, the queen having four, and each of the others at least one attendant or valet.

Chapter XX. Washington—The White House—Mount Vernon

A few days after our arrival the Queen signified her wish to call on the President, so we all attended Her Majesty to the White House. President Cleveland and his beautiful young bride most cordially received and hospitably entertained us; and a more recent experience of my own would prove that neither one of them has ever forgotten that their position required them to be really the first lady and the first gentleman of the land.

At two o'clock in the afternoon of the same day our call was returned by Mrs. Cleveland, accompanied by the ladies of the cabinet. No person could have shown in her presence a fairer type of youth and loveliness than the wife of the President, and her manner was graceful and dignified in a rare degree for so young a lady. She impressed us with a conviction, since most abundantly justified, that she was well chosen for the duties and responsibilities of an exalted position. On the day following her call we were invited to dine at the executive mansion. The Queen occupied the seat of the guest of honor at the right of President Cleveland, the Secretary of State, Mr. Endicott, attended me to my seat on the President's left; the Hawaiian

Minister, Hon. H. A. P. Carter, was assigned to a seat on Mrs. Cleveland's right; while General Dominis, my husband, waited upon Mrs. Endicott, and was at Mrs. Cleveland's left. The remaining members of the Queen's party were disposed of in proper order, and the dinner passed off with cheerfulness and in due form; it was a grand affair, and arranged with the best of taste. The apartment where it was held had been decorated to do honor to the occasion. The toilet of Her Majesty Queen Kapiolani was of white silk brocade of the choicest Japanese manufacture, artistically embroidered with heavy raised and richly worked designs; it was cut in Hawaiian fashion, a loosely flowing robe of a pattern or mode very becoming to our women, whether made of inexpensive calico or print, or of the finest of silks or most lustrous of satins. A description of this dress was given by all the newspapers, and attracted so much attention that on our arrival abroad the Queen was requested to wear the dress at court, with which solicitation she was happy to comply.

Next to the courtesies extended by the President and the ladies of the executive, perhaps the consideration shown to us by dignitaries of the Masonic order most deserves my notice. General Albert Pike, accompanied by thirteen members of the Supreme Council, thirty-third degree, Scottish Rite, called on the Queen and myself. He was a person of most impressive appearance, a venerable gentleman with long flowing beard and silky white hair resting on his square shoulders, and with the kind, benevolent character and charming manners so appropriate to his official position as the head of the order of fraternity and charity. He greeted us with dignity and cordiality, and left with Queen Kapiolani and myself written evidences of the consideration with which we were regarded by his order. These were certificates, of which mine is always carried with me, giving us the privilege of an appeal to the brethren of the fraternity in any part of the world wherever or whenever they could be of use to us. Both General Pike and the members of his staff were well acquainted with my husband, because General Dominis was of the same Masonic rank, and had maintained frequent correspondence with them on subjects of interest to the world-wide and useful society. While it has now been a joy to me to find my husband still remembered by the Masons of Washington, and to receive from them on my own part evidences of continued interest, I have sorrowed to find some places vacant in the number of those who greeted me so cordially ten years ago, notably that of General Pike.

Many other visitors and social attentions caused the time to fly past most agreeably, several entertainments where the Queen and her party were the guests of honor having been arranged for by the Minister of Hawaii to the United States, the Hon. Henry A. P. Carter. On one of these we were taken to the barracks, and invited to a careful inspection of the quarters for the officers and men. We were received with honors by the commanding officers and their wives, and taken all over the buildings, while the numberless comforts and conveniences of the establishment were exhibited and explained to us. After this an artillery drill was ordered for our special benefit, and we had the pleasure of seeing how expeditiously both men and horses could work the great and destructive field-pieces. After a few hours pleasantly spent in this manner, we returned to our hotel, intending to visit the great historic spot of the American Union on the day following.

So, at as early an hour as was convenient for Her Majesty to be ready, carriages were taken for the wharf, where a boat was awaiting us, placed as our disposal by the courtesy of the United States government. A number of prominent ladies and gentlemen were already on board to be our companions and entertainers, amongst whom I recall the names of Mr. John Sherman, then senator, now Secretary of State; Mr. Evarts, the celebrated lawyer; and many senators, whose names I do not now recall, with their wives. When we were all on board, the lines were cast off, and the little steamer started on her way down the river. It was in the beautiful month of May. The trees were out with their fresh green leaves, the early flowering shrubs were in blossom, and the banks at the riverside were lined with verdure.

The different points of interest, forts, monuments, and public buildings, were pointed out to us, and places we had often heard mentioned identified as we passed along. Near to the grounds, however, the band which had accompanied us, discoursing the sweetest of music, changed to more solemn cadences; and, as the edifices which mark the sacred spot came in sight, the American flag was lowered, the steamer's bell was tolled, the gentlemen removed their hats, and the air of the "Star Spangled Banner" was rendered with impressive effect. The steamer then came to a standstill, and boats were lowered. Into the first the Queen entered; and the whole party disembarked, occupying in all five boats in their transportation ashore. There was but one vehicle at the boat-landing, into which those of us who wished to ride entered, and the party was conveyed to the mansion house.

On arriving we were requested to register our names in the book kept for the purpose in the great central hall; from there we were conducted to the banquet-hall, passing through a smaller room where there was a little, old-fashioned square piano, said to have been the property of George Washington.

The rooms which had been used by General Washington, General Lafayette, and by Martha Washington were opened to us; and we were permitted to enter, and, further, to pause in the lady's bedroom to listen to the story of her constancy to the memory of her husband, whose grave she watched, as she sat daily at her window, from the day of his interment to that of her own death. This story, with the scene of its happening around me as I listened, was most touching to my heart; the simple four-posted, old-fashioned bedstead, with its chintz curtains, the arm-chair with valance and chintz-covering, the well-worn steps descending to a lower floor—these homely souvenirs all spoke to me of the sister woman who had sat and reflected over the loss of that heroic life which it was her privilege to share, and rendered the visit almost too sadly interesting for the accompaniment of a pleasure tour. Why is it, by the way, that she is now "Martha Washington," when even in that day she was always mentioned as "Lady Washington"? Is it a part of the etiquette of the new woman's era, or of the advancing democratic idea?

Another change I noticed in a recent visit was that bars are now placed at the doorways where then we were allowed to enter with perfect liberty to examine everything in the rooms. As time has passed, and the means of visiting the sacred shrine have become more available to the many, it has been found necessary to exclude the crowds that go to Mount Vernon; for the relic-hunter shows no respect to that which is the common property and the priceless heirloom of the people of the United States. So the ladies of the association having the care of this estate are obliged to protect the antique furniture and ancient ornaments from too close inspection.

After spending many interesting moments in the examination of the house and its contents, we went out upon the lawn, and had our photographs taken in a group, Mr. Sherman being the Queen's escort, and Mr. Evarts performing a like gallant duty for me. The next point of interest was the tomb where lie the mortal remains of that great man who assisted at the birth of the nation which has grown to be so great. Although it is but an humble resting-place for one so honored in the remembrance of mankind, yet the sight of the sarcophagus of the general and his wife as they lay side by side, the fresh, warm sunlight streaming through the iron bars which formed the gateway or entrance to the tomb, made a great impression on me; and although the Queen's party were silent, and exchanged no comments, it seemed to me that we were one in our veneration of the sacred spot and of the first President of his country. After this lull in the conversation, the party turned as if by common consent to retrace their steps toward the river, where our boats awaited us. The wild-flowers were blooming beside our footsteps, the birds were chirping in the budding trees, or chasing each other through the branches. Mount Vernon was at its loveliest. There was more of the real face of nature there then than is found today, for now the wild flowers are notably absent. We returned to the city with the consciousness of taking with us the pleasantest of memories of our excursion, and a renewed appreciation of the hospitality of the nation whose capital city we were visiting.

Chapter XXI. Boston And New York—En Route For England

Leaving Washington, we next visited the city of Boston, where on arrival we found that apartments had been engaged for us at the Parker House. We considered these the pleasantest rooms we had seen, and enjoyed excessively the liberality and good taste with which the city council had arranged for our comfort and pleasure. A committee from that body waited upon us, and did everything possible to make our visit a success. Receptions were given to us by His Excellency Governor Ames, and by His Honor Mayor O'Brien, to which cards of invitation were sent to well-known and prominent citizens. But besides these there was a general reception held at the Mechanics' Pavilion, an audience chamber capable of holding some twelve thousand persons; and it seemed as though everybody came, for it was packed with dense masses of people of either sex, to its farthest corner. We shook hands with multitudes. They seemed to enjoy it; and I know we took its fatigues most good-naturedly, as a delightful experience of democratic good-will.

Many pleasant excursions were arranged for our party while in Boston; amongst these was one to the Waltham Watch

Factory, in which we were very much interested. To see each part of so delicate a piece of mechanism as a watch made from its very beginning until the perfect timepiece was ready for the wearer, afforded us much pleasure, and gave a new enjoyment to the possession of these indispensable articles.

We were shown the harbor or port of Boston, by means of a trip to Deer Island, and made visits to the city institutions for the care of criminals and paupers, and to other localities of interest. A small steamer was provided for our party and the invited guests of the city; refreshments were served on board, and everything was done to make the afternoon pleasant for us. Queen Kapiolani was much interested in the quarters assigned to the women at Deer Island, and went through them with careful inspection. There was one inmate with whom the Queen spoke most kindly; she was a woman said to be over a hundred years old, and was yet in the possession of her faculties.

Mr. and Mrs. Benjamin Keola Pitman, formerly residents of the Hawaiian Islands, accompanied us that day. From Mr. Benjamin Pitman, Sr., we had already received a visit at the Parker House. Which sudden reversion to personal friends leads me naturally to say, that, apart from the hospitalities received from the city of Boston, a day was reserved in which we received the relatives of my husband in a family gathering. At the hour appointed we descended to the reception room, and I found myself indeed amongst friends. There were the Lees, the Snellings, the Joneses, the Jabcobses, the Emersons, and others whose names I cannot at this moment recall. I also remember one most welcome guest, not of our own family, Mr. George W. Armstrong.

There were a hundred or more, old and young, relatives of whom General Dominis had often spoken to me, and even some whom he himself now met for the first time, but all cordially happy to recognize their relations from those distant Sandwich Islands of which they had so often heard. There were kisses, affectionate embraces, and many other expressions of regard which made me feel that I was at home with my own family rather than with strangers in a foreign land. The day passed speedily and pleasantly away.

But the time arrived when we must bid adieu to our hospitable entertainers, and depart for the city of New York. In New York we remained eleven days before sailing for England; but I was ill during this time, apparently from a severe cold, and obliged to rest quietly in my rooms at the hotel. During my illness Mrs. James B. Williams was very attentive to me, often calling to see me, accompanied by her husband and daughter. She even sent her own family physician. The Queen and the rest of the party improved the time in the great metropolis, seeing as much as possible of all there was to be seen, and receiving many attentions from prominent individuals. Admiral Gherardi's ship was lying in port, to which Queen Kapiolani and her party made a visit, being received by the gallant sailor with all the honors due to her rank and station. She was also much interested in her visit to the Metropolitan Museum, the mummies exciting her curiosity and wonder, as speaking of the people of a remote antiquity.

My interest was also aroused, and in spite of illness I accompanied the party. I recall a queer little mummy, centuries old, of whose history we learned some most peculiar details. After yards and yards of linen cloth had been unrolled, there was exhibited to us a prettily formed little hand; it was very lifelike, dark-colored, but appearing as that of a person who had but recently died; we were told that the mummy was of a woman, and that the writings with it signified she had been the mother of three children. It was very wonderful how perfectly everything had been preserved by the embalmer's art, even the cloth in which the form had been wrapped being in a perfect state of preservation. But the naturalness of the hand made the curiosity almost too startling for enjoyment, and I turned away from the sight because it spoke too plainly of death and burial.

We met many pleasant people in the city of New York, yet it is natural that I should recall best those of whose history I knew something in my own country. We visited Mrs. Kaikilani Graham, a lady of Hawaiian birth, who had married a resident of this city. She and her husband received us very cordially in a convenient little suite of rooms, or "flat," just cozy enough for the newly wedded pair. She took great pride in showing to us their child, a pretty baby; and she was happy in the fact that it was born on American soil.

But our eleven days' visit was drawing to a close, and the steamer by which we were to embark for our destination was ready for our reception. This was the *City of Rome*, the largest steamship I had ever seen, and at that time about the largest afloat in the world. As we stood on the deck to bid farewell to the land, it was very amusing to me to see the four little steamers plying about our slowly moving hull, pushing the bow this way and that, so that our course might be directed towards the broad ocean; finally it would appear that their purpose was accomplished, and drawing away from us, they allowed the huge ship to make her own way down the harbor and off to sea.

She was crowded with passengers, at least a thousand souls being on board, all sorts and conditions of men and women. There were a large number of musical people — well-known singers or musicians — going abroad for study, or leaving for their homes after professional engagements in America; the usual number of health seekers; those tourists who may be found everywhere intent on seeing the world; then a few like ourselves, to whom the Queen's Jubilee was the grand attraction abroad. A strange mixture of humanity, and just at the place where one has little to occupy the mind save to study those by whom one is surrounded. It was interesting to see the different methods by which each person sought to pass away the time; to me it was natural to turn to music, my usual solace in either happy or sad moments, so I composed songs, one of which certainly was written in anticipation of meeting in the person of the good queen all that was greatest and noblest in a woman or a sovereign. These hopes were fully realized during our stay in London.

Many of the passengers had recourse to the ship's library, which was well supplied with books from the best authors; and with these they beguiled the time away reading, while reclining in their steamer chairs on the decks. Some with less of literary taste played games; while there were also the languid or lazy, who did nothing but lounge about the decks and wish the time away. By the kindness of the musical part of our company, some two or three concerts were given in the main saloon of our great ship, and were well attended. Through them quite a sum was raised for sundry charitable objects. Although the names of the performers have passed from my memory, yet I remember that it was asserted at the time that these voices, of which they made a gift to the cause and a pleasure to us, were of great value in the musical or operatic world.

There was one purpose for which an entertainment was given which was peculiar to this ship and this voyage. It was for the benefit of a shipwrecked crew we had on board. Just outside of the port of New York there had been a frightful collision, and the *City of Rome* had been fortunate enough to rescue a goodly number of those who otherwise might have found a watery grave. Their condition, however, was pitiable; for they had saved nothing of their effects, and in the confusion of the wreck had lost husbands, wives, or traveling companions. After their rescue some were lying in pain and suffering on board our ship, uncertain what had become of those dear to them. Their desolate condition appealed to all hearts, and we were only too glad to attend the concert and contribute our share to their relief. Then there was the regular concert which is held aboard all the steamships which ply the Atlantic route, that for the British sailors, whose widows and orphans look to the multitude of tourists for funds to aid them in the hour of need.

There was but one hindrance to our enjoyment of the passage across, and this was not to be avoided. For a few days the weather was thick and misty, so that the dismal sound of the great fog-horn of the *City of Rome* never ceased by day or night. But, after all, the delights and troubles of the trip were soon over. In about five days we were told to prepare to see the coast of Ireland; in another twenty-four hours we had landed the mails at Queenstown, and were on our way from thence to our port of destination, Liverpool.

Chapter XXII. Arrival—Liverpool—Some English Towns

Our earliest greeting came from Col. George W. Macfarlane, who sent off two magnificent bouquets, one for Queen Kapiolani and one for myself. There were received in the stream, because our steamer was of such immense size that she did not proceed immediately to the dock, but lay off a distance of about five miles. But while we were at lunch a small steamer was seen approaching our vessel; and as we were told that this was intended to transfer us to the shore, we at once made preparations to leave the *City of Rome*. But there was to be quite a state reception before we were permitted by our friends to land. For by the "tender," or steam-tug, there came many passengers to greet us, and these had been conducted to the grand saloon. It was the intention of Queen Kapiolani to go there in order to bid the captain of the ship farewell, but on our arrival we were met by quite a company. Amongst these were the Hon. Theodore H. Davies, the British Consul to Hawaii; Mr. R. H. Armstrong, the Hawaiian Consul at London; Rt. Rev. Bishop Staley, formerly Anglican Bishop of Honolulu; Mr. Janion of the mercantile house of Janion, Greene, & Co., long in mercantile relations with the Hawaiian Islands. These all bent the knee, kissed the hand of the queen, and saluted the rest of us with proper form; after which the conversation became general, and some most pleasant moments passed in cordial greetings with these our friends. Finally we were transferred to the little steamer, and started towards the shore. On our way we were much interested in the great stone piers, the walls, the fortifications—all of which were pointed out and explained by those who welcomed us. On passing the forts we were told that the salutes to the royal party had been fired, as was ordered the moment it was telegraphed that we were safely across the great oceans of the Pacific and Atlantic.

A half-hour's sail brought us to the pier selected for our landing. The little steamer was made fast, and we prepared to disembark. Looking up the wharves all along the piers, just as far as the eye could reach, on the right or on the left, could be seen thousands of heads; the populace generally had heard of the expected landing of Her Majesty the Queen of the far-off Sandwich Islands, and there had been a grand rush of the curious of the city to meet her and her suite. As we landed from the steamer, directly on our left was a military escort which consisted of about one hundred of the soldiers of Her Majesty Queen Victoria. These had arrived from Southampton that very day, and were specially detailed to do us honor. They were a splendid body of men; and as we passed along in front of them to our carriages, they presented arms and saluted the queen while the band which was with them played the well-known strains of the British national anthem, "God Save the Queen." Then the party moved up the dock, at the gateways of which, or entrance to the city, we were met by the lord mayor of Liverpool, with his attendants. He was decorated with the insignia of his office, and welcomed us to the city of which he was the official head.

Here our party was increased by the addition of a larger number of our friends, amongst whom I recollect Mrs. Janion with two young nieces; Mr. John Macfie, son of Mr. R. A. Macfie; Mrs. R. H. Armstrong; and also an official representative of Her Majesty Queen Victoria, who was assigned to us during our stay. This was Mr. R. T. Synge, a gentleman of the Foreign Office, whom Lord Salisbury, then Premier of England, had intrusted with the charge of our party. I think our retinue consisted of five carriages with outriders on each side. Queen Kapiolani and I occupied the coach in which was the lord mayor. My husband, Colonel Iaukea, and Colonel Boyd had a carriage to themselves, attended by one of the city officials. As I looked through the windows I could not refrain from remarking on the splendid appearance of the cavalry by which we were escorted. The men were all tall, square-shouldered, muscular looking fellows, of equal height and similar appearance. The horses, too, were just as carefully matched, being alike in color, a rich brown, splendidly caparisoned, and with all their accoutrements of the neatest and most carefully burnished materials. They rode along proudly by our sides; but, although it was scarcely the season for it, I remember noticing that the steam came from the nostrils of the horses as if it were cold weather. I was told that the peculiar atmosphere of the city of Liverpool, damp to saturation, made this phenomenon quite usual.

Arriving at the Northwestern Hotel, we were conducted from our carriages to the quarters which had been reserved for us. After rest and dinner, the queen and most of the party went to the theatre; but I had not fully recovered from the severe cold taken in New York, and did not consider it prudent to go out.

About eleven that night the queen's party returned from the theatre, and the next morning there was an elaborate breakfast given to us by the lord mayor; he himself escorted the queen. Lord Derby was assigned to me; he was a most agreeable gentleman. There were many other persons of prominence present, and the entertainment passed off very delightfully. Later we were taken to an organ recital given for our enjoyment by a gentleman who was said to be the best organist in all England. On the day following we took a train, intending to go to Norwich to visit a country gentleman by the name of Stewart. On our way we passed by fields covered with the richest blossoms of yellow gold; the display extended over acres and acres of fertile lands, and was indeed lovely to the sight, even had there not been an element of usefulness connected with it. We were told that these were mustard fields, from whence the seed is raised that is ground and used so extensively on our tables the world over. We also passed through pretty villages, their neat dwellings surrounding the parish church with its tall steeple; in fact, we were charmed with our introduction to the country life of a land of which we had always heard, Old England.

Finally, there was pointed out to us a picturesque castle which had been owned by some celebrated family somewhere about the sixteenth century. But the family to whom it had descended becoming extinct, or unable to maintain there a proper state, the estate had been purchased by Mr. Stewart, who was a man of great wealth, and it had been made a most attractive country-seat. The grounds were extensive, and taken care of with the utmost attention. The occupant had but one child, a son, heir to not less than a couple of millions on his attainment of majority, and the probable successor of his father to this great and beautiful estate. Prior to our arrival at the mansion, while we were at Ipswich, the mayor of the city came forth to welcome us; he was clothed with the robes of office, and was attended by others bearing the insignia of power. He gave us a most cordial greeting; and in his company we met our host, who, with his amiable wife and only son, did all that was possible to make us at home in his magnificent castle.

A dinner was arranged for that evening, and all the prominent people of the immediate vicinity were invited to be present to meet us. During the evening the mace of Queen Elizabeth was exhibited to us by the lady in whose charge and keeping it was; her name has escaped me for the moment, but she fully realized the importance of the trust. She told us that it had been handed down in her family from the time of Queen Elizabeth; that it had been delivered to her by her father, whose proud privilege it had been to have especial care of it, and that since he resigned the charge it had never been suffered to go out of her keeping. Others had aspired to its possession, amongst them members of the royal family itself; but she had maintained that, as it was originally delivered to her family, none had a better right than they to its care and custody. We were also conducted outside the house, or castle, and shown its beautiful and spacious grounds. Here the queen was requested to plant a tree. A silver spade with ebony handle was given to her, and she cheerfully complied with the request of our host. Near by there was one of the most perfect trees that could have been imagined; it was a beech with dark brown glossy leaves. It was celebrated far and near for its beauty, and was certainly one of the handsomest trees which it has ever fallen to my lot to behold.

Bidding our genial hosts adieu, we passed on to the next town, where we were handsomely entertained at another old castle to which the people of prominence in the neighborhood had been invited. Amongst these were the dean and his wife from the neighboring cathedral, and Mr. Colman, the celebrated manufacturer of mustard; he was also a member of parliament. The people of the district, hearing of our arrival, came in crowds to meet us, and were much interested in all that was going on. Amongst the guests at the Castle was an elderly lady who appeared to be particularly interested in the Anglican or Episcopal Church at Honolulu, and made special inquiries in regard to Mr. Gowan, one of the preachers there, who then was one of the youngest of our clergymen and quite a favorite, but who has since married and settled at Victoria, Vancouver's Island. The next place of interest visited was St. Peter's Church, the chimes of which were rung for our enjoyment. It was a new harmonic experience, and very delightful; although I noticed that the men who rang seemed to do it with the greatest effort, but in chiming one man is assigned to each bell-rope. The method of ringing the bells by playing upon keys, very much as one would produce the tones from a piano or organ, may be less fatiguing, but a more metallic sound is produced, and it is far less artistic and melodious to the lover of music.

After visiting many other points of interest, at all of which everything was done for our entertainment, we prepared for our departure to London, arriving there a few days prior to the 20th, the day of the celebration, which was also Monday. The whole city was in commotion in view of the coming great event—the Jubilee of the sovereign. Rooms were assigned to us at the Alexandra, where there were many other members of the royal families of the distant world. Amongst these were Prince Komatzu of Japan; the Siamese Prince, brother of the King of Siam; the Prince of India; and the Prince of Persia. At other leading public houses were quartered the princes and princesses of the nations of Europe.

Chapter XXIII. Sovereign Of England And India

Immediately after our arrival Queen Kapiolani sent messages of congratulations to Her Majesty Victoria, Queen of Great Britain and Empress of India; and arrangements were made for us to present our felicitations in person at Buckingham Palace on Monday at one o'clock in the afternoon. At twelve precisely of that day, Queen Victoria and her suite entered London, coming from Scotland where she had been residing for some time. The streets were thronged with people anxious to catch a glimpse of their beloved sovereign. Strange it seemed to me at the time to learn that many who had grown from youth to age in London during a whole lifetime had never seen their queen. Accompanied by her favorite daughter Beatrice and her husband, Prince Henry of Battenberg, the queen was driven to Buckingham Palace, preceded by a detachment of her celebrated Life Guards, outriders from the same regiment being detailed for each side of Her Majesty's carriage.

When the hour approached for us to go and meet her, an officer came from the palace; and Queen Kapiolani and I, attended by Colonel Iuakea and Mr. Synge, took our departure for the hall of reception. We were shown into a large room, where some of the princes had already arrived; and our first greeting came from the Premier, Lord Salisbury. He was then a fine-looking gentleman of imposing presence. He seemed to me to be some sixty-eight years of age, tall and large, with a slight stoop at the shoulders, but with fire and brilliancy in his eyes which spoke of an active mind. I could not help being impressed with the man, the scope of whose mind must command the vast widely spread problems of the government of the empire of Great Britain. Mr. Gladstone has been called "The Grand Old Man," yet this thought was strongly emphasized to me also in the presence of Lord Salisbury. He has always appeared to me to be the greater man of the two. If his rule has been less popular and more conservative, it has required no less devoted patriotism and lofty abilities. I attribute the present prosperity of the British Empire very largely to the consummate wisdom and stanch loyalty of Lord Salisbury.

While Lord Salisbury was entertaining with his conversation the royal guests, two ladies entered the room where we were, and curtsying to me, stood by my side a little in the rear of my chair. I hinted to them that the queen was sitting at my side; but they pleasantly acknowledged the information with a bow, and said that they were sent in to attend me, to which I responded with a salutation. While this was going on we saw a trifling occurrence, which, however, proved to us that human nature is about the same in the palace as in the cottage. Several of the ladies of the royal household passed through the hall, and stopped just long enough, as they went by the door, to get a peep at the strangers from over the sea. So it would appear that even royalty can forget strict etiquette under the impulse of feminine curiosity.

We were not kept waiting much longer; for Lord Lathom, accompanied by the Honorable Secretary Ponsonby, appeared, and led the way to the audience chamber. They carried their batons of office. Queen Kapiolani arose, greeted, and, with her suite, followed them. We were perhaps twenty-five feet apart as we entered the reception room, the queen attended by Colonel Iaukea, and I by the Hon. Mr. Synge, the two ladies-in-waiting following me. At the end of the hall there was an official whose business it was to open and shut the door of the audience chamber. As it was now open, he held his baton of office across it, but at the approach of Queen Kapiolani and Colonel Iaukea he removed it, and allowed them to pass in; then I entered alone, and our party stood in the presence of the British Queen.

The room was of very moderate size, with a sofa at one end on which Her Majesty sat; besides this there were only two chairs, all the other furniture, if ever there were any, having been removed. At a farther window stood H. R. H. the Duke of Connaught and T. R. H. the Prince and Princess Henry of Battenberg. Her Majesty Victoria greeted her sister sovereign, Kapiolani, with a kiss on each cheek, and then, turning to me, she kissed me once on the forehead; we were asked to be seated, the two queens sitting together on the sofa and engaging in conversation, which was translated by Colonel Iaukea. In the meantime I occupied one of the chairs. Queen Kapiolani expressed her congratulations on the great event of the day, and her gladness that the Jubilee found Her Majesty in good health, and added her expressions of hope that she might live many years to be a blessing to her subjects. The Queen received her good wishes with a like spirit of cordiality, thanking her for coming so far to see her, and then went on to speak with enthusiasm of the pleasure she had taken in meeting her husband, my brother, King Kalakaua. She said she had been much pleased with him, and had never forgotten his agreeable visit. In the meantime the Duke of Connaught was at my side, and we exchanged a few pleasant words. Next came the Princess Beatrice, who, after an expression of kindly interest, returned to her former station. Queen Victoria then entered into a little conversation with me, confining her remarks chiefly to educational matters, and asked me with some detail about the schools of the Hawaiian Islands. We then rose to make our adieus.

The End of Hawaii's Independence

The two queens exchanged kisses as before, and the Queen of England again kissed me on the forehead; then she took my hand, as though she had just thought of something which she had been in danger of forgetting, and said, "I want to introduce to you my children;" and one by one they came forward and were introduced. After this I hesitated a moment to see if she had anything further to say to me, and finding that she had not, I curtsied to her and withdrew. By the time I had reached the door of the audience chamber, Queen Kapiolani had arrived at the farther end of the hall, and thinking I was alone, I hastened my steps to rejoin her; but soon I was conscious of the presence of the ladies-in-waiting by hearing the whispered words, "Their Majesties." On looking about me I saw at the door to my left two very fine-looking gentlemen standing side by side in the doorway, one in a gray suit and the other in black, both carrying canes. They acknowledged my presence by a most gallant salutation, as I slightly bowed to them in passing; then they resumed the subject of their conversation. These were His Majesty the King of Denmark, and His Imperial Highness the Crown Prince, father of the present Emperor of Germany. On finding myself again with my sister-in-law, we prepared to enter our carriage and return to our hotel. Thus terminated my first interview with one of the best of women and greatest of monarchs.

Chapter XXIV. The Reception At The Foreign Office

That evening an entertainment was given at the Foreign Office at which we were expected to be present. I expressed a wish on leaving the hotel to go in a carriage with my husband, which naturally placed the duty of escort to Queen Kapiolani on Colonel Iaukea and Hon. Mr. Synge. According to etiquette, by taking this step I was obliged to ride in one of the carriages belonging to the legation of Hawaii; and, as only the royal carriages could go to the principal entrance, the carriage in which I was would be obliged to present itself at the side entrance. But when we got there, and Colonel Boyd, our attendant, was asked whose carriage it was, he replied, "It is the carriage of the Crown Princess of Hawaii." Then the officer said that we had made a mistake by coming to that entrance. However, we passed in, and I was conducted to the waiting-room which had been assigned to the royal ladies for their exclusive use, while my husband and Colonel Boyd were taken to the room assigned to the use of the generals.

In the room I entered, what was my surprise to see my sister-in-law, Queen Kapiolani, standing almost alone and unattended, as though she were at a loss what to do next. Near me was a fine lady, a Grand Duchess from one of the small German principalities. She had entered the room about the same moment with me; and comprehending the situation at once, and knowing that I spoke English, while the queen did not, she turned to me and said; "Why does not the queen sit down, so that we may all be seated?" Upon receiving from me a hint in our native language, the queen complied with this wish, and we were all soon at our ease. Then there entered several gentlemen of royal blood—the King of Hanover, and princes and princesses of European countries—and we adjourned to the grand reception room. We were ushered into a large hall, well filled with ladies of rank, and all of them most magnificently dressed to do honor to the occasion.

It would seem that each of these had brought out the family heirlooms in precious stones. There were duchesses with shining tiaras, marchionesses with coronets of flashing stones, noble ladies with costly necklaces or emerald ear-drops, little women who seemed almost bowed down under lofty circlets of diamonds over their brows, tall women bearing proudly off their adornment of stones of priceless value. I have never seen such a grand display of valuable gems in my life. There was such a profusion of brilliant and handsome jewels before my eyes, that to compute its worth would be to lose one's self in a maze of confusing calculation. Yet there was amidst the shining throng one young lady, tall and of commanding presence, whose sole ornament was a single glittering star fixed in her hair. It shone forth more brightly, attracted my gaze more quickly, and its elegant simplicity excited my admiration above all others. She was a lady of high rank, and it is a matter of regret to me that I did not learn her name.

While conversing with some of the duchesses who advanced to speak with me, Lord Salisbury made his appearance; and approaching Queen Kapiolani, offered her his arm, leading the way to the centre of the room, my husband and I following. Very soon we were joined by H. R. H. the Duke of Connaught, with Lady Salisbury. As this couple came up I waited a moment with my husband that they might pass in front of us; but the prince motioned to me to assume the precedence, and seeing him pause for us, we passed on, while he and his fair companion followed in our wake. Passing thus through the crowds, who made way as we approached, we were conducted to a side room, where refreshments were served. Here Lord Salisbury placed the queen on his right, and I was notified to be seated on his left, my husband standing behind my chair. The Duke of Connaught addressed him, and asked him to be seated, using as the form of salutation the title of governor. At first Governor Dominis declined, but on being urged by the prince, complied with his polite invitation. This is worthy of mention, because on this occasion the position of honor in the very centre of the room was assigned to our party. On the left of my husband was Lady Salisbury, and by her side the Duke of Connaught; then the Maharajah, Prince of Indore; and so on. The moments sped by very agreeably in general conversation; but as the Duke of Connaught glanced across the apartment, his eye caught sight of Lady Aylesbury, who was at one of the more remote tables. The prince very politely arose, went across the room, and greeted her most gallantly, informing us as he did so, that she was the only one of the ladies of rank now living who had been present at the coronation of his royal mother, whose Jubilee we were then celebrating. She was an elderly lady, with little curls each side of her brow; and this act of courtesy and gallantry to her impressed me as one of the prettiest and pleasantest things seen that evening. From her cordiality to the prince, I doubt not that it was highly appreciated by Lady Aylesbury. After we rose from the tables, we mingled in social conversation with the guests of the evening for a few minutes, and then retiring from the rooms returned to the hotel.

Chapter XXV. The Jubilee—At The Abbey—At The Palace

On the following, or great day of the Jubilee, we were to be present in the morning at the historic church of Westminster Abbey; and the hour of half-past ten had been appointed for General Dominis and Colonel Boyd to take their positions there. Our party, consisting of the members of royal families, left at eleven o'clock, the procession being led by the Japanese Prince; then followed the Prince of Persia, the Prince of Siam, and then the Indian Prince.

Succeeding these came the Queen of the Hawaiian Islands with myself, and to us was accorded the most unusual honor of an escort drawn from the Life Guards of Her Majesty Queen Victoria. This was scarcely expected, but we were told that it had been especially granted to the Queen and Crown Princess of Hawaii. When we spoke of the high appreciation we felt of this and all the attentions we had received, we were assured in response, that, as we had come such a long distance to do honor to the occasion, Her Majesty had thought that the least she could do was to provide for us special honors. We were given one of the queen's own carriages, with horses and drivers, during our stay in London. Our drive to Westminster Abbey was a short one. We passed through crowds and crowds of people, both sides of the street being thronged, but there was perfect order; besides which, the Life Guardsmen were on each side of our carriages. Detachments from the British navy, and members of the metropolitan police, were stationed at every point. But it was a happy, good-natured crowd (eleven millions, so I heard it estimated), assembled in the great city of London to congratulate the sovereign on her semi-centennial anniversary. As we passed from the Alexandra to the beautiful Abbey, cheering could be heard on every side; the fronts of the houses were a living mass of humanity. Benches were placed along their fronts, on which the people stood or sat, and every party that passed received enthusiastic salutations.

On reaching the doors of the Abbey, our party was met by Lord Lathom and Sir Henry Ponsonby, as representatives of Queen Victoria; and by them we were conducted to the seats reserved for our use. Colonel Iaukea and Hon. Mr. Synge disappeared at once as though swallowed up in the vast crowd which had been gathering in the place since the early hours of the morning. As the people arrived, they were arranged by the ushers in charge according to their rank. As delegation after delegation came in, each was quietly and properly assigned to its appropriate station.

In the centre of the great edifice, there was a raised platform or dais, to which we were conducted. Soon after us a most prominent party arrived, and were also seated on the dais. We found them to be the kings, queens, princes, and princesses from several of the European countries. There was a little lady who made her appearance accompanied by her husband, who was blind; she seated him on a bench back of that we occupied; then she proceeded to adjust his necktie, she pulled down his coat and smoothed it out, and arranged other parts of his uniform to suit her own taste. Finally, when his appearance seemed to her satisfactory, she left him, and coming towards us took a seat directly between Queen Kapiolani and myself. This lady was none other than the Grand Duchess of Mecklenburg-

Strelitz, whose royal cousin, Queen Victoria, was celebrating the Jubilee of the day. On the left of my sister-in-law sat the Queen of the Belgians.

    While we were awaiting the opening ceremonies, the grand duchess turned to me and said, "*Parlez vous Français?*" Upon my response in the negative, she addressed to me a similar question, only this time asking if I spoke English; to which I replied, "Yes, a little." Then, much to my amusement, she motioned to the princesses opposite to us that her companion understood English, and we were very soon in a most agreeable and animated conversation on the topics of the day. Soon the band began the grand and solemn strains of "God Save the Queen," and all but a few arose under the impression that it announced the entrance of Her Majesty Queen Victoria. The little duchess inquired of me why I was rising, and without awaiting a reply volunteered the information that the anthem was probably in honor of the arrival of some members of the royal family. And this proved to be the fact; for almost immediately there appeared a company of ladies, these being the daughters, granddaughters, and daughters-in-law of Queen Victoria. They advanced, and took their seats on the left side of the dais.

    Their entrance was followed by another blast from the bugles and a further measure of the national anthem, to which there responded a company of the sons and grandsons of the reigning sovereign, led by His Royal Highness the Prince of Wales. These took their seats on the right of the dais, and thus we were surrounded by the royal household. After all was tranquil, there followed a final flourish of the trumpets; and for the third time the band gave us "God Save the Queen," and at this salutation there appeared Her Majesty Queen Victoria, preceded by the Archbishop of Canterbury and four other bishops. Slowly they proceeded to the stations which had been reserved for them, in the centre of the great church at the end farthest from the people, but quite near to where I sat, so that I could watch them to my perfect satisfaction.

Queen Victoria ascended the dais, and advanced to her seat at its very centre, where there was a plain-looking, old-fashioned armchair, said to have once belonged to St. Peter himself. She stood at a spot just opposite to this seat. All the rest of us had risen, and remained standing during her approach. Before seating herself, she made a little curtsy, which salutation was returned by all those who had awaited her coming from the opposite dais or platform. She was simply attired in a neat, black dress, wearing a bonnet very small and unobtrusive, while about her neck she wore a handsome necklace composed of single stone diamonds. After she was in her seat, and the rest of us had followed her example, the religious services were begun, and most impressive they seemed.

The Archbishop of Canterbury opened the ceremony with prayer. Then followed the Te Deum; and the music must have had an especial charm of tender regret for the queen, for it was the composition of the Prince Consort, her deceased husband. Thus the grand pageant of religious worship proceeded; and while up rose the prayers of the vast assembly, involving the blessing of the Almighty upon the head of the great British Empire, a gleam of God's sunshine penetrated through one of the windows, and finding its way from the casement across the grand temple, illuminated with its radiance the bowed head of the royal worshipper. It was a beautiful emblem of divine favor, and reminded me of the coincidence of which mention has been made that occurred at the moment of the coronation of my brother in Hawaii.

The inspiring anthems, as they were so grandly and harmoniously rendered by the great choir, lifted all hearts up to the Ruler of the Universe, and the solemn tones of the great organ hushed every thought inconsistent with the devout worship of the occasion. When this part of the ceremony came to a close, Her Gracious Majesty received the homage of her daughters and granddaughters, tenderly kissing each one in turn. They responded by a respectful kiss on the royal hand. The sons and grandsons next went through a similar manifestation of affection and respect, after which the procession began to form for leaving the Abbey. Its order in departing was exactly the reverse of that at the entrance, those preceding who had been last to arrive; finally, the last of the lords and ladies, dukes and duchesses, princes and princesses, kings and queens, were out of doors and on the way back to Buckingham Palace. The crowds had never left the streets and sidewalks, but had remained in position so as to get another view as we passed along. The sea of heads on both sides of the royal party had not diminished perceptibly by so much as one individual, the gay decorations were all in place, and flags and streamers floated from every point. Never could there have been a day when London was more lavish of its holiday attire.

When we arrived at Buckingham Palace, I was waited on by the Duke of Edinburgh, whilst Queen Kapiolani was under the escort of the heir to the British throne, the Prince of Wales. In the banquet hall was a long table through the centre, which took up the entire length of the room; this was assigned exclusively to the visiting kings and queens from every part of the world, many of whom had traveled long distances to be present at this Jubilee. Two smaller tables were attached at each end of the long one, and these were set apart for the princes and princesses who were also the guests of the nation. To one of these tables, and towards its centre, my escort, H. R. H. Prince Alfred, Duke of Edinburgh, and now of Saxe-Coburg, conducted me, and gave me a seat; on my right was the present Emperor of Germany, who proved to be a most sociable neighbor, and an agreeable conversationalist, so that we kept up quite an animated flow of words. Truthfully speaking, I think the Duke of Edinburgh was not quite easy in his mind. He was the Lord High Admiral, and was naturally thinking of the long line of officers and men which had been drawn up to do honor to the royal visitors, and who could only be relieved from guard duty by his order. He excused himself to us a few minutes, probably to give some preliminary command to this effect, but soon returned, and still appeared as though he were anxious that the lunch and its ceremonies should be over. I suppose it was the natural uneasiness of the sailor, and a sense of the responsibility he felt for the comfort, and release from duty, of those under his authority.

During the course of the lunch, Prince William of Prussia asked me if I recognized a gentleman sitting opposite to us. I responded that I thought I did, and went on to say, that, to my remembrance it was Prince Henry of Prussia. He said that I was correct, and complimented me warmly on my strength of memory. This was the same prince who had once visited our Islands many years before this date, and whose delightful visit was unexpectedly shortened by the death of his brother Waldemar.

The naval forces were drawn up in a line a short distance from the palace, and as soon as possible after the repast they received the thanks of their royal commander; the officers and the men were assured of the queen's appreciation of their loyalty and devotion, and then all were permitted to retire, each body to its own vessel. I am confident that not a man there was more relieved at the change than the sailor-prince himself, who then became more animated, and more like the duke of whom I had such delightful reminiscences when he visited me in Hawaii—as I have said in a previous chapter of these memoirs.

From the banquet hall Her Majesty, followed by her royal guests, adjourned to a larger room in the palace, commanding a fine view of the streets and squares about us. Here from the windows we watched the marines and the naval forces as they filed past on their way back to the ships from whence they had come. They were a superb body of men, of whom their royal commander, and indeed all England, might well be proud.

After they had marched away, we were shown into a side room where were displayed the presents which had been sent to the queen in recognition of this her jubilee year. They were too many and too varied for me to attempt anything like an enumeration; yet there were one or two pieces which I will mention. Hawaii had sent a unique frame placed on an easel, in the centre of which was an embroidered piece, with the letters "V. R." worked in the rare royal feathers, while the frame itself was studded with diamonds. Then there was a very perfect representation of St. George and the Dragon in the traditional form, but wrought of gold. This had been presented by the Crown Prince of Prussia, husband to the Princess Royal of England, the daughter of Queen Victoria, who was soon after this epoch left a widow by her husband's untimely death. At present she is the Dowager Empress of Germany. I now learn that her afflictions have been increased by a loss sustained in the recent conflagration at the Paris charitable bazaar, a calamity which put more than one household in Europe of royal connections into deepest mourning. After spending some time with us in the examination of her presents, Her Majesty Victoria retired. This was the signal for us to do likewise, so one by one we withdrew to our respective hotels.

As we drove homeward, and passed over the route by which we had come, scarcely a man or woman of all that vast crowd which had congregated there so recently was to be seen; the avenues of travel seemed to have been deserted. Yet the throng had dispersed in so orderly a manner that there had been no confusion, and no accidents were ever reported to mar the joy of the Jubilee.

Chapter XXVI. The Prince Of Wales, "Grand Master" Mason

We were all too much fatigued to think of going out again that evening. Entertainment after entertainment followed in an endless variety, and on too grand a scale to think of enumerating them all, or even of mentioning the many ways in which the royal family of England showed its hospitality towards us. Amongst those who attended me personally, besides the Duke of Edinburgh, I must not forget to notice attentions from Prince Louis of Battenberg and the Grand Duke Sergius of Russia. One evening, after a grand reception, a ball was given at the palace, to which all royalty went to pay their respects to the first gentleman of England, the Prince of Wales, and his amiable wife.

Queen Kapiolani and I were conducted to seats on the dais, where the Princess of Wales, Princess Louise of Lorne, and other members of Her Majesty's household, were seated. It was an excellent point from which to see the dancing, which soon began. While watching the dance, I happened to glance down to the farther end of the hall, and saw the Marquis of Lorne bend his arm cordially about that of my husband, Governor Dominis, and pace to and fro with him about the hall, the two gentlemen seemingly much interested in each other as they engaged in prolonged and pleasant conversation. The entertainment went gayly on until a late hour, and as usual the first movement to retire was made on the part of the royal family; after which the guests began to take leave of each other, and we returned to our hotel.

There was one day set apart during the Jubilee for a Masonic Celebration; and from the grand crowd of visitors assembled in London to do honor to the occasion, invitations were sent to all members of that fraternity. The response was general, and at eleven o'clock of the day appointed the visiting brethren met at Prince Albert Hall. The arrangements were carried to such perfection that each person was conducted without the least confusion to a seat which had been assigned to him. My husband, Governor Dominis, wearing the regalia to which his rank as a Mason of the thirty-third degree entitled him, upon reaching the entrance indicated by the terms of the invitation he had received, found an usher in attendance to escort him to his place. After exchanging the signs and tokens of mutual recognition, he passed into the hall, and his guide conducted him through the vast assembly of the brotherhood. He had not the least idea as to what part of the chamber he was assigned, but followed in the footsteps of the gentleman in whose care he had been intrusted.

Soon they passed in front of the dais, or raised platform, commanding a view of the noble audience. On this was seated the Grand Master of the assembled representatives of the Freemasonry of the world, none other than H. R. H., the Prince Royal, Albert Edward of Wales. As Governor Dominis passed in front of the Grand Master, still ignorant of his own position, Masonic salutations were exchanged; and much to his surprise my husband found himself conducted up to the platform, where on the right of the Prince of Wales the third seat had been assigned to him. His astonishment was succeeded by emotions of pride. Governor Dominis was always a most unassuming man; not at all eager to put himself forward, never presuming in the least to encroach on the rights or privileges of others. But when he found himself thus placed in one of the highest and most honorable positions, it was undoubtedly enough to make his bosom glow. But he valued the honor as a Mason more than as a man; for it was the recognition of his place in an organization whose bond of union was that of brotherly love, and whose ancient and noble rites these high-born or royally connected persons from every part of the globe had assembled to celebrate.

In that great assembly over which the royal prince presided, and into whose upturned faces my husband had the joy of looking, were more than ten thousand men of the different degrees of the order. Prayer was offered by one of the grand chaplains; and the princely Grand Master then rose and initiated the ceremonies by giving out the national anthem, "God Save the Queen", which was sung by all present with an ardor and fervor seldom excelled. United in their bond of affection and brotherly kindness, their hearts were also filled with the spirit of the Jubilee which had allowed them to meet in this grand assembly. It was an occasion to fill all present with a sense of its grandeur and importance; and when my husband returned to me his feelings and sentiments were too profound for expression, too lasting to allow him ever to forget. The usual forms and ceremonies of a Masonic gathering, known and understood only by those of the fraternity itself, had been, I was told, most impressively rendered, and gave great satisfaction to all.

My husband was always a most conscientious Mason, and fulfilled to the letter his duties as a friend and a brother to his order. Many a charitable deed towards the poor of the fraternity was done by him of which no one ever spoke, because no one knew anything about them at the time. Large sums of money have been contributed by him for the purpose of extricating brethren of the Masonic order from financial or other difficulties. These amounts were rarely returned to him; perhaps he had not expected that they would be paid. At any rate, nothing was said of them; but when his papers fell into my hands for examination at his death, they were disclosed to me, and I recognized what a great amount of good had been done, and what a true and faithful Free Mason Governor Dominis had been his life long. At this time the parties he had assisted had left Hawaii, and possibly had retained no thought of him or their obligation; yet a good action is never lost, and his many and beautiful deeds of generosity are precious to my remembrance, and remain a source of consolation to me to this day.

Chapter XXVII. England's Homes And Hospitality

On one of the days when we were free of other engagements, the party of Queen Kapiolani took carriages, and drove out to the residence of Lady Aberdeen, where Mr. Gladstone was staying for a few days. We were received most cordially by himself and his good wife out under the trees on the ground. The weather was favorable, it was a lovely afternoon for social pleasure, and everything was done to make us feel at home in the society of the "Grand Old Man". As I remember his appearance, he was a tall, large-framed man, with broad, high forehead, dark piercing eyes, and a nose which was the most prominent feature of a striking and intellectual face—certainly a countenance and a presence, once seen, not easily to be forgotten. When he spoke, there was a serious thoughtfulness in his remarks, and words of world-wide significance seemed as ready with him as those of common import are with any other. There were a number of visitors claiming the honor of an interview; he listened patiently to anyone's questions, but directed his replies to all those by whom he was surrounded. Mrs. Gladstone was a tall, stylish woman of rather advanced years, of dignified mien and intelligent countenance; she stood by her husband's side during most of the time while he was conversing with his visitors, and from her attentive manner one could not but receive the thought that in the eventful life of the great statesman she must have been a valuable counselor and a sympathetic confidant.

One Sunday soon after this interview, Mr. And Mrs. R. H. Armstrong called at our hotel, and took Governor Dominis and myself, attended by Colonel Boyd, on a little outing in their good company. Mrs. Newman, and her daughter, now Mrs. John Fowler, were also with us. Arriving at the railroad station, we entered the train, by which we were conveyed some distance out of town to a pleasant place called Richmond, situated on the banks of the river Thames.

There we were conducted to a house exhibited to us as the type of an English inn. I was much interested in the edifice; for I had always read from my earliest days glorious descriptions of English inns, where the pleasures of the chase culminated, and to whose doors the trophies of the hunters were brought. But on entering this house there was a little bit of disappointment, or at least wonder, as I surveyed its contracted quarters. The rooms were low-studded and of small size, so that probably no more than fifteen persons could have found accommodations therein. I could have almost reached the ceiling, had I stretched forth my arm and pointed it upward. Then, where were the banquet halls? Surely the inns of which the English novelists had told me must have been on a grander scale than this one to which I was conducted!

From the inn we went on board a steamer, which the forethought of Mr. Armstrong had secured for our comfort, and started out on an excursion which was to introduce a novel experience; for, after steaming up the river a short distance, we came to a lock; to pass it there were in waiting many other water-craft of all kinds, steamers and tow-boats, little vessels propelled by sails, or even small boats by oars and poles. When the gates of the lock were opened, that, and that only, was the moment when these could pass through; so there was such a scrambling in the water about us, such a jostling, such a pushing ahead to see who would get within the lock first, or, more important, that their boat should not be left in the outer waters when the gates closed. It was a lively contest, and often it appeared as though some of the craft would be hopelessly swamped; but the affair passed without accident, for indeed, with all their rivalry, everybody was good-natured, and the occupants of the boats took the matter very cheerfully when passed by a competitor.

But there was one phase of the exhibition which excited my attention, not to say surprise and wonder. This was the indifference of the men in the smaller boats, who lounged in the stern, cigar in mouth, book or paper in hand, while the poor girls with poles exerted their strength to the utmost to shove their boats along into the waters of the lock. Men smoking or reading while the women were doing all the work! Taking their ease, while from those called the weaker sex came the exertions necessary to get the boat into her place amongst the crowd of others. It was not a pleasant picture, nor did it speak of gallantry. I had never seen anything like it.

We all finally got through the gates of the lock, and steamed up the river until we came to a landing, where our attention was attracted by a very pretty sight; this was a house-boat, very nice in appearance, with an upper and a lower veranda, the upper being trimmed with curtains of a red material edged with white. Through the convenient folding-doors, which were opened above, we caught view of a large apartment, which I took to be the reception-room, and the lower room, also thrown open, was probably the dining-room. As we watched this neat home upon the water, there appeared a small skiff rowed by a man, but on the seat in the stern was another occupant—a pretty little lady clad entirely in one prevailing color. On her head she wore a red hat; the parasol she held over it was red; she wore also red gloves and red shoes; but her fair face and golden hair made a contrast most lovely and striking with the tints of her costume and surroundings; and as she turned to look at us, the laughing blue eyes, which peeped out from under her rosy ensemble, made her indeed the picture of a charming Witch of the

Thames. We watched her until she reached her house-boat, and disappeared from our gaze.

On landing, our party wended its way to another of the English inns. It had attracted our admiration from the water as it nestled prettily under the trees by which it was surrounded. On arriving we found a charming place. The long and well-kept walks of gravel and pebbles encouraging us to stray into its grounds; and one by one we followed this inclination, while Mrs. Newman and some others, impressed with the same desire, climbed a neighboring hill. It was not a very difficult one, nor at all high; but it was a conspicuous object, because covered with tempting verdure and dotted with flowers, chiefly of the species of the rhododendron, whose vari-colored blossoms stretched out, all over the hillsides, in charming profusion.

But the wanderers were soon called to return, and the party reunited, because an omnibus had driven up by which we were to be taken to Clifton House, an estate owned by the Duke of Westminster. A short drive brought us to its doors, where we were welcomed, and shown through the apartments. This was nearer to my ideal of an English country-house; for here were lofty ceilings, and a spacious banquet hall, opening out on a lawn of richest and most luxuriant green. Looking out over this verdant foreground could be seen far away in the distance the blue line of the River Thames, winding in and out through the forest trees which rose along its border. The view was most beautiful, and I could well believe that in the past it had been the lordly estate of the Duke of Buckingham. With the aid of a lifelike portrait of a noble lady, which from its place on the walls of the manor looked silently down, I could picture to myself the days in which she had been the charming hostess of the reception-room in which we stood. I could see her doing the honors of this beautiful residence, and making guests welcome to her handsome estate, receiving the grand lords and lovely ladies who met there after the fatigues and excitements of the chase. The element of sport, and the thirst for pleasure, largely influenced the customs of that former epoch in English country life; and yet, with all their gayety, they were able to provide for the sustenance and happiness of a large number of retainers and tenantry without enormous expense. For these, their people, lived under their lords and mistresses with loving submission and loyal devotion, understanding the duties of their station in life, and therewith content; they looked to them for their maintenance and kind consideration, and asked for no more. The relation between master and retainer was one of love on both sides, of pure affection for a trusted and faithful vassal, of devotion and desire to please from the man to the master.

But at the present day all this has gone, the changes introduced by an entirely different civilization have made the former life impossible; the laws of trade, the demands of mercantile life, the advancement of commerce, of which London is the grand centre, have effected a revolution, which has entirely overthrown the relationship existing at other times between the country gentleman and his retainers. Now the lord of the manor rises early, and hurries away to the city, where important matters at the bank, or the shipping-office, or the lawyer's desk, are waiting for him; the places on his old-time estate, which long ago were filled with trusty retainers, are desolate, and often large halls stand permanently vacant. Walls are bare of ornament or picture because there is no one to keep up the establishment. Is England better and happier for the extinction of a style of life read of in history but not today existing? At least, by such souvenirs as this manor house, are pictures brought back to one's mind of a past, that had much in it of sufficient worth to awaken emotions of sadness that it has gone forever.

We again boarded the little steamer which had awaited our return to her decks; and when we were comfortably settled, she steamed away up the river. On the picturesque banks of the Thames we saw, as we passed, many pretty pictures of modern life. The water, too, was alive with moving craft, pleasure-boats and toiling steamers, while at several points were stationed bands of music, the strains of which came softly over the waters to our ears. All these sights and sounds added to the pleasure of our outing; and yet most of the actors in this vivid pageant were, doubtless, only intent on the business of making a livelihood. We went about as far as the depth of the water allowed the steamer to ascend, and then turning, steamed back to the landing. I must not forget to notice that our enjoyment and understanding of the places we passed was increased by the presence of two entertaining young men of leisure invited as guests. They were strangers to us, but contributed much to our pleasure and information. One was a Mr. Skinner, but the name of his associate has for the moment escaped my memory. Disembarking from our steamer, we entered the cars, and were soon again at our hotel, and with the added happiness of having stored away the memory of a most delightful day on the celebrated River Thames, as well as of Mr. And Mrs. Armstrong's charming hospitality.

Chapter XXVIII. Ill News From Hawaii — Our Return

The final entertainment, given to the party of royal visitors from all quarters of the globe, was a garden party, tendered by Her Majesty Queen Victoria, at which she herself and all her good and beautiful children were present. Punctually at the appointed hour the Queen of England, attended by the heir apparent to the throne, H. R. H, the Prince of Wales, accompanied by the princess, his lovely wife, made their appearance; following them came the other members of the royal family. The procession moved along the graveled walks of the palace garden, led by the great and good lady whose jubilee year we were celebrating. It was made up of kings and queens, princes and princesses, from most of the reigning families of the world; on each side of us as we passed stood the crowds of eager and respectful observers; the greensward in the gardens at each side of the walk was a solid mass of people. These were of many ranks and conditions in life, and principally persons of note. Among them were well-known actors and celebrated actresses; naval officers, and other holders of official positions; representatives of almost every class over whom the good queen rules. Here and there, as we advanced, were heard strains of music, tents having been erected for the accommodation of the bands which were in service for the day. I think there were four of these at different points in our march, each composed of the best and most skillful musicians that could be enlisted for the occasion.

We finally paused before two tents which had been assigned to the party. Into one of these entered Her Majesty Victoria, no one going into her tent, excepting only the Prince of Wales. Even the princess, his wife, accompanied the other ladies into the tent which had been provided for our reception. Queen Kapiolani and I had the honor of being directly with this accomplished lady, while her husband, with a son's devotion such as he has always so commendably shown, had gone to attend his royal mother. Close to us was a table sumptuously furnished with all that taste could desire; but however attractive to the eye, I noticed its viands were not liberally consumed.

As we had passed along in the light of day, I had had an opportunity to impress upon my mind the appearance of the Queen of England, and to look at her as a woman, under circumstances far more favorable for permanent impression than in some of the pageants where she had officially appeared. She was sixty-eight years of age at this time, and seemed to be in the best of health. In walking she carried a little ebony cane on which she scarcely leaned. She had been represented to me as short, stout, and fat, and not at all graceful in appearance; but I did not at all agree with the truth of this representation. She was a well-proportioned, gracious, queenly woman. I would not call her handsome; yet she had a kind, winning expression on her face which gave evidence of the gentle spirit within. This was to be our final interview, and the afternoon with its pleasures soon passed away; we bade adieu to our royal hostess, wishing her with all our hearts many, many more years of prosperity as a sovereign, and content and peace as the woman whose name is respected and loved wherever the sun shines throughout the wide, wide world.

Returning to our hotel, we received news which changed at once the current of our thoughts. This was of the revolutionary movement, inaugurated by those of foreign blood, or American birth, in the Hawaiian Islands during our absence. It was indeed a case of marked ingratitude; for this rebellion against constituted authority had been brought about by the very persons for whose prosperity His Majesty Kalakaua had made such exertions, and by those to whom he had shown the greatest favors. On receipt of the intelligence, we decided that, instead of continuing our proposed tour, and visiting the continent of Europe, we would return at once to Honolulu. Mr. and Mrs. Armstrong proved themselves faithful friends, and through their kindness all was speedily arranged for the return voyage. They were ably assisted in their hospitable work by Mr. and Mrs. Sigismond Hoffnung and their son, Mr. Sidney Hoffnung. The last-named had been chargé d'affaires at Hawaii at one time in place of Mr. Abraham Hoffnung, who left him in that office during his own absence in Australia. The Hoffnungs while we were in London gave a grand entertainment and dinner in honor of the visit of Queen Kapiolani, and we then had the pleasure of meeting Lord Roseberry and his wife. This lady was a daughter of one of the Rothschilds, a large woman of fine appearance and commanding presence, and of a style which made her noticeable in company. Then she wore around her neck a string of single pearls which was a wonder in itself, for I was told that its value was about three hundred thousand dollars. We had the pleasure of meeting her again at an afternoon tea, which passed off very charmingly, given to us at her residence, at which there were many interesting people.

But after the news we received from home, our minds would not be at rest to further enjoy the kind attentions which had been tendered us during the month of our stay; so we bade adieu to the beautiful city of London, and took our departure from Liverpool. There we parted with Mr. and Mrs. Armstrong, and went on board the *Servia*, Captain McKay, of the Cunard Line, by which steamer we made a pleasant passage of nine days to New York. Resting only enough to get our accommodations on the overland train, in six days more we were in San Francisco; and six days' farther travel, this time by water, found us nearing our home. The weather on our westward way had been excessively hot; for it was midsummer, and we had suffered some inconvenience from the heat in crossing the continent. Our own climate is so equal in temperature that we feel extremes of heat even more than excessive cold.

As our vessel was entering the harbor of Honolulu, a smaller steamer came off to meet us; and being made fast alongside, we were transferred, and at once made for the shore. Here we found the people assembled to give us a royal welcome. The wharves were lined with throngs of men and women. The shipping, too, had been utilized for points of observation, and the decks and rigging of all the vessels were filled with those eager to watch the coming of the royal party. And yet, mingled with all the joy felt at our safe return, there was an undercurrent of sadness as of a people who had known with us a crushing sorrow. There were traces of tears on the cheeks of many of our faithful retainers, which we noticed, and of which we knew the meaning, as we passed by. They knew, and we knew, although no word was spoken, the changes which had been forced upon the king.

We were received by the members of the new cabinet of the king, by name Mr. Godfrey Brown, Minister of Foreign Affairs; Mr. L. A. Thurston, Minister of the Interior; Mr. W. I. Green, Minister of Finance; Mr. C. W. Ashford, Attorney-General—all men of foreign birth; while of the ministry directly preceding, three members had been native Hawaiians.

Mr. Brown shook us warmly by the hands, and attended us to the royal carriage which had been waiting; and then, accompanied by the royal staff of His Majesty, we were quickly driven past the assembled multitudes to Iolani Palace, where King Kalakaua—my brother and the husband of Queen Kapiolani—was prepared to receive us. He appeared bright, and glad to welcome us back; yet we could see on his countenance traces of the terrible strain through which he had passed, and evidences of the anxiety over the perilous position, although this was only the commencement of the troubles preparing for our family and nation.

Chapter XXIX. "The Bayonet Constitution"

It is necessary now to briefly review the events which had taken place in our absence of about three months abroad. We arrived in Honolulu on the twenty-sixth day of July, 1887. A conspiracy against the peace of the Hawaiian Kingdom had been taking shape since early spring. By the 15th of June, prior to our return, it had assumed a no less definite shape than the overthrow of the monarchy.

For many years our sovereigns had welcomed the advice of, and given full representations in their government and councils to, American residents who had cast in their lot with our people, and established industries on the Islands. As they became wealthy, and acquired titles to lands through the simplicity of our people and their ignorance of values and of the new land laws, their greed and their love of power proportionately increased; and schemes for aggrandizing themselves still further, or for avoiding the obligations which they had incurred to us, began to occupy their minds. So the mercantile element, as embodied in the Chamber of Commerce, the sugar planters, and the proprietors of the "missionary" stores, formed a distinct political party, called the "down-town" party, whose purpose was to minimize or entirely subvert other interests, and especially the prerogatives of the crown, which, based upon ancient custom and the authority of the island chiefs, were the sole guaranty of our nationality. Although settled among us, and drawing their wealth from our resources, they were alien to us in their customs and ideas respecting government, and desired above all things the extension of their power, and to carry out their own special plans of advancement, and to secure their own personal benefit. It may be true that they really believed us unfit to be trusted to administer the growing wealth of the Islands in a safe and proper way. But if we manifested any incompetency, it was in not foreseeing that they would be bound by no obligations, by honor, or by oath of allegiance, should an opportunity arise for seizing our country, and bringing it under the authority of the United States.

Kalakaua valued the commercial and industrial prosperity of his kingdom highly. He sought honestly to secure it for every class of people, alien or native, in his dominions, making it second only to the advancement of morals and education. If he believed in the divine right of kings, and the distinctions of hereditary nobility, it was not alone from the prejudices of birth and native custom, but because he was able to perceive that even the most enlightened nations of the earth have not as yet been able to replace them with a ruling class equally able, patriotic, or disinterested. I say this with all reverence for the form of government and the social order existing in the United States, whose workings have, for more than a century, excited the interest of the world; not the interest of the common people only, but of nobles, rulers, and kings. Kalakaua's highest and most earnest desire was to be a true sovereign, the chief servant of a happy, prosperous, and progressive people. He regarded himself as the responsible arbiter of clashing interests, and his own breast as the ordained meeting-place of the spears of political contention. He was rightly jealous of his prerogatives, because they were responsibilities which no civic body in his kingdom could safely undertake to administer. He freely gave his personal efforts to the securing of a reciprocity treaty with the United States, and sought the co-operation of that great and powerful nation, because he was persuaded it would enrich, or benefit, not one class, but, in a greater or less degree, all his subjects.

His interviews with General Grant, his investigations into the labor problems, which the success of the Hawaiian plantations demanded, were all means to the same end—an increase of domestic prosperity. He succeeded, and the joy of the majority was great. The planters were elated, the merchants were encouraged, money flowed into their pockets, bankrupt firms became wealthy, sugar companies declared fabulous dividends; the prosperity for which my brother had so faithfully worked he most abundantly secured for his people, especially for those of foreign birth, or missionary ancestry, who had become permanent residents of Hawaii.

The king did not accomplish these things without some native opposition; although it was respectful and deferent to his decision, as the ideas and customs of our people require. Some foresaw that this treaty with the United States might become the entering wedge for the loss of our independence. What would be the consequences should the Islands acquire too great a commercial attraction, too large a foreign population and interests? Would not these interests demand the protection of flag backed by a great military or naval power? But Kalakaua, aware that under the provisions of international law no nation could attack us without cause, and relying on the established policy of our great ally, the United States, fully assured that no colonial scheme would find acceptation there, boldly adventured upon the effort which so greatly increased the wealth and importance of his kingdom—a wealth which has, however, owing to circumstances which he could not then foresee, and which none of his loyal counselors even dreamed of, now gone almost wholly into the pockets of aliens and foes.

For years the "missionary party" had, by means of controlling the cabinets appointed by the king, kept itself in power. Its leaders were constantly intriguing to make the ministry their tool, or to have in its organization a power for carrying out their own special plans, and securing their own personal benefit. And now, without any provocation on the part of the king, having matured their plans in secret, the men of foreign birth rose one day en masse, called a public meeting, and forced the king, without any appeal to the suffrages of the people, to sign a constitution of their own preparation, a document which deprived the sovereign of all power, made him a mere tool in their hands, and practically took away the franchise from the Hawaiian race. This constitution was never in any way ratified, either by the people, or by their representatives, even after violence had procured the king's signature to it. Contrary entirely to the intent of the prior constitution drawn by a Hawaiian monarch (under which for twenty-three years the nation had been conducted to prosperity), this draft of 1887 took all power from the ruler, and meant that from that day the "missionary party" took the law into its own hands.

It may be asked, "Why did the king give them his signature?" I answer without hesitation, because he had discovered traitors among his most trusted friends, and knew not in whom he could trust; and because he had every assurance, short of actual demonstration, that the conspirators were ripe for revolution, and had taken measures to have him assassinated if he refused. His movements of late had been watched, and his steps dogged, as though he had been a fugitive from justice. Whenever he attempted to go out in the evening, either to call at the hotel, or visit any one of his friends' houses, he was conscious of the presence of enemies who were following stealthily on his track. But, happily, Providence watched over him, and thus he was guarded from personal harm.

He signed that constitution under absolute compulsion. Details of the conspiracy have come to me since from sources upon which I can rely, which lead to the conviction that but for the repugnance or timidity of one of the executive committee, since risen very high in the counsels of the so-called republic, he would have been assassinated. Then they had planned for the immediate abrogation of the monarchy, the declaration of a republic, and a proposal for annexation to be made to the United States. The constitution of the republic was actually framed and agreed upon; but the plot was not fully carried out—more moderate counsels prevailed. They therefore took the very constitution of which I have spoken, the one which had been drafted for a republic, hastily rewrote it so as to answer their ends, and forced Kalakaua to affix thereto his official signature.

It has been known ever since that day as "The Bayonet Constitution," and the name is well chosen; for the cruel treatment received by the king from the military companies, which had been organized by his enemies under other pretences, but really to give them the power of coercion, was the chief measure used to enforce his submission. They had illegally come out against him, bearing arms; and it is openly stated that they had prepared measures to be a law unto themselves. Whatever the faults of Mr. Gibson, so long prime minister of Kalakaua, he was an able man, and his only public crime was his loyalty to his king. And it was for this reason that he, and his son-in-law, Mr. Fred H. Hayselden of Lanai, were seized by a mob composed of the "missionary party" armed with rifles, and marched down the public streets to the wharves; not an atom of respect being shown to the gray hairs of the old man who had occupied for years the highest position in the king's cabinet. Who was the man, and where is he now, who knocked off the hat, and struck the loyal old man, as he silently accepted his changed position?

So these two citizens were forced along into a small structure on the wharf, where hung two ropes with nooses already prepared, and a man of widely known missionary ancestry, led the outcry, vociferating loudly and lustily, "Hang them! Hang them!" Could it be possible, I thought, that a son of one of my early instructors, the child of such a lovely and amiable Christian mother, could so far forget the spirit of that religion his parents taught, and be so carried away with political passion, as to be guilty of murder?

Yet he was not the only one, by any means, who seemed to have forgotten those principles of our Lord, to teach which their parents had come to our shores. For while this was going on in the city, another missionary boy rode out to the country residence of Mr. Gibson, at Kapiolani Park, and entering abruptly into the presence of his daughter, Mrs. Hayselden, threw a lasso over her head, as though the gentle woman had been a wild animal, and avowed his intention of dragging her into town. While he held her, those with him searched the house, hoping that they might discover arms or some other evidence by which Mr. Gibson and the members of his family could be convicted and hung, but they were disappointed. After subjecting her to this brutality, which she bore most bravely, the ruffians left her to await the return from Honolulu of her natural protectors. But, alas! Instead of their presence, what sorrow was to be hers! She received news of the manner in which they had been treated, and how doubtful it was whether they would ever be allowed to meet again this side of the grave; for after keeping their victims some days in terror of life, on the fifth day of July, 1887, the two men, against whom no charge, political nor criminal, was ever made, were placed on board a sailing-vessel and landed at San Francisco. The treatment received was too much for the elder sufferer; and although the conspirators had not directly assassinated him, he died soon after. His son returned to Hawaii, and became sheriff of Lanai during my reign. He was one of the first persons selected for dismissal by the present government; he had taken no part in public manifestations, but was informed by the attorney-general, Mr. W. O. Smith, that he was removed from office, "simply because you are a friend of the queen."

A contemporary painting of Hawaiian King Kamehameha I

Engraving of King Kamehameha II.

King Kamehameha III.

King Kamehameha IV.

King Kamehameha V.

Queen Emma

King Kalakaua

Liliuokalani as Regent

Queen Liliuokalani

Lorin A Thurston, the American who forced King Kalakaua to sign the "Bayonette Constitution", stripping the Hawaiian Monarchy of power and placing Hawaii under the control of the American-dominated Cabinet and Legislature.

Robert Wilcox, who led an abortive uprising to restore the powers of the Hawaiian monarch

American diplomat John L Stevens. He led the clique of Americans who worked to overthrow the monarchy and annex Hawaii to the US.

The American members of the Royal Cabinet, who called themselves "The Committee of Public Safety".

American troops from the US Navy ship *Boston* seize Hawaii and depose Queen Liliuokalani

Sanford Dole became the first President of the Hawaiian Republic.

James Henderson Blount. Upon discovering that Stevens and other Americans had conspired to use American troops to overthrow the legitimate Queen of Hawaii, Blount was sent by President Grover Cleveland to demand that the Queen be reinstated.

President William Mckinley. Reversing Cleveland's demands, Mckinley incorporated Hawaii as a US possession.

Americans on Hawaii celebrate the official annexation to the United States in 1900.

Chapter XXX. Invited To Conspire Against The King

Turning from this narration of the events which had transpired before the return of the queen's party from abroad, I will resume the thread of my personal narrative from the moment of meeting with my brother. After exchanging a few words of salutation and family greeting, we left the queen to listen to her husband's account of what had taken place during their three months' separation and returned to our home, very glad indeed to be again settled at Washington Place.

There we found the good mother of my husband delighted to meet us, and filled with gratitude at our safe return. Her expressions of joy at once more meeting her son were but natural, for had he not always been devoted to her comfort? There was a little English lady who had been staying with Mrs. Dominis during our absence, and both my husband and I were glad to have the opportunity of expressing to her our sense of obligation for all she had done for his mother's needs while we were gone. She had been very attentive and considerate. Her name was Miss Davis, and she was a sister of Rector Davis of South Kona.

At this time, nearly a month after the revolution and change of constitution, everything seemed to settle down into quiet again; but appearances are deceptive, and "the devil never sleeps." So, having achieved so much of their desires, the conspirators worked day and night to keep the city in a ferment. Plans were made, and committees were formed; the extreme views of some of the members caused others, more scrupulous, to retire, and to say that they could not willingly consent to be tools in the hands of wicked men, instruments of evil to their fellows. So these committees were organized over and over again, without fixed purpose, without stability, until finally all other elements had withdrawn from connection with the conspirators, save a small number of agitators whose sole rallying-point was annexation to the United States.

During the session to the legislature for the year 1888, Mr. James I. Dowsett, Jr., a young man, came to my house at Muulaulani, Palama, to inform me that he had been commissioned by those members who belonged to the missionary party to inquire if I would accept the throne in case my brother should be dethroned. To my indignation at the proposition was added astonishment that the request should come from a mere boy eighteen years of age; and I responded at once to his remark by saying, with some emphasis, that such a proposal was not to be considered. My answer would be "No," and this final. He then, with an air of apology, added that he hoped I would not be offended with him personally, because he had only been the bearer of the message. Then he volunteered the intimation that, since his errand had been unsuccessful, I might receive a repetition of the same proposition in the course of a few days. I then asked him what was the intention of the missionary party? What did they propose to do to my brother? How was he to be dethroned? Were they going to murder him? To these interrogatories he replied that he knew nothing more about it, and bade me adieu.

But, in conformity with his words, about a week from that day my telephone was rung by Mr. W. R. Castle, who wished to know if I would be at home that morning; if so, he would like to call and see me on an important matter, and would arrive in about half an hour. He was told that I would see him, and at the appointed time he appeared. He indicated that our conference should be held in some place selected for its privacy, where we would not be overheard nor interrupted. I chose a side room, or corner, where I generally attended to my correspondence or did my literary work. But in a room adjoining there happened to be, at the moment of his visit, a party of girls who had met to consult on a little social matter — the arrangements for a picnic. Just as soon as they heard me enter my writing-room, and recognized from the conversation that someone was with me, their voices hushed, and they remained as still as mice; and so listened to every word which passed between myself and Mr. Castle.

He announced to me that he had come to propose that I should accept the throne, to which I should at once ascend, and receive the support of the missionary party. I demanded of him how my brother could be dethroned. Did they mean harm to his person? He denied that there was any such intent, but declared that King Kalakaua must retire, and that I should assume his position as the reigning sovereign. Perhaps they imagined at this time that I would be a willing tool to carry out all of their projects. It was true that I was always an active member of all the associated plans for carrying on missionary works, and was never appealed to in vain by the missionaries to give money or sympathy to all that was to be done in the name of Christianity. Whatever was to be undertaken by their church, or by any of their societies, had received my hearty co-operation from my earliest womanhood. I was about the first one to whom they went for subscriptions, nor did they ever go empty away. I was a member of the Fort-street Benevolent Society, also of the Strangers' Friend Society; and at the very time of the landing of the United States troops to overthrow my government, was a member of the Woman's Board of Missions. In fact, I was concerned with the missionary party all my lifetime, in more measures of organized benevolent work than I have the space to mention here. Perhaps it was because I had gone hand in hand with them in all good works that they thought I would cast in my lot with them now for evil—give my consent to their plans, so frankly avowed, of conspiracy for my brother's overthrow, and thus profit by their rebellion against his lawful authority. If so, they found themselves much mistaken. I allowed Mr. Castle to explain as fully as he pleased their designs, and then I told him with firmness and decision that I would have nothing to do with them in this matter. Seeing that I firmly declined the proposal, Mr. Castle retired; and as that was the last I heard about it, I infer that, having made their plots, they lacked the courage, or the heart, to put their plans into execution. I will do the missionary party the justice to state that their confidence in my aid for every good word and work was not destroyed by my refusal to join in their conspiracies. About the time that the old Fort-street congregation was getting settled in their new and beautiful building, now called the Central Union Church, which is directly opposite my residence known as Washington Place, I received from my former instructor, Rev. E. G. Beckwith, a most flattering letter; and Mr. Charles Cook asked me to take a pew there at five hundred dollars a year. I was pleased to know that the reverend gentleman, who had known me throughout my whole life—and at this time I was some years past my fiftieth birthday—should entertain so favorable an opinion of his ancient pupil. Although I was at this time quite a regular attendant at the Kawaiahao church, yet I had this proposal of Mr. Cook under consideration. Just what I might have done I cannot now say; for the political events which ultimately led to the overthrow of my government by his friends and his party, came upon me so thick and fast, that I had little time for the consideration of anything but the most important matters.

In the month of April, 1889, Mrs. Dominis became very ill; and one day the candle of life, which had been flickering in the socket, went gently out. But the troubled political atmosphere was such that even my domestic sorrow was not respected.

For it had been proposed that the king should take a trip to San Francisco, in regard to some commercial matter. It was a new scheme; some novel proposal to be made for closer relations with the United States, by which, of course, the missionary party was to be benefited, and of the terms of which my long-suffering brother was to be the bearer and the promoter. On Sunday, when my husband's mother was borne up the Nuuanu Valley to her last resting-place, the cabinet, notwithstanding the sacredness of the day, was in session, making plans and discussing the means for the projected trip of His Majesty to America.

In the midst of our sorrow a message arrived directed to me. It was from Mr. Jonathan Austin, the Minster of Foreign Affairs, asking me if I would be one of a council of regency to take charge of the government during the expected absence of the king. I immediately sent my husband, Governor Dominis, to inform His Majesty and his cabinet that I would accept the regency, but only to be sole regent in the king's place and stead; that the cabinet had full power to act upon all measures relating to the administration of government; that were I one of a council of regency there would be no executive; and that this was the second time I had been obliged to state my position and decline such an arrangement. While my husband was delivering this message; the funeral ceremonies of his mother were suspended; and on his return the last sad rites of respect to her remains were rendered, and the procession wended its way up the valley to her place of burial.

Chapter XXXI. The King Threatened And Oppressed

After all, the anticipated trip was never taken. I am at a loss to explain the causes of its failure, but I understood that there was some friction in the cabinet. That body was now the absolute monarch of the kingdom of the Hawaiian Islands. Its members, Messrs. Austin, Damon, C. W. Ashford, with L. A. Thurston as its chief, defied the king to his face, and openly insulted him in his own palace. In one of their official documents they use to him the following language:

"The government in all its departments must be conducted by the cabinet. Your Majesty shall, in future, sign all documents and do all acts which, under the laws of the constitution, require the signature or act of the sovereign, when advised so to do by the cabinet, the cabinet being solely and absolutely responsible for any signature of any document or act so done or performed by their advice."

As His Majesty very naturally demurred to such construction of even their own constitution, the cabinet appealed to the supreme court, who to the number of five justices, the first named being Albert F. Judd, and the last Sanford B. Dole, very consistently with the public record of these gentlemen, declared that the king was wrong, and that all power was placed in the hands of the cabinet. It was by such acts as this that the missionary party sought to humiliate my brother in the estimation of his own people; so that it has well been said by those conversant with the history of these days, that His Majesty Kalakaua died in reality of a broken heart — broken by the base ingratitude of the very persons whose fortunes he had made.

On the 10th of May, 1889, the Princess Kaiulani, being then in her fourteenth year, left Honolulu under the charge of Mrs. Thomas Rain Walker, wife of the British vice-counsul, for England. It was the intention of her father, Hon. A. S. Cleghorn, that she should remain abroad a short time for educational advantages; but owing to the changes which have taken place since her departure, she is still living with him in Europe.

In June, 1889, grand preparations were made for the celebration, on the eleventh, of Kamehameha Day. All who were interested in the races turned their steps in the direction of Kapiolani Park. Twelve o'clock was the hour appointed for the salutes to be fired, and all was to be done to make the day one of enjoyment. But a special invitation had been sent to me by the committee of the Sunday-school of the Congregational church to attend a picnic of the Sunday-school children, who were to assemble at the house and grounds of Mr. John Thomas Waterhouse, Jr., up the Nuuanu Valley; so after the salute, or soon after twelve, I left the gay company at Kapiolani Park, and with two lady companions went up to the picnic, where I found myself most cordially welcomed, and made the guest of honor of the pleasant occasion. Young and old seemed to be very much gratified that I had willingly excused myself from other scenes of social enjoyment, to be present at the reunion of these interesting classes of children; and as for myself, I enjoyed the company, as I always take pleasure with children and in educational gatherings.

In the early part of July, 1889, I made a trip to Kauai; but before speaking of this journey, on which I was absent about a fortnight, I find it is necessary to go back a little, and give an account of my connection with Mr. Robert W. Wilcox.

Mr. Wilcox, in early youth, was sent abroad by King Kalakaua to be educated for future service to the state. But the revolution of 1887 compelled the king to cut off his income; and so he was recalled, arriving at Honolulu about the date of our return from the Victorian Jubilee. During his absence, however, he had met and married an Italian lady, the Countess Sobrero; and the young wife accompanied him on his return. For a while they were domiciled at the Arlington Hotel; but their means were nearly exhausted, and the party in power resolved to do nothing for them. Aware of the facts, in pity for their situation I offered them quarters under my roof until they could provide for themselves.

They were very glad to accept my proposal, and I gave them comfortable rooms in the long building attached to the main house at my Palama residence. I tried to make it as pleasant for them as I could, and devoted my attention especially to the newly married wife. She was excessively homesick, and was constantly making efforts to get together money sufficient to enable them to leave the Islands. Through the kind assistance of Mr. F. A. Schaefer, the Italian consul, and a few others, after residing with me for two months, they were at last able to leave Honolulu, and reached the city of San Francisco. From thence I heard from her that they were comfortably settled, that she had found pupils in foreign languages, and that her husband had also secured employment as a surveyor of lands. But early in the year 1889 I received word from Mr. Wilcox that he was again making up his mind to come to Honolulu; that he intended to enter the political arena, and run as a candidate for the legislature.

I wrote him at once, using all my influence to dissuade him from the very thought of it, telling him plainly that he was far better off where he was. I trusted that he had listened to my advice, but what was my astonishment when he appeared at Honolulu. As the rooms formerly occupied by him and Mrs. Wilcox were not at that time used, and I was then living in Washington Place, I told him that he was welcome to go to Palama, and remain there until such time as he should be able to provide for himself elsewhere. I could not foresee that my kindness and hospitality to these persons in need would be used by suspicious parties to connect my name with a foolish and ill-organized attempt subsequently made by Mr. Wilcox to restore some part of the authority of which the missionary party had deprived the king. All unconscious of any such scheme, I started on my journey to visit friends in Kauai.

It was midsummer in 1889 when I arrived at the island of Kauai, and at first took up my residence with Governor Kanoa. He was one of the few chiefs of the olden times and earlier manners who had not yet passed away from earth. Although of lesser grade than some of those mentioned in these memoirs, yet he was conversant with all forms of his duty, and observant of that etiquette handed down from ancient days towards the chiefs of rank superior to his own. It was, therefore, natural to him to open his house to me, and to receive my suite with that generous hospitality and cordiality typical of the Hawaiian of high birth. After spending a few days at his estate, he provided horses and carriages for my party, and accompanied by his wife, a good Hawaiian lady, we proceeded to "Eleele," where I had received an invitation from a young couple to be their guest. From a brief but pleasant visit there, we went on to Waimea, and took up our abode with Mr. and Mrs. Levi Kauai. When it was known that the heir to the throne was at their house, many people of that district called, and during my stay we received numerous pleasant attentions. From here we made preparations for retracing our steps, but stopped on our return to visit at a pretty little estate, situated in a quiet valley just outside of Waimea, where resided Mrs. Gay and her daughters. Mr. Robinson and Mr. Francis Gay also made their home with this amiable lady. All of these had ever been noted for their patriotic attentions to any of the chiefs who from time to time visited the district. This reputation was ably sustained, and I retain the most pleasing recollections of their courtesy and kindness on this occasion. My regard for this family extended even one generation farther back, their grandmother, Mrs. Sinclair of the island of Niihau, being also one of my warm friends.

On this visit I made careful inquiries as to the success of Mr. Gay's efforts to raise the "Oo" bird on this island. This is a bird about the size of a robin, under whose wings may be found the choice yellow feathers used in the manufacture of cloaks or collars exclusively pertaining to the Hawaiian chiefs of high rank. It is not the mamo bird, from which also feather capes and cloaks are made.

I had succeeded in getting from Hawaii, the largest island, some specimens expressly for their island. Twenty pairs had been brought as far as the island of Oahu. Of these, three pairs originally were sent to Kauai, but on making inquiry I found that only one pair was now known to be living there. These seemed to be thriving. Perhaps one cause of their content was a shrub or bush of the mimosa family growing near to the house, which bore fragrant blossoms very similar to those of the lehua, from which, in its own native island, this bird sucks the honey on which it subsists. They are true Hawaiians; flowers are necessary for their very life. This single pair of birds kept near to the house, and were often seen on this fragrant mimosa-tree. Ten years have flown by since I had the pleasure of looking at them there; but it is to be trusted that they have been thriving, laying their eggs year by year, and have by this time a flourishing colony. There is a bird on Kauai very similar in some points to the Oo, but they have a white feather under the wing instead of the much-prized yellow tip from which the celebrated leis and cloaks are made.

After the parting with this agreeable family we turned our steps toward Niumalu, the residence of the governor; and having also exchanged with him our greetings and farewells, we took passage on the schooner *James Makee* for Honolulu. I arrived in due time, refreshed by the journey, and with my party also delighted with the manifestations of kindly interest and loyal love which we had received throughout our trip.

Chapter XXXII. Attempted Revolution

On returning to Washington Place, greatly to my regret I found my husband suffering much from the attacks of his old enemy, the rheumatism. But he bore his sufferings patiently, and was pleased to know that I had had so pleasant a journey. On the day following my return, I went to my out-of-town residence at Palama, in order to look over my garden, in which I have never ceased to take a keen interest. After satisfying myself that the faithful old gardener had given everything proper care, I turned my attention toward the house itself, and found matters there also satisfactory.

I had finished my examinations, and was just on the point of leaving, when I heard steps on the front staircase; and knowing that some person was without, I advanced to the door, which I did not open, but drew down the grating, and met the gaze of a young man with haggard, anxious countenance. It was Mr. Robert W. Wilcox who was standing before me, trying with all his self-control to appear calm, but evidently much excited. He told me in a few words that he was ready to release the king from that hated thralldom under which he had been oppressed, and that measures had already been taken. I asked him at once if he had made mention of so important a matter to His Majesty. He replied that he had not.

I then charged him to do nothing unless with the full knowledge and consent of the king. To this he responded that he had counted the cost, and would most gladly lay down his life for my brother's sake. He then proceeded to inform me that it was on this very night that the step would be taken; that every preparation had been made, and the signal for decisive action would soon be given. This was the first intimation of any kind which had been brought to my knowledge of the initiation of the movement. At the time he was speaking with me I had not the least idea of the use which subsequent events proved had been made of my Palama residence, and my old gardener had been kept in equal ignorance. Our lack of suspicion is easily explained; for the entire building can be traversed when the shutters are kept closed, and no observer on the outside would be any the wiser, whatever his position. Knowing this as well as I, Mr. Wilcox and his associates had held their secret meetings there; and always observing due caution, their occupancy or manner of using the place was known only to themselves.

It turned out just as I had been warned by my visitor; and on the very night of the disclosure the outbreak occurred, and Mr. Wilcox made his unsuccessful attempt to overthrow the missionary party. The king that night was not at the palace, but at his boat-house. I was in Washington Place. As I have always been in the habit of rising early, I awoke at my usual time, and saw that my husband was quietly sleeping, and having a respite from his pain. I dressed without disturbing him, and strolled out into the garden, where I was in the habit of taking a morning walk before breakfasting.

I was not long there before I noticed that something unusual was transpiring. Members of the rifle companies were to be seen hastening from every direction; some of them fully dressed and carrying their arms in proper form, but some appeared to have left their homes in haste, so that they did not have the various parts of their uniform adjusted, but were dressing themselves as they ran past. They were all going in the direction of the armory on Punch-Bowl Street. Young Harry Auld, who was employed in the custom-house, went by while I stood near the gate to my grounds; and I asked him at once what was the meaning of the commotion at this early hour.

He informed me that Mr. Wilcox had taken possession of the palace, and was supported there by a company of soldiers. Naturally I connected this information with what I had heard the night before, and all became clear to me. Towards ten o'clock in the forenoon firing began, and soon shots went whizzing past our house. There were occasional outbursts of musketry throughout the day; but towards evening all became tranquil again, or nearly so. We heard that Mr. Wilcox had been deserted by his men, and had therefore surrendered. The rifle companies were stationed at the music hall opposite the palace; but their gallant commander kept out of harm's way at the Hawaiian Hotel, from whence he sent his orders by an orderly to his executive officer. Late in the afternoon Mr. Hay Wodehouse, and the purser of the steamer *Australia*, climbed onto the roof of the hotel stables to have their share of the fun, taking with them a small mortar or other contrivance for firing bombs. They discharged these missiles into the palace grounds, aiming at the bungalow with such effect as to shatter the furniture of the Princess Poomaikalani, and do much other damage. This was the time when Mr. Wilcox sent word to Colonel Ashford that he would lay down his arms; and being arrested for the useless riot, he was led to the station-house. His punishment was a moderate imprisonment, and it has been said that he was released from the consequences of his act because he had in his power certain persons who would have been much terrified had he been inclined to tell all he knew. However this may be, it is evident that out of gratitude he had perhaps some plans or purposes for being of service to my brother, because the king had tried in the past to do something for him. His enthusiasm was great, but was not supported by good judgment or proper discretion. His efforts failed; and indeed, it is not easy to see how under the circumstances it could have been otherwise.

Chapter XXXIII. The King's Departure — Again Regent

I have spoken of the pleasant Sunday-school picnic of the 11th of June, 1889. My entertainers, it seemed, were sufficiently gratified with my presence not to forget me in their next invitations; and the year following I was invited out to Punahou, where the Sunday-schools of all the Congregational societies were to assemble. I first drove out to Kapiolani Park to see the races. These went on finely. The assembled multitude cheered on the winning horse, the sweet strains of the band floated out on the air of the beautiful day, and the people seemed inspired by their surroundings to forget all their political troubles or their domestic necessities. After I heard the salute denoting the noon hour, again, as on the previous occasion, accompanied by two lady companions, I proceeded to the picnic at Punahou. For some reason as yet not explained, the assembled worthies of the Congregational church did not seem as cordial as they were a year earlier. However, I did not allow any to know that I noticed the change; and besides, there were many sincere friends present who treated me most hospitably and kindly. While engaged in conversation with some of these, Mr. Albert F. Judd, the chief justice, approached me, and inquired if I could descry a vessel which was making her way slowly out of the port and gaining an offing. I replied that I saw the one to which he referred. Then he went on to volunteer the information that on board that craft was Colonel Ashford, who had escaped from prison, and was secretly taking his departure.

A few days prior to this celebration, in one of those turns of the tide of politics by which the Ashfords have more than once found themselves in strange company, Mr. V. V. Ashford, on some charge of seditious conduct toward the governing party, found himself in prison.

I mention this as but one amongst many instances I might recall where those charged with political, or, indeed any other offence, have, for reasons best known to the missionary party, been allowed or even constrained to leave the Islands. Of some of these, nothing more has ever been heard.

The 18th of November of that same year was celebrated with much display and many congratulations as the birthday of His Majesty Kalakaua. During the afternoon a reception took place at the palace, in which the societies organized by the king, the queen, or by myself had a general reunion. These were the Hooulu Lahui, the Liliuokalani Educational Society, and the Naua Society, the last named under the special patronage of the king. After paying their respects to His Majesty and the queen, the whole company adjourned to the wharves. As usual there was a fine regatta, in which many pretty water-craft took part. We are always favored with fresh and regular breezes, and the little white-sailed yachts made a neat and inspiring picture as they contested for the prizes. Those who won went home happy in their trophies of victory; those who did not had, at any rate, a delightful sail. The boat-houses were turned into places of entertainment, and fine lunches were given at that of the king as well as at many others. My riding society had been specially invited to take their refreshments at the boat-house of Dr. Trousseau.

As we were all gayly going to lunch after viewing the sport, general attention was attracted to a balloon which was at the moment ascending from the foot of Punch-Bowl Hill. Scarcely had the light globular object reached the upper currents of the atmosphere, when it was whirled away with fearful speed, for it was a very windy day. On watching the car under the balloon, we noticed that the man had cut himself adrift, and was descending from mid-air in a parachute. He was coming down bravely; but what was the horror of all of the spectators to observe that instead of landing on the wharf, or even in the port, he was being carried far out to sea, beyond the breakers, where the waters were alive with sharks. Steamers and boats were immediately got under way to effect his rescue, but he was never seen again. The balloon from which he had made his fatal leap also disappeared, and no trace of either was ever discovered. The poor man probably met his fate from the jaws of the monsters of the deep the moment he touched the water.

In the evening there was a grand display of fireworks, and a procession of the fire companies of the city. There was also a new organization which paraded this evening, called the "Sons of Hawaii," at whose head was Mr. John Cummins. It was to be reviewed by His Majesty Kalakaua. The men were mounted on the finest horses which could be found in the city, and were manly fellows and good riders. At eight in the evening Their Majesties, the king and queen, the members of the cabinet, with many who held office under the government, assembled in front of the palace to receive the organization.

I was not at that hour present, because I was making a tour of the city in order to inspect the decorations and see the fireworks. But just as I finished my drive, and entered the palace yard, the "Sons of Hawaii" came up the avenue with their horses on the full gallop, making a most inspiriting display. How well they sat their steeds, and how gracefully they rode! Each man held aloft a lighted torch, adding much to the effect of the cavalcade. They drew up in front of the king, and were most profound in their salutations. I paid particular attention to their behavior, because amongst them were a number of the missionary boys, who seemed to act as though they would outdo those of native birth in their manifestations of loyalty and respect. There was a sad interest to me afterwards in recalling this evening, because it was about the last celebration in which my brother made a public appearance.

The fatigues of this day, several sources of worry, and the responsibilities which I felt were approaching, brought on a slight fever; and for three weeks I was confined to my rooms, at times not leaving my sick-bed.

Three days before his departure the king came to see me, and told me of his intention to visit the United States. I did all I could to dissuade him from the journey. I reminded him of his failing health, and informed him that I was not in my usual vigor. Cold weather, too, to which he was unaccustomed, was fast approaching; and if anything should happen to him, how would I, with my feeble health, be able to meet the increasing burdens of my station. He replied that he would leave those behind who would look out for the government. His only errand at this moment was to notify me that I was to be appointed regent during his absence. He really did need change, after what he had borne in recent years; and this consideration doubtless entered into his resolution.

But the principal motive of his journey was to have an interview with Mr. H. A. P. Carter, the Hawaiian minister at Washington, in order to give him instructions in view of the McKinley Bill, which had just passed the American Congress, the influence of which was supposed to be dangerous to the interest of the foreign element at Honolulu, and destructive to the profits of the sugar planters. So the king went cheerfully and patiently to work for the cause of those who had been and were his enemies. He sacrificed himself in the interests of the very people who had done him so much wrong, and given him such constant suffering. With an ever-forgiving heart he forgot his own sorrows, set aside all feelings of animosity, and to the last breath of his life he did all that lay in his power for those who had abused and injured him.

If ever there was a man who was pure in spirit, if ever there was a mortal who had perfect charity, he was that man. In spite of all the revilings uttered against him, he never once opened his lips to speak against another, whomsoever it might be. And so my poor brother said good-by to us all, and bade farewell to his beautiful Islands, which he was never to look on again.

Just before he sailed I went to the palace. There he called together his cabinet, and addressing to the gentlemen a few pleasant words, he placed me in their charge, hoping for the best, and expressing the wish that under our care the burden of the government might be lighter than it had proved to him since he had been the reigning sovereign. At eleven o'clock he exchanged his last words with Queen Kapiolani and myself, and then hastened rapidly away to the wharf, where a boat from the United States man-of-war *Charleston* was in waiting to convey him on board that vessel. Crowds witnessed his departure, all the shipping was gay, the vessels saluted the out-going ship, a royal salute was fired, and he was gone.

Chapter XXXIV. The King's Return—My Accession

Thus again began my regency. With only twenty-five soldiers to guard the palace, a feeling of uncertainty in the mercantile world, and many signs of domestic unrest, my husband thought it best for me to return to Washington Place every night; but each morning at nine o'clock I went to my official duties, and part of these was always the examination of some alarm or rumor which had come to the palace doors. Now it was the report of a secret meeting at some house up the Nuuanu Valley to debate upon an overthrow of my government, again the account of an assembling out on the plains for conspiracy. Often, even after I returned to my home, would come a telephonic message announcing that the palace was to be attacked, and the military must be called out.

On tracing these rumors, whenever there was any basis of truth in them, it was found that the agitation was always the work of that same clique who were never satisfied, always conspiring, always determined that they would either rule or ruin. Such men, having no covenant with their own consciences, suspicious even of their own shadows, in power or out of power, are always a menace to the peace of the community.

Nothing worthy of record transpired during the closing days of 1890, and the opening weeks of 1891, until in the city it was reported that the ship *Charleston* was in sight with yards cock-billed, in token of mourning. My ministers were assembled in the Blue Room of the palace; and as I entered I could see on each countenance apprehension of the fate which we feared must have befallen the king, and to which we soon gave expression in words. On the arrival of the *Charleston* in port, we were officially notified. One of the cabinet went to the wharf to inquire what plans were made for the reception of the king's remains.

He brought back word that at five o'clock of that afternoon the admiral himself would come to the palace at the head of the party which was to escort the body of the deceased sovereign. Not wishing to leave the palace, I immediately wrote to my husband, who was at home suffering from rheumatism, to inform him of all that had been brought to my knowledge. On learning of my brother's death, in spite of his indisposition he came at once to the palace, so as to be near me at this critical moment. I was so overcome by the death of my dear brother, so dazed with the suddenness of the news which had come upon us in a moment, that I hardly realized what was going on about me, nor did I at all appreciate for the moment my situation. Before I had time to collect myself, before my brother's remains were buried, a trap was sprung upon me by those who stood waiting as a wild beast watches for his prey.

The ministers, who were apparently of one mind with the justices of the supreme court, called together the members of the council, and when all had taken their seats, sent for me. I turned to Governor Dominis before entering the chamber, and inquired of him, "What is the object of this meeting?" He said that they had come together to witness my taking of the oath of office. I told him at once that I did not wish to take the oath just then, and asked why such proceedings could not be deferred until after my brother's funeral. He said that others had decided that I must take my official oath then and there.

Few persons have ever been placed without a word of warning in such a trying situation, and I doubt if there was any other woman in the city who could have borne with passable equanimity what I had to endure that day. I will scarcely limit the comparison to my sex; I doubt if many men could have passed successfully through such an ordeal. Ere I realized what was involved, I was compelled to take the oath to the constitution, the adoption of which had led to my brother's death.

After taking the oath of office administered to me by the chief justice, Albert Francis Judd, the meeting dissolved, and we adjourned to the Blue Room, where all the members of the privy council came to pay to me their mournful congratulations. Of these the chief justice was the first; and as he shook my hand he said to me, "Should any of the members of your cabinet propose anything to you, say yes;" and left me quite at a loss to know what his words might portend. But it soon became apparent. After the members of the privy council departed, the cabinet remained. Mr. Cummins, Minister of Foreign Affairs, said that they wished to notify me that they would have to continue in office; and then went on with a lecture, or apology, which I could not understand, and the argument of which I do not believe he had quite mastered himself. Mr. Godfrey Brown, the Minister of Finance, came to his relief by offering the suggestion that no changes could be made in the cabinet except by the legislature. The only notice I took of their discussion was to say that I could not understand the necessity of mentioning the matter at all at such a moment. To this Mr. Petersen, the Attorney-General, rejoined that I ought to understand the situation and accept it. I replied that I had no intention of discussing situations or other political matters at all at this time, and I would defer all further notice of the matter until after the king's burial.

At five o'clock the afternoon of the 29th of January, 1891, the solemn procession began at the boat-landing, where the men from the *Charleston* had landed with the king's remains, and from whence they took up the line of their mournful march to Iolani Palace. It was a gloomy, cloudy afternoon. As they moved slowly up to the gates of the palace, there was a moment's pause; and just then a triple rainbow was seen to span with its arch the entire structure, stretching from one end to the other, and, as it were, embracing the palace. Crowds of people thronged in, respectfully following the king's remains, with hearts too full of grief to speak of the deceased sovereign even to each other. When the cortége arrived at the palace steps, the casket was placed on the shoulders of the stoutest and best-picked men of the ship, and borne to a bier in the centre of the Red Chamber, which had always been the royal reception room, where it was to lie in state.

The kind-hearted and ever-friendly officer who commanded the *Charleston*, Admiral George Brown, paid his respects to the widowed queen, and then, in company with his officers, returned to his ship. He had taken my brother as a guest of honor to San Francisco; he had shown to him the greatest courtesy and the most unaffected kindness during the passage; then, after the final scene, to him had belonged the sad office of conveying the remains of his late companion back over the same route, a silent passenger going to his final resting-place. The Hawaiian people are always grateful for tokens of respect shown to their chiefs, so on the proposed departure of the *Charleston* there was a general wish for a day to be given to the contributions of tokens of friendship to the admiral. On the day set apart for this grand expression of gratitude, men, women, and children crowded on board, each bearing some memento of Aloha to the gallant sailor. These consisted of curiosities of all kinds—old-fashioned spears, calabashes, shells, necklaces, and countless other articles of native use or manufacture, each telling its own little story of our people, recalling to whoever might see it in any part of the world some tender memory of Hawaii.

Chapter XXXV. The Last Sleep—Lying In State

In the meantime proper preparations were made for the funeral of His Majesty Kalakaua, than whom no king was ever more beloved by his people. The usual ceremonies were carried out as customary for the lying in state of a sovereign, or chief of the royal family. The casket was laid on a cloth of the royal feathers, which was spread over a table in the centre of the Red Chamber in the Iolani Palace, and guards were detailed for duty by day and by night. For this service twenty men are always selected, whose office it is to bear aloft the royal kahilis, which are never lowered during the course of the whole twenty-four hours. The attendants are divided into four watches of three hours each. Those relieving form a line, and take their positions as the stations are vacated by their predecessors, who, on resigning the plumes of state, return to their homes. The watchers are generally selected from men who can claim ancestry from the chiefs; of these there are quite a number still living, of well-known families, although now generally poor in worldly possessions. While in attendance at the side of the royal casket, some sang the death-wail or old-time mèlès or chants belonging solely to the family of the deceased chieftain; and in the meantime attendants of a younger race composed dirges which were more in accord with the lyrics of the present day. There was also detailed for my brother a guard of honor from the Masonic fraternity; two Masons always remained with the other watchers, and were relieved in a similar manner.

Three weeks constitute the period devoted to the obsequies before the burial, or the "lying in state," of the remains of a high chief of the Hawaiians. During this delay the cabinet and the privy council carried out the plans made for the details of the royal funeral. The death and burial of a sovereign is not a trivial matter in Hawaii. The people come from all parts of the islands to the funeral of the one whom they have known and loved as the head of the nation.

At last the morning for the final ceremonies arrived, and early in the day the sad exercises began with one of the most interesting and impressive ceremonies I ever witnessed. This was the honor rendered by the secret society of the Hale Naua to their head and founder. Prayers were offered, and they went through the different ceremonies, as is the custom with the Masonic or other similar fraternal organizations. The high priest, Mr. William Auld, officiated, two lay priests assisting during these parts of the ritual. Then entered twelve women with lighted candles in their hands; each one of these, bearing aloft her taper, offered a short prayer, the first words at the head, next at the shoulders, then at the elbows, then the hands, and so on to the thighs, the knees, the ankles, and the feet. There were six of the torch-bearers on each side; and after these forms they surrounded the remains, and all repeated in unison prayers appropriate to the burial of the dead. They then withdrew in the most solemn manner. This service, so far from being, as has been alleged, idolatrous, had no more suggestion of paganism than can be found in the Masonic or other worship. An excellent opportunity was given me to contrast the two on this occasion, and each seemed to me to be a most beautiful and impressive method of rendering honor to the memory of a deceased member.

At the hour appointed for the state services, each dignitary, according to his rank, took the place which had been indicated to him in the great Red Room. His Lordship the Bishop of Honolulu, wearing the robes of his office, then appeared, and began the service laid down in the Anglican ritual for the burial of the dead. At the proper time each person moved to the position which had been assigned for him in the procession which was to proceed from Iolani Palace to the royal mausoleum. And just at this point there was a slight hitch; for the diplomatic corps declared that their members should be first after the carriages of the royal family, while the members of the cabinet claimed this position of precedence for themselves. After a brief discussion over the question, it was finally settled that the cabinet might take the first position, the diplomatic corps following, and in this order the procession moved onward. On each side of the bier were the kahili bearers; and these plumes, some large, some small, of various colors, were borne aloft above the heads of the moving throng, who marched with slow step up the Nuuanu Valley towards the royal mausoleum. On arrival at Kawananakoa, the casket was placed in the centre of the tomb, and the final prayers were offered by the bishop and the clergy assisting his lordship, after which they retired. Then the Masonic brethren, embracing nearly all the members of the lodges in the city, who had marched in a body, filed in with slow and solemn step, and surrounded his bier. Clothed in the insignia of their order, they stood in saddest silence about the casket, on which was placed the regalia lately worn by my brother and their brother, and also a roll on which were the records of his rank as a Mason. Then the brethren marched around the casket, and each laid thereon a little sprig or branch of green pine as a final and personal token of his grief at parting with a brother Mason. When all had done this, they retired, leaving the members of the royal family alone with their grief in the silent recesses of the tomb. Lastly, the guns of the military escort gave the final salute to the departed, three volleys of musketry being successively fired above the grave; and the line of return was formed in proper order, the kahili bearers still waving aloft the plumes, those traditional accompaniments of royalty, and which now became the insignia of office appertaining to the former heir-apparent, who had now become the sovereign of the Hawaiian Islands.

Chapter XXXVI. My Cabinet—Princess Kaiulani

On the day following the final ceremonies of the royal funeral my cabinet was called together; and one hour before the ministers were to arrive, Mr. J. A. Cummins, who was the Minister of Foreign Affairs, made his appearance, and asked if I had any plans or purposes in regard to the approaching meeting. In reply to this I advised him of my wish that he should resign from the cabinet, and accept the appointment of governor of Oahu, to which office I thought he would be better suited, as his duties would call him out amongst the people.

I felt sure he would enjoy visiting the outside districts; while the life of a minister in the cabinet bound him to official matters of a burdensome and responsible nature not so well adapted to his character and abilities. But to this offer of consideration for him, I was told by Mr. Cummins that he preferred to remain in the ministry. "But," I suggested, "the question is, will the ministry remain?" To this he replied that he had no doubt of that; in fact, he was sure that they would not be dismissed. I did not argue the matter with him, but simply said, "Are you, then, decided, and do you decline the appointment of governor of Oahu?" "Yes," he repeated; "my determination is made, besides which I may be of use here to the down-town party."

The hour of ten arrived and the cabinet met. I inquired at the opening of the cabinet meeting what was the business of the day; to which reply was made that it was necessary that I should sign without any delay their commissions, that thus they might proceed to the discharge of their duties. "But, gentlemen," said I, "I expect you to send in your resignations before I can act." My reasoning was, that, if they were now cabinet ministers, why should they appeal to me to appoint them to the places which they already filled? They hesitated, and regarded each other. "No," I continued, "if you do not resign, I do not see how I can issue to you new commissions." This was a point to which they did not think I would call attention, a suggestion which they had not foreseen might come from me, and they scarcely knew which way to turn. They thought that, while holding their former commissions, I ought to issue to them new ones over my royal signature. As this did not agree with my views of the matter, I stated to them definitely that it must be a question for future consideration, and that it would be best to refer the point for decision to the Supreme Court. After a lengthy period of the greatest anxiety to me, it was announced by Chief Justice Judd that the decision was in my favor, and that the commissions of the present members of the cabinet expired with the death of the king.

The ground on which the ministers had based their scheme was that the constitution distinctly stated that no change of ministry should take place except by a vote of "want of confidence" passed by the majority of the legislature. But while this was true, the document did not provide in any article for the continuance of the cabinet after the decease of the sovereign. It was, therefore, held by the chief justice that the ancient custom in this respect remained in force, and that commissions held under the deceased monarch gave no authority under his successor. Messrs. Cummins, Spencer, Brown, and Peterson, accordingly tendered their resignations, which I accepted, and then appointed: Mr. Samuel Parker, Minister of Foreign Affairs; Mr. C. N. Spencer, Minister of the Interior; Mr. H.A. Widemann, Minister of Finance; Mr. W.A. Whiting, Attorney-General; their commissions all bearing date of the 26th of February, 1891. Besides these appointments the position of chamberlain, being vacant by the absence of Hon. George W. Macfarlane, was filled by Mr. J. W. Robertson, who had been his assistant, and who subsequently proved to be a most efficient officer. Mr. Charles B. Wilson was appointed marshal.

While the matter was pending, arrangements were made for the meeting of the members of the House of Nobles for receiving the nominations of an heir apparent to the throne. On the ninth day of March, 1891, Princess Victoria Kaiulani, Kalaninuiahilapalapa Kawekiu i Lunalilo, daughter of my sister, Princess Miriam Kekauluohi Likelike and Hon. A. S. Cleghorn, was duly proclaimed heir apparent, and her nomination recognized by the United States ship-of-war *Mohican* by a salute of twenty-one guns.

Chapter XXXVII. My Husband Made Prince Consort—His Death

In July I made the usual royal tour of the islands. I was accompanied by my husband, Governor Dominis, and by Hon. Samuel Parker and Hon. W. A. Whiting of my cabinet. I visited Hawaii, Maui, and Molokai. At all the places in these islands where we stopped we were most cordially greeted and royally entertained by the people. Returning to Honolulu, we started out again for Kauai, but with a larger party than on the previous portion of the royal tour. I was now accompanied by Prince Kalanianaole, Hon. Samuel Parker, Mrs. C. A. Brown, Mrs. W. A. Aldrich, Mrs. C. H. Clark, Mrs. P. P. Kanoa, attended by her husband, Mrs. C. B. Wilson and her son, J. H. Wilson, Hon. E. K. Lilikalani, Hon. John K. Richardson, Mrs. Ulumaheihei, Hon. W. P. Kanealii, Hon. D. W. Pua, Mr. J. Kekipi, and Mr. and Mrs. Joseph Heleluhe. Greatly to our mutual regret, illness prevented my husband from being one of the party.

At Kauai we were most hospitably received and royally entertained by Mr. and Mrs. W. H. Rice. They took us to their handsome private residence at Lihue, to which there came all the principal people of the islands to pay respects. It was a great pleasure to me to receive these greetings, because up to this visit I had never seen so large an assembly of the principal people of that island. There were the Eisenbergs, the McBrides, the Wilcoxes, the Rices, the Smiths, some of these the living representatives of the oldest and best known of the missionary families. It seemed to me to be more like an assembling together of our societies in the city of Honolulu. Everything was done to make my arrival a most happy occasion to me by Mr. and Mrs. Rice, whose personal friends became my friends, and added their welcome to that of my genial hosts. My visit to Hanalei was made comfortable through the energy and kindness of Mr. Rice. In crossing from Hanalei through the sands of Hoohila, it was by reason of his personal guidance that the passage was made in safety, and that we reached the top of a high hill without accident.

Under the hospitable roof of Mr. and Mrs. Titcomb we spent a restful night; and on the morning following, boarding the steamer *James Makee*, our party bade farewell to all the kind friends at Lihue. From thence we proceeded to the island of Niihau, and landing, spent a very pleasant day on shore. Every attention was rendered to us by the manager who had charge of the island under appointment from the Gays. Horses and carriages were placed at our disposal, with which we rode through the country, and on our return found that we had been provided, by the forethought of this gentleman, with a luncheon of nice fat mutton; and as we returned with excellent appetites and were a large company, it soon disappeared. When evening came on we returned by the steamer to Kalapaki, where Mrs. Rice had preceded us and had a surprise in readiness. A grand sea-bath was proposed, to which we all gladly assented; and with scarcely an exception we refreshed ourselves in the cooling waters.

Then came the surprise, for under a grove of Hau trees growing back of their mansion-house was spread a most tempting table of good things. It was literally covered with the best of all that is produced in the whole extent of these islands. Nothing seemed lacking that could gratify the taste or tempt the appetite. Can it be possible that our genial host is the same man of whom, in narrating the events of the revolution of 1887, and the political troubles of Mr. Gibson, I have had occasion to speak, as showing later traits of an almost savage character? It is sad, but only too true. Moments sped quickly by, and time for departure came ere we were aware; so, bidding farewell to our entertainers and their numerous friends, we went on our way to Honolulu, where we arrived in the early part of the day following.

I found my husband somewhat better, but not yet able to leave his bed. He had not forgotten me during my absence, and had planned some surprises for me at our Waialua residence, which he desired to show to me himself. But he was too ill to undertake the journey. I was loath to leave him, and so hurriedly made the trip around the island of Oahu. Accompanied by Hon. Samuel Parker, Hon. J. A. Cummins, and others, we spent one night at the Kaneohe plantations, two nights at the residence of Mr. W. C. Lane, and passed only a little more time at Mr. Cecil Brown's.

At all of these places the people who came to receive us were delighted to have the opportunity to show their loyalty and manifest their love. We stopped at Kahuku, at Laie, amongst the residents of the Mormon faith, and then rode on to Waialua, where I found that my husband had indeed executed a great surprise for me. A large wooden lanai, or outer room, had been built, capacious enough to accommodate some one hundred and fifty or more persons. He had thought what a pleasure it would be to have this cool and pleasant resort, where, after the heat of the day or a row up the stream of Anahulu, I might take my comfort in sitting under the grateful shade, with all the friends I might select and invite to meet and rest with me there. It proved to be all that his kindness foresaw and desired, and also served as a reception-room for pleasant dances and other festivities.

After staying at Waialua a few days, where Mrs. Halstead and her husband, a well-known planter of that locality, entertained us, and also visiting some other prominent people of the district, we turned our steps toward Ewa, where Mrs. Kahelelaukoa Brown gave a grand luau in our honor. From thence our party returned to the city, making, as we entered its streets, quite an imposing cavalcade. At Washington Place I found my husband delighted to meet me, but I noticed with solicitude that he seemed to be very feeble. He grew weaker and weaker from this time until the morning of his death.

I was not expecting the immediate event, but watching in the room, when he motioned to me to approach his bedside—I complied with the wish. Hon. Samuel Parker and Major W. T. Seaward entered about the same moment, and remained a few minutes with us. Out on the broad piazza at the farther end of the house were seated a few of my young lady friends, his faithful valet, Mainalulu, and the attendants, Mary Kamiki, Keamalu, and Kawelo. Dr. Trousseau, the physician in charge of the case, soon entered, and after a brief examination said that he thought the patient needed rest, and motioned to those who were present that they would be excused from the chamber. Accordingly they retired to the veranda, leaving me alone by my husband's bedside. This was at about one o'clock. I drew near to the foot of the bed, and stood where I could easily watch him while he was apparently sleeping. I had been thus standing but a few minutes when, noticing a slight quivering motion pass over his frame, I immediately went to his side, and then hastily called the friends in attendance and summoned the doctor. He examined the patient, and said that all was over. Just a few minutes before my husband passed away he made a peculiar motion of his hand which I have seen brethren of the Masonic fraternity use in the act of prayer. Was this the moment at which his spirit was taking its flight from earth, to enter that larger and grander brotherhood beyond the things which are seen?

The attending physician was quite affected by the death of Governor Dominis; for his friendship with my husband was one of many years standing, and they had the warmest esteem for each other. By this simple statement of fact, it will be noticed that I was entirely alone by the side of my husband when he died; but there have been words of the cruelest import uttered by those who were not there, and could have known nothing of the facts. May they be forgiven for the wrong done to me and to my husband's memory.

There was an immediate meeting of the ministers of my cabinet to decide what was to be done in regard to the obsequies of Governor Dominis. That evening the remains were removed to Iolani Palace, and were laid in state. This was on the twenty-seventh day of August, 1891. It was the general wish, and the decision of the cabinet ministers, that the honors customarily granted to the deceased sovereigns should be accorded to my husband. Consequently, the lying in state, the military guards, the watchers from the Masonic fraternity, the ladies in attendance bringing their leis, their garlands, their floral decorations, the kahili bearers with the plumes of office, all were employed in manner and detail as I have already described it in speaking of the funeral of my brother, His Majesty King Kalakaua. The day appointed for the final ceremonies arrived; and Governor Dominis was borne, with all the honors accorded to his brother the king, to his final resting-place, followed by many sincere mourners, who had, by the kind offices of which I have only made mention now, done all that could be done to soften my grief, and for whose sympathetic attentions I shall never cease to be grateful.

Chapter XXXVIII. Hawaiians Plead For A New Constitution

After my husband's death, my retainers at Waikiki (to each of whom I had set apart a lot of land, so that each family might have its own home, and, further, that these might be handed down for the use of their children and children's children), proposed to come and stay with me in the city. So I accorded to each family one week, that all might have a share in this kindly office. This rule was laid down by me, and carefully observed from the date of my husband's death.

This will be, perhaps, the place to mention a matter which has been made use of in an evil way by certain of my enemies. On my accession to the throne my husband had been made prince consort, and after my brother's burial I had proposed to him that he should move to the palace; but in his feeble health he dreaded the long stairs there, which he would be obliged to climb, so I proposed to have the bungalow put in repair, and that the entire house should be placed at his service.

With this proposition he was much pleased, and hopefully looked forward to the time when, recovering from his illness, he would be able to take possession of his new home. He asked that there might be a small gate opened near the bungalow, so that he might easily come and go without being obliged to go through the form of offering to the sentry the password required for entrance by the front gate. His wish was immediately granted, and instructions given to the Minister of the Interior to that effect. The bungalow was handsomely fitted up, and all things were made ready for his occupation; but owing to his continued and increasing ill-health he never moved into it.

Mr. C. B. Wilson and his wife (seeing that she was one of my beneficiaries, and in her younger days one for whom my husband and I had great consideration) asked if they might come and be near me. In response, I told them that they might take the room that had been occupied by the Princess Poomaikalani in the bungalow. That was all that passed between us about the matter. Mrs. Wilson and Mrs. Clark were in constant attendance upon me as ladies in waiting.

Mrs. Eveline Wilson from her childhood had professed a great fondness and love for me, and with two other young ladies, Lizzie Kapoli and Sophie Sheldon, had made my home theirs. Bright young girls, with happy hearts, and free from care and trouble, they made that part of my life a most delightful epoch to me. It was then that Mr. Wilson first sought the hand of pretty little Kittie Townsend. Thus we had known Mr. Wilson quite well as a young man when he was courting his wife. My husband and myself had warmly favored his suit; and, with his wife, he naturally became a retainer of the household, and from time to time they took up their residence with us. But one cannot always tell what a young man of promise may be when he arrives at full manhood.

Mr. Samuel Parker called on me one day, and, after discussing some cabinet affairs, asked me directly, if there was any truth in the report that I had called in the advice or sought the assistance of Mr. C. B. Wilson in public affairs. To this I very naturally demanded the reasons why he should ask such questions. He replied that Mr. Wilson had told persons down town that he knew of matters which were connected with the cabinet, and that it was through his advice that certain measures had been carried through. On the strength of these remarks, occasion had been taken by Mr. J. E. Bush and Mr. R. W. Wilcox to publish in their newspapers articles calculated to prove injurious to my reputation. I answered Mr. Parker that I consulted no one outside of my cabinet, and that no measures had ever been consummated excepting such as had been advised by the ministers. He recognized the truth of this statement, and communicated the substance of our conversation to his colleagues.

Mr. Bush and Mr. Wilcox at the very commencement of my regency had openly asked for billets of office; a favor I had scarcely the power, and certainly not the intention, to grant, because all the offices were then filled by men whom I thought were good, loyal, and true to the crown. Mr. Bush had further published articles in his paper which did not meet with my approval, for they were attacks upon my brother, the king. Was he at work with the opposition party at the time he solicited office? Whether this was so or not, his subsequent actions showed at least the deepest ingratitude towards myself, who had showered favors on him and on his family, educated his children, and kept them all from poverty. Mr. R. W. Wilcox I have spoken of elsewhere. It will be seen that he had also become one of my enemies.

I was recently told that Mr. Wilson, at the time of Mr. Wilcox's attempt in 1889, would enter the meetings which were held at the king's barracks, and then, leaving the assembly, would stealthily go around to the house of Mr. A. F. Judd, and report all that had transpired. I have had no experiences more painful than the evidences of ingratitude among those I have had reason to think my friends; and I sincerely hope that in this case I have been misinformed.

One evening, shortly after Mr. and Mrs. Wilson had moved into the bungalow, he presented himself at the Blue Room of the palace, and then first mentioned the idea that a new constitution should be promulgated. About two days after this suggestion I received a call from Mr. Samuel Nowlein, who alluded to the same matter. A few days after Mr. Joseph Nawahi, with Mr. William White, had an interview with me by their request, and called my attention to the same public need. Until these conversations, it had not occurred to me as possible to take such a step in the interest of the native people; but after these parties had spoken to me, I began to give the subject my careful consideration. Twice Mr. White spoke to me on the matter before I told him that I would like to have a conference with all, to listen to an expression of their views.

Accordingly a meeting was called to be held at Muolaulani Palace, at which there was to be an opportunity for them to compare their opinions and discuss them in my presence. I heard what the opinions of the gentlemen were, but gave them no intimation of my own ideas or intentions, for I had really come to no definite conclusion. When the assembly was opened, I noticed that Mr. Wilson was not present, nor did he attend any of the meetings which were held for the consideration of the matter of constitutional reform, but came singly and alone to speak to me on the subject. But it seems that all this time, while I was simply reflecting on the situation, each of them was going forward and engaging in the preparation or draft of a new constitution.

When completed, I was handed by one party a copy of that it proposed, and by Mr. Wilson I was given a copy of the one on which he had been engaged. After reading both over, I employed a young man, simply because he was a very neat penman, to make copies; his name was W. F. Kaae, but he was usually called Kaiu. This is worthy of mention, because I subsequently discovered that, while upon this work for me, he took copies to Mr. A. F. Judd for the examination of that gentleman. It can readily be seen by what kind of persons I was surrounded; it must be remembered that I now write with a knowledge of recent events, but that then I had the fullest confidence in the loyalty of those who professed to be my friends.

The election of 1892 arrived, and with it the usual excitement of such occasions. Petitions poured in from every part of the

Islands for a new constitution; these were addressed to myself as the reigning sovereign. They were supported by petitions addressed to the Hui Kalaaina, who in turn indorsed and forwarded them to me. It was estimated by those in position to know, that out of a possible nine thousand five hundred registered voters, six thousand five hundred, or two-thirds, had signed these petitions. To have ignored or disregarded so general a request I must have been deaf to the voice of the people, which tradition tells us is the voice of God. No true Hawaiian chief would have done other than to promise a consideration of their wishes.

My first movement was to inquire of the parties active in the matter what they had to propose. I asked the Hui Kalaaina if they had any draft of a constitution prepared for my examination. The committee replied that they had not. After leaving my presence, they applied to Mr. W. R. Castle, and requested him to draw one out for them. Soon after the committee again entered my presence, this time bearing a neatly written document; but whether it had been drawn by Mr. Castle or by others, it is difficult for me to say. This I handed back to the committee, telling them to keep it until some future day, when I would ask them for it; because I did not intend at that moment to make any announcement of my purposes.

September 1st, 1892, witnessed the opening of the legislative assembly. There was nothing lacking of that pomp and display which had been first inaugurated in the days of Kanikeaouli, the third of the Kamehamehas. These forms and ceremonies were suggested and taught to the Hawaiian people by Dr. G. P. Judd, Mr. W. Richards, and Mr. R. Armstrong, men who originally came to Hawaii with no other avowed object than that of teaching the religion of Jesus Christ; but they soon resigned their meagre salaries from the American Board of Commissioners for Foreign Missions, and found positions in the councils or cabinets of the Kamehamehas more lucrative and presumably more satisfactory to them.

Lunalilo had an official staff, and many of his aids-de-camp were white men, as also happened with Kamehameha V.,

Kalakaua, and all the recent Hawaiian sovereigns. Dr. E. Hoffman, Mr. W. F. Allen, Mr. M. T. Monserrat, Mr. Prendergast, and many others whose names I might mention, have been perfectly willing to wear the uniform of the crown, to display their gilt lace and brass buttons on state occasions, and to ride richly caparisoned horses with shining accoutrements through our streets; and as long as the missionary party chose the men that were to be thus decked out, honored, and exhibited, it was never alleged that the Hawaiian kings loved display, and sought pomp and fuss and feathers. Yet what had our earlier monarchs ever done for the public good? Individually, nothing. They had acquiesced in the course laid down for them by the missionaries. The government established by these pious adventurers was the government of the day.

Those of their number who were able to get into government service drew their salaries faithfully, and spent or saved as they saw fit, but observed a truly "religious" silence as to the folly of spending money on public displays. This is the more remarkable, because there were other ways, even then, of securing treasury deficiencies. I remember that when G. P. Judd, W. Richards, and R. Armstrong were cabinet ministers, a deficiency so inexplicable occurred that the cabinet was required to resign immediately, and to one of the retiring members the popular appellation "kauka-kope-kala" subsequently adhered pretty tenaciously. I refrain from translating, as the title is not one of honor; but it still clings to the family as an heirloom.

It is more to the point that Kalakaua's reign was, in a material sense, the golden age of Hawaiian history. The wealth and importance of the Islands enormously increased, and always as a direct consequence of the king's acts. It has been currently supposed that the policy and foresight of the "missionary party" is to be credited with all that he accomplished, since they succeeded in abrogating so many of his prerogatives, and absorbing the lion's share of the benefits derived from it. It should, however, be only necessary to remember that the measures which brought about our accession of wealth were not at all in line with a policy of annexation to the United States, which was the very essence of the dominant "missionary" idea. In fact, his progressive foreign policy was well calculated to discourage it.

And for this reason, probably, they could not be satisfied even with the splendid results which our continued nationality offered them. They were not grateful for a prosperity which must sooner or later, while enriching them, also elevate the masses of the Hawaiian people into a self-governing class, and depose them from that primacy in our political affairs which they chiefly valued. They became fiercely jealous of every measure which promised to benefit the native people, or to stimulate their national pride. Every possible embarrassment and humiliation were heaped upon my brother. And because I was suspected of having the welfare of the whole people also at heart (and what sovereign with a grain of wisdom could be otherwise minded?), I must be made to feel yet more severely that my kingdom was but the assured prey of these "*conquistadores.*"

As I have said, the legislature was opened, and began its daily sessions. The usual measures were brought in, one after another, for consideration by the representatives of the people. But all other matters were persistently thrust aside in order to give time for the repeated dismissals of cabinets. By the account given by me of the revolution of 1887, it will be noticed that the constitution forced upon my brother at that date made the sovereign inferior to the cabinet. The ministry must be appointed by the monarch, but once appointed had absolute control over every measure, nor could the monarch dismiss them, and only a vote of the legislature could deprive them of their portfolios. That provision made the cabinet, as I have shown in previous pages, a perpetual football in the hands of political parties.

Therefore, this session of the legislature, instead of giving attention to measures required for the good of the country, devoted its energies to the making and unmaking of cabinets. I think there were four rapidly commissioned by me and voted out. But at this point I call attention to the statement which I made to Hon. James H. Blount, the commissioner charged with the work of investigating the circumstances of the over-throw of the constitutional government of the Hawaiian Islands. In that statement will be found the matter which properly supplements this chapter, and need not be again detailed in this memoir. It naturally, together with some review of events already related, forms the connecting link between the opening ceremonies of the legislature and the enforced abdication of my authority.

Selected by reason of his perfect impartiality and long acquaintance with foreign affairs, this gentleman was sent out by His Excellency Grover Cleveland, President of the United States, and arrived in Honolulu on the twenty-ninth day of March, 1893. In July Mr. Blount made his final report, to which I need only allude to say that, as is well known, after digesting a mass of testimony on both sides, he decided that I was the constitutional ruler of the Hawaiian Islands. It was at this time that I made to him the statement which will be found in the closing pages of that volume.

Of the manner in which Hon. J. H. Blount conducted the investigation, I must speak in the terms of the highest praise. He first met the parties opposed to my government, and took down their statements, which were freely given, because they had imagined that he could be easily turned in their favor. So they gave him the truth, and some important facts in admission of their revolutionary intentions, dating from several years back. Mr. Blount afterwards took the statements of the government, or royalist side. These were simply given, straightforward, and easily understood. Compare the two statements, and it is not difficult to explain the final report of Mr. Blount. All the evidence can be reviewed by any person who may wish to do so, and a judgment formed of the men who caused this revolution, as it has been bound in volumes, and can be seen at the Library of Congress in the Capitol at Washington.

Chapter XXXIX. The "Crimes I Am Charged Withal."

The three "intolerable" measures with which my government stands charged by those who succeeded in enlisting the aid of so powerful an ally as the United States in this revolution are as follows:

First—That I proposed to promulgate a new constitution. I have already shown that two-thirds of my people declared their dissatisfaction with the old one; as well they might, for it was a document originally designed for a republic, hastily altered when the conspirators found that they had not the courage to assassinate the king. It is alleged that my proposed constitution was to make such changes as to give to the sovereign more power, and to the cabinet or legislature less, and that only subjects, in distinction from temporary residents, could exercise suffrage. In other words, that I was to restore some of the ancient rights of my people. I had listened to whatever had been advised, had examined whatever drafts of constitutions others had brought me, and promised but little.

But, supposing I had thought it wise to limit the exercise of suffrage to those who owed allegiance to no other country; is that different from the usage in all other civilized nations on earth? Is there another country where a man would be allowed to vote, to seek for office, to hold the most responsible of positions, without becoming naturalized, and reserving to himself the privilege of protection under the guns of a foreign man-of-war at any moment when he should quarrel with the government under which he lived? Yet this is exactly what the quasi-Americans, who call themselves Hawaiians now and Americans when it suits them, claimed the right to do at Honolulu.

The right to grant a constitution to the nation has been, since the very first one was granted, a prerogative of the Hawaiian sovereigns. The constitution of 1840 was drawn at Lahaina by a council aided by missionary graduates, but promulgated by the king without any appeal to other authority. That of 1852 was drawn by Dr. Judd, John II., and Chief Justice Lee. It was submitted to the legislature, not to the people, and, as amended by the members, became the law of the land. In 1864 there was an attempt to hold a constitutional convention: but, as I have shown in this history, Prince Lot, or, as he then was, Kamehameha V., dissolved the convention, because dissatisfied with its inaction, and in a week's time declared the former constitution abrogated; and, without asking a vote from anybody, gave the land a new and ably drawn constitution, under which the country was prosperously ruled for twenty-three years, or until it was overthrown by aliens determined to coerce my brother. Then followed their own draft of 1887, which also was never ratified by any deliberative assembly.

Such, in brief, is the history of constitution-making in Hawaii; and from this mere statement of the facts it will be seen that of all the rulers of the Hawaiian Islands for the last half-century, I was the only one who assented to a modification of the existing constitution on the expressed wishes, not only of my own advisers, but of two-thirds of the popular vote, and, I may say it without fear of contradiction, of the entire population of native or half-native birth. Yet, with the above historical record before them in a book written and printed by one of their own number, the missionary party have had the impudence to announce to the world that I was unworthy longer to rule, because on my sole will and wish I had proposed to overthrow "the constitution."

Second—I am charged by my opposers with signing a lottery bill. I have already shown, in the communication of the cabinet to my brother, and the ruling of the Supreme Court supporting their view, that, according to the "bayonet" constitution, made and enforced by the missionary party, the sovereign shall and must sign such measures as the cabinet presents for signature. This is, in another form, an absolute denial of the power of the veto. But even had I held veto power, it may be noted here that on many accounts the bill was popular. No one would have been more benefited than my accusers. The government of Hawaii was to take no part in the lottery, but was to receive a fixed and openly stated sum of money for its charter. Among the advantages guaranteed was that the projectors should build a railroad around the large island of Hawaii, thus employing the people and benefiting land-holders.

We were petitioned and besought to grant it by most of the mercantile class of the city—shopkeepers, mechanics, manufacturers—in fact, all the middle class of the people. Nor is the reason at all difficult to state by any one who knows our community. When the people of native and part native birth prosper, business is good and the community is prosperous. The prosperity brought by the reciprocity treaty and the sugar plantations had disappointed our expectations. The money went into the hands of the few, who safely invested in foreign interests and enterprises every dollar of it, save the amount of wages paid to foreign and Mongolian labor. But the advantages to be received from the charter of this, which in some American localities is called a "gift enterprise," would be immediately put in circulation among our own people, because spent on much-needed public works, and thus would bring some little prosperity to them parallel to that enjoyed by foreigners.

I am not defending lotteries. They are not native productions of my country, but introduced into our "heathen" land by so-called Christians, from a Christian nation, who have erected monuments, universities, and legislative halls by that method. I am simply explaining what this bill intended, because, by the reports sent to their correspondents in the United States, the missionary party represented me as a grand vender of lottery tickets, by which I was to become rich and powerful; whereas the scheme, be it good or bad, would not have been to my individual profit, but to that of my native people.

Third—I proposed to issue licenses for the importation and sale of opium. I did think it would be wise to adopt measures for restricting and controlling a trade which it is impossible to suppress. With a Chinese population of over twenty thousand persons, it is absolutely impossible to prevent smuggling, unlawful trade, bribery, corruption, and every abuse. There were more scandals connected with the opium traffic than I have the time to notice here. Some of the most prominent citizens have been connected with these affairs, and frauds have been unearthed even in the custom-house itself. The names of Mr. Parks, of Mr. W. F. Allen, and more recently of Mr. Henry Waterhouse, have been associated with some very questionable dealings in this drug; and it may be doubted whether the practice of hushing up such matters is favorable to good morals in any community. The Provisional Government seems to have had no scruples in the matter; for the sons of the missionaries exported a large quantity of confiscated opium, and sold it for fifty thousand dollars in British Columbia.

The British government has long since adopted license instead of prohibition, and the statute proposed among the final acts of my government was drawn from one in use in the British colonies; yet I have still to learn that there has been any proposition on the part of the pious people of London to dethrone Her Majesty Queen Victoria for issuing such licenses.

I have thus, for the first and only time, reviewed the position of my opponents in regard to the only public charges which they made against my administration of government; and the reader can judge if all or any of them are of a nature to justify revolt against authority, and the summoning of aid of a foreign vessel of war, as they outrageously stated at the time—"to protect American life and property!"

My appointments of cabinet officers were never given the test of experience; because the ministry was invariably voted out by the legislature "for want of confidence" without just cause, and in one notable instance within an hour or so from the time when I sent in the names. It is a matter of great satisfaction to me when I look back at the actions of that legislature, to reflect that none of the ministers of my selection have ever been voted out for any crime, for any defalcation in their accounts, or for failure in the exercise of their duties in public office. But it is a source of sincere regret to me that the members of that legislative assembly should have so forgotten themselves, the dignity of their position, and the responsibility with which the people had intrusted them as representatives, as to permit themselves to behave in such an unpatriotic manner.

The Macfarlane cabinet was one of the greatest popularity amongst the Hawaiian people on account of the stand Mr. Macfarlane took in the House, and his courage in replying to the false and uncalled-for speeches of J. L. Stevens, the American Minister resident.

Chapter XL. Overthrow Of The Monarchy

After the so-called Provisional Government had been recognized by Minister Stevens, and I had referred in writing my case to the United States, there was no more for me to do but retire in peace to my private residence, there to await the decision of the United States government. This I did, and cautioned the leaders of my people to avoid riot or resistance, and to await tranquilly, as I was doing, the result of my appeal to the power to whom alone I had yielded my authority. While in Washington in 1897, I had prepared for me as brief a statement as possible from official documents there of the reference of my case to the decision of the United States government as arbitrator in the matter.

It has been my endeavor, in these recollections, to avoid speaking evil of any person, unless absolutely demanded by the exigencies of my case before the public. I simply state facts, and let others form their own judgment of the individuals. But of Minister John L. Stevens it must be said that he was either mentally incapable of recognizing what is to be expected of a gentleman, to say nothing of a diplomatist, or he was decidedly in league with those persons who had conspired against the peace of Hawaii from the date of the "Queen's Jubilee" in 1887. Several times in my presence, to which he had access by virtue of his official position, he conducted himself with such a disregard of good manners as to excite the comment of my friends.

His official dispatches to his own government, from the very first days of his landing, abound in statements to prove (according to his view) the great advantage of an overthrow of the monarchy, and a cession of my domains to the rule of the United States. His own daughter went as a messenger to the largest one of the islands of my kingdom to secure names for a petition for the annexation of the Hawaiian Islands to the American Union, and by an accident lost her life, with the roll containing the few names she had secured. All this took place while he was presumed to be a friendly minister to a friendly power, and when my minister was under the same relation to his government. Of his remarks regarding myself personally I will take no notice further than to say that, by his invitation, I attended a very delightful lunch party at his house a few months before the United States troops were landed.

Mr. Albert F. Willis arrived in Honolulu on Saturday, the fourth day of November, 1893. He came from San Francisco on the same steamer with Rev. Dr. C. M. Hyde, the local representative or agent of the American Board of Missions. By this gentleman Mr. Willis was approached and informed, until he became imbued with Dr. Hyde's own prejudices against the native people of the Hawaiian Islands and against their queen. That clergyman's propensity to speak evil of his neighbor may be recalled by those who read his remarks about the late lamented Father Damien. One of the first acts of Mr. Willis was to send for me to come to his residence, which I did, accompanied by my chamberlain, Mr. Robertson. Was it the place of the lady to go to the house of the gentleman, or for the latter to call on the lady? I leave it for others to decide. As for myself, I simply felt that I would undertake anything for the benefit of my people.

At this time men were going about town with firearms; shots were at times flying about the city, whistling through the air, or penetrating houses to the great danger of the occupants; and no one was responsible for the local disorder. Words of harm towards my person had been openly spoken by the revolutionists; spies were in my household, and surrounded my house by day and by night; spies were also stationed at the steps of the Congregational church opposite my residence, to take note of those who entered my gates, how long they remained, and when they went out. My respect for true religion prevents my stating the active part one of the preachers of God's Word took in this espionage. It was under these circumstances that I prepared to visit Mr. Willis in accordance with his request.

On entering the house of Mr. Willis, Mr. Mills directed me into the parlor, while he and Mr. Robertson entered the opposite room. A Japanese screen divided the apartments. I was seated on the sofa when Mr. Willis, entering, took a chair, and sat down just in front of me, near the screen. He informed me that he was the bearer of the kindest greetings from President Cleveland, and that the President would do all in his power to undo the wrong which had been done. He then asked if I would consent to sign a proclamation of general amnesty, stating that I would grant complete protection and pardon to those who had overthrown my government. I told him that I would consult my ministers on that matter. The suggestion did not seem to meet with his approval.

I well knew, and it has been conclusively shown in this history, that my actions could not be binding or in any way recognized unless supported by the ministers in cabinet meeting. This was according to law, and according to the constitution these very persons had forced upon the nation. Perhaps Mr. Willis thought that all he had to do was to propose, and then that my place was to acquiesce. But he asked again for my judgment in the matter as it stood, and seemed determined to obtain an expression of opinion from me. I told him that, as to granting amnesty, it was beyond my powers as a constitutional sovereign. That it was a matter for the privy council and for the cabinet. That our laws read that those who are guilty of treason should suffer the penalty of death.

He then wished to know if I would carry out that law. I said that I would be more inclined personally to punish them by banishment, and confiscation of their property to the government. He inquired again if such was my decision. I regarded the interview as an informal conversation between two persons as to the best thing for the future of my country, but I repeated to him my wish to consult my ministers before deciding on any definite action. This terminated the consultation, excepting that Mr. Willis specially requested me not to mention anything concerning the matter to any person whomsoever, and assured me he would write home to the government he represented.

He did so. It was a long month before he could receive any reply; but when it came he communicated the fact to me, and asked for another interview at his house. This time he also inquired if there was any other person I would like to have with me. I suggested the name of Mr. J. O. Carter, at which the American minister seemed to be highly pleased. So at the stated hour we met. This time Mr. Willis had present as his stenographer Mr. Ellis C. Mills, afterward American consul-general at Honolulu. He first read me what he said were some notes of our former interview. From whence did these come? By Mr. Willis's own proposition we were to be entirely alone during that interview, and to all appearance we were so. Was there a stenographer behind that Japanese screen? Whatever the paper was, Mr. Willis finished the reading of it, and asked me if it was correct. I replied, "Yes."

Doubtless, had I held the document in my hand, and had I been permitted to read and examine it, for the eye perceives words that fall unheeded on the ear, I should then have noticed that there was a clause which declared that I was to have my opponents beheaded. That is a form of punishment which has never been used in the Hawaiian Islands, either before or since the coming of foreigners. Mr. Willis then asked me if my views were the same as when we met the first time; and I again said "Yes," or words to that effect. Mr. Carter inquired if I rescinded so much of Mr. Willis's report as related to the execution of the death penalty upon those in revolt. To this I replied, "I do in that respect."

Yet, notwithstanding the fact was officially reported in the despatches of Mr. Willis, that I especially declared that my enemies should not suffer the death penalty, I found to my horror, when the newspapers came to Honolulu from the United States, that the President and the American people had been told that I was about to behead them all! There is an old proverb which says that "a lie can travel around the world while the truth is putting on its boots." That offensive charge was repeated to my hurt as often as possible; although I immediately send my protest that I had not used the words attributed to me by Mr. Willis in our informal conversation, and that at my first official interview with him I had modified (so far as my influence would go) the law of all countries regarding treason.

At the interview held Saturday, Dec. 16, I did decline to promise executive clemency, and gave as my reason that, this being the second offence of these individuals, they were regarded as dangerous to the community. That their very residence would be a constant menace; that there never would be peace in my country, or harmony amongst the people of different nations residing with us, as long as such a disturbing element remained, especially after they had once been successful in seizing the reins of government. But on Monday, Dec. 18, Mr. Willis came to Washington Place; and again acting under the advice of Hon. J. O. Carter, I gave to him a document recognizing the high sense of justice which had prompted the action of Mr. Cleveland, and agreeing that, in view of his wishes, the individuals setting up or supporting the Provisional Government should have full amnesty in their persons and their property, if they would work together with me in trying to restore peace and prosperity to our beautiful and once happy islands.

It was most unfortunate that the American minister should have so misrepresented me, or that I should have so misunderstood him, or that his stenographer (if there was one concealed at that interview) should have blundered, or that I should have been so overburdened by the many aspects of the painful situation as to be ignorant or unconscious of the importance of the precise words read in my presence. The only official communication made by me was to the effect that there should be perfect amnesty, and this was made in recognition of President Cleveland's courtesy and justice.

Events proved that it would not have made the least difference what I had said or what I had not said; for these people, having once gained the power, were determined never to relinquish it. Mr. Dole wrote to the American minister charging him with being in correspondence with me, and demanded of Mr. Willis if he was acting in any way hostile to his, that is, the Provisional Government. The very next day Mr. Willis sent word to Mr. Dole that he had a communication to make to him. So, Dec. 20, Mr. Willis went to President Dole, and delivered his message from President Cleveland, in which Mr. Dole was asked to resign that power which he had only obtained through the acts of Minister Stevens and the United States troops. Mr. Willis's speech is a full and explicit confession of the ground taken by my government, that it was overthrown by a conspiracy to which the United States, through its minister, was a party; and after assuring Mr. Dole that I had granted full amnesty to all parties, asked him to resign and restore the old order of things. Mr. Willis says in his latest utterance on the subject:

"It becomes my duty to advise you of the President's determination of the question which your action and that of the queen devolved upon him, and that you are expected to relinquish to her, her constitutional authority. In the name of and by the authority of the United States of America, I submit to you the question, 'Are you willing to abide by the decision of the President?'"

Could there be any plainer recognition than this that I was the constitutional ruler of my people?

And yet I cannot help calling attention to the difference in the treatment accorded to the two parties, and their reference to the United States. Three days were given to Mr. Dole to consider Mr. Cleveland's decision, as announced by Mr. Willis. The documents were placed in his hands to study over; and were he disposed he could call together his associates, compare their opinions, and then return a carefully written and diplomatic answer. This he did, under the date of the 23rd of December, at midnight, when he himself delivered his response to Mr. Willis. In contrast, I, a lone woman, was sent an order to go to the residence of a gentleman until that moment a stranger to me. Without the least warning of the nature of the communication to be made to me, and without a moment's deliberation or consultation with friendly counselors, I was urged to give my opinion as to matters which in any government should be decided only after careful consideration; and then my first immature impressions of the claims of my people and of justice were telegraphed broadcast, while my official and subsequent proclamation of the entire amnesty was hardly noticed. And yet, all this time, by Mr. Willis's own words, I was recognized by the United States as the constitutional sovereign of the Hawaiian Islands.

The Hawaiian people almost worship the name of President Cleveland; for he has tried to do what was right, and it was only because he was not supported by Congress that his efforts were not successful. Mr. Dole's answer, as could have been predicted by any who know the men composing the missionary party, was a refusal to comply with the request of President Cleveland. But, none the less, my grateful people will always remember that, in his message to Congress and in his official acts, Mr. Cleveland showed the greatest anxiety to do that which was just, and that which was for the honor of the nation over which he had been elected chief ruler. He has always had from me the utmost respect and esteem.

Chapter XLI. Some Important Inquiries

The first annexation commission was sent to Washington by the parties who had been prominent in the overthrow of the monarchy during the closing days of the administration of President Harrison. When Mr. Carter and his fellow-commissioners, Messrs. Thurston, Wilder, Castle, and Marsden, arrived in Washington, President Harrison and Secretary Foster had received my letter of protest, so that they had ample time to consider the situation before the so-called commissioners were presented at the executive mansion. Yet, after having been fully warned by the statements in my letter, these men were received diplomatically.

I was the constitutional ruler the last time the Department of State had heard from the Islands.

The minister bearing my commission and seal was at that moment residing at the national capital.

I had informed President Harrison and his Secretary of State of the unjust and fraudulent actions of the revolutionists, of the well-known aid and counsel they had received from Mr. John L. Stevens, the American minister, and the substantial assistance given by the forces of the United States ship *Boston*, under command of Captain Wiltse, through which agencies, and those alone, my government had been overthrown.

I had asked that justice should be done, and that the rights of my people should be restored.

President Harrison chose to set aside my statement and petition, and give audience to these irresponsible commissioners, sending to the Senate a treaty which, without the least authority, they offered to him.

These commissioners were self-chosen; but even allowing that they had been selected by the missionary party, with whom they were in sympathy, yet that was a mere petty minority — only 637 voters against 9,500 of Hawaiian birth and nationality. Yet their proposition was certainly sent to the Senate, while no action whatever was ever taken upon mine, although in this I did not represent myself individually, but the constitutional government and the real people of Hawaii. I have been informed, since I visited Washington in 1897, that the Senate decided that these acts of President Harrison amounted to a recognition of the Provisional Government. Why should this be so, when it was a mere proposal placed before the President, and by him transmitted as such to the Senate? It was there simply for their consideration. No vote was taken on the question up to the day when it was withdrawn by his successor, President Cleveland. The pretence of recognition to these irresponsible commissioners was unjust to me, as well as a wrong to the Hawaiian people.

In contrast to this, the wise step taken by President Cleveland in sending a commissioner to investigate the situation was fair to both sides, and carried out by the man of his choice in a thoroughly impartial manner. When Mr. Cleveland was finally forced into some kind of recognition of the missionary party, he used these words, that he recognized "the right of the Hawaiian people to choose their own form of government." My people have had no choice since the Provisional Government came into power.

Nothing of importance seems to have transpired during the early part of the year 1894. All this time, however, the Hawaiian people were waiting with patience to hear from the American continent that justice was to be done, and their constitutional rights restored by the great power to which they had trusted.

No messages or communications of any kind were made to me all this time by the American minister, and none were sent to me from Washington by the Department of State. Why was this? By Mr. Cleveland's decision, by Mr. Gresham's despatches to Mr. Willis, by the declarations of that gentleman publicly made to Mr. Dole, I, Liliuokalani, was the constitutional sovereign of the Hawaiian Islands; why should I have been kept in complete ignorance of all that was taking place at Washington, while the petty minority of alien residents, who had been summoned by the American minister "in the name of the United States of America to resign power and authority," should receive official despatches which ought to have been delivered to me?

Just before he left the Islands, Mr. Blount impressed upon me with great solemnity the importance of the continuance of the peaceful attitude of the Hawaiian people, assuring me that if any disturbance should take place on our part it would prompt the United States to send vessels of war to the port, men would again be landed, and the result would be the loss of the independence of our country. Believing that he spoke by authority, and that the day of release from the oppression of the stranger was near, I continued from the day of my retirement at Washington Place to impress upon all the necessity for abstaining from riot or disturbance.

The people listened to my voice, and obeyed my will with a submission that kept the community free from disorder far more than any law or restraint of that which has called itself a government. Many a time I have heard that the Hawaiians would no longer submit to their oppressors, that they were about to appeal to fire and the sword; but I have always dissuaded them from commencing any such measures. This discontent was not confined to the people of native or even part native birth. Those of foreign ancestry not in sympathy with the revolutionists, those whose daily comfort had been disturbed or whose business had been made unprofitable or ruined by the rich and powerful missionary party, appealed to me and my friends to restore the old order of things, that prosperity might again smile on the majority, instead of being locked up in the bank accounts of a very few.

It subsequently became known to me through other sources, although not until long after the date about which I now write, that the Senate had taken matters out of the hands of President Cleveland, and had conducted an independent investigation in the city of Washington, at which O. P. Emerson, Peter C. Jones, Z. S. Spalding, W. D. Alexander, Lieutenant Lucien Young, Mr. E. K. Moore, L. G. Hobbs, W. T. Swinburne, Lieutenant Laird, Mr. A. F. Judd, W. C. Wilder, J. H. Soper, A. S. Wilcox, C. Bolte, Geo. N. Wilcox, John Emmeluth, C. L. Carter, F. W. McChesney, W. B. Oleson, J. A. McCandless, Minister John L. Stevens, James F. Morgan, William R. Castle, L. A. Thurston, Dewitt Coffman, M. Stelker, William S. Bowen, P. W. Reeder, Charles L. Macarthur, Admiral George Belknap, N. B. Dalameter, Francis R. Day, Rev. R. R. Hoes, W. E. Simpson, N. Ludlow, and S. N. Castle, gave either by affidavit or in person their testimony against me.

So far as the above individuals knew anything whatever about the affairs of Hawaii, they were conspirators against my government; the obscurely known amongst the number were from those who had been, as one of them stated, simply rusticating at the Islands a while, and had been poisoned against the native people by my enemies. Not a single witness on the side of constitutional government was examined by the committee, if I except Hon. James H. Blount, who was called, and courageously repeated all the statements of his report to Mr. Cleveland.

Yet on such ex parte testimony as this, the Senate made a lengthy and partisan report, which I never had an opportunity to examine until my residence in Washington during the winter of 1897. It is altogether too long to find admittance here, but its meaning can be expressed in a very few words. It says that, rightfully or wrongfully, the native monarchy had been overthrown, the parties who succeeded in this fraud and imposition had been acknowledged as a government by the administration of Mr. Harrison, and therefore the question would not be reopened nor the facts reviewed by the United States!

Where was proper consideration given to my own statement to President Harrison, made through my commissioner, Mr. Paul Neumann? Why were not the petitions of the patriotic leagues of my people put into the inquiry? Why was not the fact that there was such an inquiry going on communicated to me? Why were my enemies informed of that which was in progress, so that they could hurry to Washington, or send their testimony, while not one of my friends was given the opportunity to raise a voice on behalf of the disfranchised Hawaiian people or their persecuted queen? Whatever may be the answers to these questions, it is true that no message ever reached me. No further communication was ever made to me by the American minister, nor did I even hear, except through the most vague kind of rumor, that probably no more would be done in the cause of justice. Even the fact of the decision of the Senate was not communicated to me; yet it seems that it was all settled the last week of February, 1894, on the testimony of the above aliens.

Since the bold admissions of members of the missionary party made to Minister Blount of their own guilt, since the confession, by those who had established themselves at the head of a provisional government, of the intended crime of which my brother was to be the victim, all of which appears in black and white on the pages of their own testimony, the scornful title of "P. G." has clung to them, to their children, and will be passed down to their children's children. After the truth was made public they became ashamed to hear themselves called "P. G.'s," and, repudiating the name, called themselves instead "Annexationists."

The so-called Provisional Government began in the spring of 1894 to consider again a change of name. So they allowed a few of their chosen tools to vote for what was called a constitutional convention, of which the original conspirators, to the number of nineteen, who had no warrant for their position save their own self-given nominations, and eighteen others in sympathy with them, enacted what they called a constitution; and in order to have some guns fired at its adoption, and to curry favor with the United States, they announced the so-called Republic on the fourth of July, 1894, and it was declared from the steps of Iolani Palace, while the vessels of war in the harbor were saluting for a totally different occasion.

During that same month, Mr. Samuel Parker had mentioned to me the necessity, in his opinion, of sending a Hawaiian commissioner to the United States to see what could be done for our people. Mr. Cornwell also consulted me upon the same matter. By conference with these gentlemen, it was decided that, instead of sending five commissioners, as we had at first designed to do, that Hon. Samuel Parker, Mr. John A. Cummins, Judge H. A. Widemann, with Major W. T. Seaward as secretary, should visit the capital of the United States, and represent those in Hawaii, whether native or foreign, opposed to the missionary party, that so the government of the majority might get a hearing in the councils of that great nation to which alone I yielded my authority.

What was the result of this commission? That is impossible for me to say. They went and they returned. They brought me no papers giving an official account of their proceedings or actions while on the mission. Each had some bit of information to communicate verbally. About the only definite remark which recurs to me now is that Secretary Gresham had informed them that Mr. Cleveland was suffering from a slight illness, and would be unable to see them for three or four days, at which intelligence they became discouraged, and left Washington. They had absolutely nothing to show me for their time and the expenditure of my money.

A month after word was sent to me that the merchants of Honolulu, who were in sympathy with the monarchy, had decided to send Judge Widemann on a foreign mission in our interests, at which I was pleased, and acquiesced in the choice. He was gone about three months, and again returned with only a verbal statement to the effect that, while on his way to England, he had heard that that nation was sending a message of recognition to the Republic of Hawaii. He continued on his journey as far as Germany, where he reported that the minister to whom he meant to present the statement of our side of the case was absent from the country on a tour of business or pleasure. So Judge Widemann returned without any favorable results.

All the expenses of these commissions from the very commencement, when I sent Mr. Paul Neumann to follow the original commissioners of the first supporters of the rebellion, were paid by me from my private purse. And from the seventeenth of January to the present hour, that remains true of every effort which has been made to induce the government of the United States to act under the righteous decision of its President, Grover Cleveland, supported by the impartial report of Hon. James H. Blount. No one, outside or inside the Hawaiian Islands, has contributed a cent to the repeated outlays I have made for the good of the Hawaiian people.

Further, from the date of the overthrow of the constitutional monarchy to the present day, I have never received from the Provisional Government, nor from its successor, the "Republic of Hawaii," a single cent of income from any source whatever. Even those revenues of the crown lands which had been collected prior to the seizure of the public treasury by the insurgents, and which remained in the hand of the commissioner at the time of my retirement from public life, were never paid to me. What became of these moneys I do not say, but not a dollar of it was ever handed to me.

For four years and more, now, these people have confiscated and collected the revenues reserved from all time in order that the chief highest in rank, that is, the reigning sovereign, might care for his poorer people. Never were the revenues of these lands included in government accounts. They comprised 915,000 acres out of a total extent of four millions, or about one-quarter, and yield an income of about $50,000 a year. They are by legislative act and rulings of the Supreme Court my own property at this day. But notwithstanding this, the doctrine that might makes right seems to prevail; and not content with depriving me of my income, and employing it to forward their own schemes, the present government is now striving to cede these lands, which they do not own and never can own, to the United States.

Chapter XLII. Attempt To Restore The Monarchy

At the time of the return of Mr. Widemann from abroad, the intensity of the feeling was at its height amongst the Hawaiian people that something should be done to save the country. Of their own accord they bought rifles, pistols, and other arms, stealthily keeping these for future use. During this time, too, they were privately informed where arms belonging to the men in power were kept; for although it is generally conceded all over the world, and common sense would seem to show how one should act towards one's enemies, yet there was the strangest intermingling of those of the two parties, which were called the "Royalists" and the "P. G.'s." Instead of recognizing each other as enemies, and keeping apart as such, they associated as in former days.

Visiting went on just the same, exchanges of thought and opinion were the same. The Royalists, open hearted and free of speech, socially ignored the fact that the P. G.'s were, in every material sense, their enemies. These latter kept the situation in view, and with soft words studied to worm out of the unsuspecting all that they could in the way of information as to

Royalist hopes and plans, that the particulars might be communicated to the P. G. government.

Moreover, many who swore allegiance to the "Republic of Hawaii" began to regret bitterly that they ever permitted themselves to support the revolutionary party. They had been in comfortable circumstances, had even laid aside for a rainy day, and felt that the savings of their years of prosperity would find them independent in life's decline. But since the overthrow of honest government they had lost, or been forced to spend, all they had accumulated, and the little business left to them would scarcely sustain their families.

Weary with waiting, impatient under the wrongs they were suffering, preparations were undoubtedly made amongst some in sympathy with the monarchy to overthrow the oligarachy. How and where these were carried on, I will not say. I have no right to disclose any secrets given in trust to me. To the time of which I now write their actions had been peaceful, out of respect and obedience to their queen. If, goaded by their wrongs, I could no longer hold them in check with reason; if they were now, by one accord, determined to break away, and endeavor, by a bold stroke, to win back their nationality, why should I prohibit the outburst of patriotism? I told them that if the mass of the native people chose to rise, and try to throw off the yoke, I would say nothing against it, but I could not approve of mere rioting.

On Jan. 6, 1895, came the beginning of a revolt. For three months prior to that date my physician, Dr. Donald McLelan, had been in attendance on me, and, as I was suffering very severely from nervous prostration, prescribed electricity. For two years I had borne the long agony of suspense, a terrible strain, which at last made great inroads on my strength.

The knowledge of the secreting of arms on my premises, the distribution of munitions of war amongst the people who were guarding my house and grounds, has been imputed to me. Whether any arms were brought there, where they were, or what they were, I never took occasion to inquire. I never saw a single pistol or rifle by day or by night. I remember that I had occasion to scold my gardener for the disturbed condition in which I often found my plants. It seemed as though some persons had been digging up the ground, and replacing disturbed soil. But no arms were secreted by me or by my orders about the place, from the roof to the cellar, or from one end to the other of the garden, nor were any kept there to my knowledge, save parlor rifles and harmless old-fashioned muskets.

My husband had a passion for collecting ancient specimens of firearms, and for this purpose he set apart in the yard a small cottage which had once been a favorite retreat of his bachelor days. He had everything arranged prettily, and on its walls was a formidable show of antiquated instruments of war. I recall the appearance of one very old Arabian musket, which he took special pride in exhibiting to his friends. There was also an old-fashioned flute, and a sword which, so it was said, had formerly belonged to General Washington.

There were many other relics of antiquity in this line, which had been contributed by his friends—large pistols and small pistols, loading with ramrods from the muzzle, clubs and spears from the South Sea Islands; and, in fact, it was quite a cabinet of curiosities of obsolete warfare.

He had, during his lifetime, rifles and shotguns of modern style of manufacture, which he took with him on his visits to the estates of Hon. Samuel Parker, or when we went to our country residence at Waialua. But these latter, after his death, were appropriated by his personal friends; and there was therefore nothing on the place by which the least harm to anyone could be done. Yet it was on the opening of this curiosity shop, as harmless as any gallery of family portraits, that the word was passed around town that a large quantity of firearms of different styles had been found secreted in a small house on the grounds of the queen.

I slept quietly at home the night of the outbreak. The evening before Captain Samuel Nowlein came in, and told me that his party was in readiness. This must have been about eight o'clock in the evening, as the meeting in the Congregational church had just begun as Captain Nowlein bade me farewell. He had not been gone very long when there seemed to be quite a commotion amongst the church members. They appeared to be hastening from the building. By this time it was quite dark. I retired, and heard nothing more about the uprising until the morning following. When Captain Nowlein went, he had left the premises under guard of one Charles H. Clark. The men who were usually on duty about my estate were still at their stations, without any firearms, without the least appearance of anticipated disturbance.

Now, as to the disturbance itself. At six o'clock in the afternoon of the sixth day of January, it was telephoned from Diamond Head that there was a conspiracy developed into action, and that the parties engaged therein would be found at the house of Mr. Henry Bertelmann. Captain Robert Waipa Parker took some half dozen native policemen with him, and started for the locality. On their way they stopped at the house of Mr. Charles L. Carter, son of the Hon. H. A. P. Carter, whom they informed of the nature of their errand. Upon hearing it, Mr. Carter immediately said that he would like to go with them, and "have a little fun too," and suited the action to the word by clapping two pistols into his belt. When they arrived at the Bertelmann place there was some resistance, and shots were exchanged between the police and the persons assembled there. In the course of the fray Mr. Carter was shot. It was reported that the wound was not in a locality where it would be likely to be at all dangerous, yet he soon expired. A policeman received a shot through the lungs at the same time, but he is alive and well today. These, I believe, were all the serious casualties of the day.

Chapter XLIII. I Am Placed Under Arrest

On the sixteenth day of January, 1895, Deputy Marshal Arthur Brown and Captain Robert Waipa Parker were seen coming up the walk which leads from Beretania Street to my residence. Mrs. Wilson told me that they were approaching. I directed her to show them into the parlor, where I soon joined them. Mr. Brown informed me that he had come to serve a warrant for my arrest; he would not permit me to take the paper which he held, nor to examine its contents.

It was evident they expected me to accompany them; so I made preparations to comply, supposing that I was to be taken at once to the station-house to undergo some kind of trial. I was informed that I could bring Mrs. Clark with me if I wished, so she went for my hand-bag; and followed by her, I entered the carriage of the deputy marshal, and was driven through the crowd that by this time had accumulated at the gates of my residence at Washington Place. As I turned the corner of the block on which is built the Central Congregational church, I noticed the approach from another direction of Chief Justice Albert F. Judd; he was on the sidewalk, and was going toward my house, which he entered. In the meantime the marshal's carriage continued on its way, and we arrived at the gates of Iolani Palace, the residence of the Hawaiian sovereigns.

We drove up to the front steps, and I remember noticing that troops of soldiers were scattered all over the yard. The men looked as though they had been on the watch all night. They were resting on the green grass, as though wearied by their vigils; and their arms were stacked near their tents, these latter having been pitched at intervals all over the palace grounds. Staring directly at us were the muzzles of two brass field pieces, which looked warlike and formidable as they pointed out toward the gate from their positions on the lower veranda. Colonel J. H. Fisher came down the steps to receive me; I dismounted, and he led the way up the staircase to a large room in the corner of the palace. Here Mr. Brown made a formal delivery of my person into the custody of Colonel Fisher, and having done this, withdrew.

Then I had an opportunity to take a survey of my apartments. There was a large, airy, uncarpeted room with a single bed in one corner. The other furniture consisted of one sofa, a small square table, one single common chair, and iron safe, a bureau, a chiffonier, and a cupboard, intended for eatables, made of wood with wire screening to allow the circulation of the air through the food. Some of these articles may have been added during the days of my imprisonment. I have portrayed the room as it appears to me in memory. There was, adjoining the principal apartment, a bath-room, and also a corner room and a little boudoir, the windows of which were large, and gave access to the veranda.

Colonel Fisher spoke very kindly as he left me there, telling me that he supposed this was to be my future abode; and if there was anything I wanted I had only to mention it to the officer, and that it should be provided. In reply, I informed him that there were one or two of my attendants whom I would like to have near me, and that I preferred to have my meals sent from my own house. As a result of this expression of my wishes, permission was granted to my steward to bring me my meals three times each day.

That first night of my imprisonment was the longest night I have ever passed in my life; it seemed as though the dawn of day would never come. I found in my bag a small Book of Common Prayer according to the ritual of the Episcopal Church. It was a great comfort to me, and before retiring to rest Mrs. Clark and I spent a few minutes in the devotions appropriate to the evening.

Here, perhaps, I may say, that although I had been a regular attendant on the Presbyterian worship since my childhood, a constant contributor to all the missionary societies, and had helped to build their churches and ornament the walls, giving my time and my musical ability freely to make their meetings attractive to my people, yet none of these pious church members or clergymen remembered me in my prison. To this (Christian?) conduct I contrast that of the Anglican bishop, Rt. Rev. Alfred Willis, who visited me from time to time in my house, and in whose church I have since been confirmed as a communicant. But he was not allowed to see me at the palace.

Outside of the rooms occupied by myself and my companion there were guards stationed by day and by night, whose duty it was to pace backward and forward through the hall, before my door, and up and down the front veranda. The sound of their never-ceasing footsteps as they tramped on their beat fell incessantly on my ears. One officer was in charge, and two soldiers were always detailed to watch our rooms. I could not but be reminded every instant that I was a prisoner, and did not fail to realize my position. My companion could not have slept at all that night; her sighs were audible to me without cessation; so I told her the morning following that, as her husband was in prison, it was her duty to return to her children. Mr. Wilson came in after I had breakfasted, accompanied by the Attorney-general, Mr. W. O. Smith; and in conference it was agreed between us that Mrs. Clark could return home, and that Mrs. Wilson should remain as my attendant; that Mr. Wilson would be the person to inform the government of any request to be made by me, and that any business transactions might be made through him.

On the morning after my arrest all my retainers residing on my estates were arrested, and to the number of about forty persons were taken to the station-house, and then committed to jail. Amongst these was the agent and manager of my property, Mr. Joseph Heleluhe. As Mr. Charles B. Wilson had been at one time in a similar position, and was well acquainted with all my surroundings, and knew the people about me, it was but natural that he should be chosen by me for this office.

Mr. Heleluhe was taken by the government officers, stripped of all clothing, placed in a dark cell without light, food, air, or water, and was kept there for hours in hopes that the discomfort of his position would induce him to disclose something of my affairs. After this was found to be fruitless, he was imprisoned for about six weeks; when, finding their efforts in vain, his tormentors released him. No charge was ever brought against him in any way, which is true of about two hundred persons who were similarly confined.

On the very day I left the house, so I was informed by Mr. Wilson, Mr. A. F. Judd had gone to my private residence without search-warrant; and that all the papers in my desk, or in my safe, my diaries, the petitions I had received from my people—all things of that nature which could be found were swept into a bag, and carried off by the chief justice in person. My husband's private papers were also included in those taken from me.

To this day, the only document which has been returned to me is my will. Never since have I been able to find the private papers of my husband nor of mine that had been kept by me for use or reference, and which had no relation to political events. The most important historical note lost was in my diary. This was the record made by me at the time of my conversations with Minister Willis, and would be especially valuable now as confirming what I have stated of our first interview.

After Mr. Judd had left my house, it was turned over to the Portuguese military company under the command of Captain Good. These militiamen ransacked it again from garret to cellar. Not an article was left undisturbed. Before Mr. Judd had finished they had begun their work, and there was no trifle left unturned to see what might be hidden beneath. Every drawer of desk, table, or bureau was wrenched out, turned upside down, the contents pulled over on the floors, and left in confusion there. Some of my husband's jewelry was taken; but this, in my application and offer to pay expenses, was afterwards restored to me.

Having overhauled the rooms without other result than the abstraction of many memorandums of no use to any other person besides myself, the men turned their attention to the cellar, in hopes possibly of unearthing an arsenal of firearms and munitions of war. Here they undermined the foundations to such a degree as to endanger the whole structure, but nothing rewarded their search. The place was then seized, and the government assumed possession; guards were placed on the premises, and no one was allowed to enter.

Chapter XLIV. Imprisonment—Forced Abdication

For the first few days nothing occurred to disturb the quiet of my apartments save the tread of the sentry. On the fourth day I received a visit from Mr. Paul Neumann, who asked me if, in the event that it should be decided that all the principal parties to the revolt must pay for it with their lives, I was prepared to die? I replied to this in the affirmative, telling him I had no anxiety for myself, and felt no dread of death. He then told me that six others besides myself had been selected to be shot for treason, but that he would call again, and let me know further about our fate. I was in a state of nervous prostration, as I have said, at the time of the outbreak, and naturally the strain upon my mind had much aggravated my physical troubles; yet it was with much difficulty that I obtained permission to have visits from my own medical attendant.

About the 22d of January a paper was handed to me by Mr. Wilson, which, on examination, proved to be a purported act of abdication for me to sign. It had been drawn out for the men in power by their own lawyer, Mr. A. S. Hartwell, whom I had not seen until he came with others to see me sign it. The idea of abdicating never originated with me. I knew nothing at all about such a transaction until they sent to me, by the hands of Mr. Wilson, the insulting proposition written in abject terms. For myself, I would have chosen death rather than to have signed it; but it was represented to me that by my signing this paper all the persons who had been arrested, all my people now in trouble by reason of their love and loyalty towards me, would be immediately released. Think of my position—sick, a lone woman in prison, scarcely knowing who was my friend, or who listened to my words only to betray me, without legal advice or friendly counsel, and the stream of blood ready to flow unless it was stayed by my pen.

My persecutors have stated, and at that time compelled me to state, that this paper was signed and acknowledged by me after consultation with my friends whose names appear at the foot of it as witnesses. Not the least opportunity was given to me to confer with anyone; but for the purpose of making it appear to the outside world that I was under the guidance of others, friends who had known me well in better days were brought into the place of my imprisonment, and stood around to see a signature affixed by me.

When it was sent to me to read, it was only a rough draft. After I had examined it, Mr. Wilson called, and asked me if I were willing to sign it. I simply answered that I would see when the formal or official copy was shown me. On the morning of the 24th of January the official document was handed to me, Mr. Wilson making the remark, as he gave it, that he hoped I would not retract, that is, he hoped that I would sign the official copy.

Then the following individuals witnessed my subscription of the signature which was demanded of me: William G. Irwin, H. A. Widemann, Samuel Parker, S. Kalua Kookano, Charles B. Wilson, and Paul Neumann. The form of acknowledgment was taken by W. L. Stanley, Notary Public.

So far from the presence of these persons being evidence of a voluntary act on my part, was it not an assurance to me that they, too, knew that, unless I did the will of my jailers, what Mr. Neumann had threatened would be performed, and six prominent citizens immediately put to death. I so regarded it then, and I still believe that murder was the alternative. Be this as it may, it is certainly happier for me to reflect today that there is not a drop of the blood of my subjects, friends or foes, upon my soul.

When it came to the act of writing, I asked what would be the form of signature; to which I was told to sign, "Liliuokalani Dominis." This sounding strange to me, I repeated the question, and was given the same reply. At this I wrote what they dictated without further demur, the more readily for the following reasons.

Before ascending the throne, for fourteen years, or since the date of my proclamation as heir apparent, my official title had been simply Liliuokalani. Thus I was proclaimed both Princess Royal and Queen. Thus it is recorded in the archives of the government to this day. The Provisional Government nor any other had enacted any change in my name. All my official acts, as well as my private letters, were issued over the signature of Liliuokalani. But when my jailers required me to sign "Liliuokalani Dominis," I did as they commanded. Their motive in this as in other actions was plainly to humiliate me before my people and before the world. I saw in a moment, what they did not, that, even were I not complying under the most severe and exacting duress, by this demand they had overreached themselves. There is not, and never was, within the range of my knowledge, any such a person as Liliuokalani Dominis.

It is a rule of common law that the acts of any person deprived of civil rights have no force nor weight, either at law or in equity; and that was my situation. Although it was written in the document that it was my free act and deed, circumstances prove that it was not; it had been impressed upon me that only by its execution could the lives of those dear to me, those beloved by the people of Hawaii, be saved, and the shedding of blood be averted. I have never expected the revolutionists of 1887 and 1893 to willingly restore the rights notoriously taken by force or intimidation; but this act, obtained under duress, should have no weight with the authorities of the United States, to whom I appealed. But it may be asked, why did I not make some protest at the time, or at least shortly thereafter, when I found my friends sentenced to death and imprisonment? I did. There are those now living who have seen my written statement of all that I have recalled here. It was made in my own handwriting, on such paper as I could get, and sent outside of the prison walls and into the hands of those to whom I wished to state the circumstances under which that fraudulent act of abdication was procured from me. This I did for my own satisfaction at the time.

After those in my place of imprisonment had all affixed their signatures, they left, with the single exception of Mr. A. S. Hartwell. As he prepared to go, he came forward, shook me by the hand, and the tears streamed down his cheeks. This was a matter of great surprise to me. After this he left the room. If he had been engaged in a righteous and honorable action, why should he be affected? Was it the consciousness of a mean act which overcame him so? Mrs. Wilson, who stood behind my chair throughout the ceremony, made the remark that those were crocodile's tears. I leave it to the reader to say what were his actual feelings in the case.

Chapter XLV. Brought To Trial

So far was my submission from modifying in any way the course of the government, that the principal prisoners were, after all, condemned to death. Their sentences were passed the same as though my signature had not been obtained. That they were not executed is due solely to a consideration which has been officially stated: "Word came from the United States that the execution of captive rebels would militate against annexation. That about settled it."

Proceedings against me, personally, were not modified. Every day thereafter papers were brought to me from the office of President Dole, a legal service, I suppose it is called, being made on me by Major George C. Potter, an aid-de-camp of the president's staff. In the first of these I found myself charged with the crime of "treason." After about a week had gone by, the accusation was changed to "misprision of treason." The substance of my crime was that I knew my people were conspiring to re-establish the constitutional government, to throw off the yoke of the stranger and oppressor; and I had not conveyed this knowledge to the persons I had never recognized except as unlawful usurpers of authority, and had not informed against my own nation and against their friends who were also my long-time friends.

The names of those who had informed, and by whose testimony I was to be convicted, were Captain Samuel Nowlein, Charles H. Clark, W. W. Kaae, Charles Warren, Keahikaauwai, George H. Townsend, and Captain Davies of the steamer *Waimanalo*.

February 5th was to be the day of my trial. After the summons had been served, Mr. Paul Neumann, in consultation with Mr. Wilson, called to consult with me, as it had been a question whether or not I should personally appear in court, as it would be undignified and humiliating. Humiliation! What had I left? It was the intention of the officers of the government to humiliate me by imprisoning me, but my spirit rose above that. I was a martyr to the cause of my people, and was proud of it. So I told them that I would attend; and on the morning of the 8th, at the hour appointed, Sergeant Kenake appeared, and conducted me, attended by Mrs. Wilson, to the court-room.

It was the former throne room of the palace, and was crowded with curious spectators. The diplomatic corps, Mr. Albert F. Willis, Minister of the United States, A. G. S. Hawes, British Commissioner, Monsieur De Verlet, French Commissioner, Senior Canavarro, Portuguese Commissioner, and Mr. F. Schmibu, the Japanese Consul, were all present. There were also ministers of the gospel, and a liberal representation from all classes, including many ladies of Honolulu society. In the centre of the room was the table before which the Military Commission (as it was called) was convened. It was before such an audience and by such a tribunal that I was to be tried for treason.

At one end of the table sat Mr. W. A. Whiting, as president of the court. He had once, early in my reign, been Attorney-general, and a member of my cabinet. Opposite to him was Mr. W. A. Kinney, the Judge Advocate. Besides these there were some half-dozen young men—Colonel Fisher, Messrs. Zeigler, Camara, Pratt, Wilder, W. C. and J. W. Jones—none of them names of any prominence or responsibility in the community.

The trial proceeded, Mr. A. F. Judd being the first to give his testimony against me. I cannot recall all that was said or done, nor is it necessary; but I know that, to make complete the work of saving the lives of my friends, I was compelled to testify as in the statement, and to affirm that it was through the advice of other friends I abdicated.

The only charge against me really was that of being a queen; and my case was judged by these, my adversaries, before I came into court. I remember with clearness, however, the attack upon me by the Judge Advocate, the words that issued from his mouth about "the prisoner," "that woman," etc., uttered with such affectation of contempt and disgust. The object of it was evidently to humiliate me, to make me break down in the presence of the staring crowd. But in this they were disappointed. My equanimity was never disturbed; and their own report relates that I throughout preserved "that haughty carriage" which marked me as an "unusual woman."

I said nothing to their taunts and innuendoes, and showed no emotion; but when the proper time came, I denied that I had been guilty of any treasonable action, and asked my counsel to submit the following statement:

"In the year 1893, on the fifteenth day of January, at the request of a large majority of the Hawaiian people, and by and with the consent of my cabinet, I proposed to make certain changes in the constitution of the Hawaiian kingdom, which were suggested to me as being for the advantage and benefit of the kingdom, and subjects and residents thereof. These proposed changes did not deprive foreigners of any rights or privileges enjoyed by them under the constitution of 1887, promulgated by King Kalakaua and his cabinet, without the consent of the people or ratified by their votes.

"My ministers at the last moment changed their views, and requested me to defer all action in connection with the constitution; and I yielded to their advice as bound to do by the existing constitution and laws.

"A minority of the foreign population made my action the pretext for overthrowing the monarchy, and, aided by the

United States naval forces and representative, established a new government.

"I owed no allegiance to the Provisional Government so established, nor to any power or to any one save the will of my people and the welfare of my country.

"The wishes of my people were not consulted as to this change of government, and only those who were in practical rebellion against the constitutional government were allowed to vote upon the question whether the monarchy should exist or not.

"To prevent the shedding of the blood of my people, natives and foreigners alike, I opposed armed interference, and quietly yielded to the armed forces brought against my throne, and submitted to the arbitrament of the government of the United States the decision of my rights and those of the Hawaiian people. Since then, as is well known to all, I have pursued the path of peace and diplomatic discussion, and not that of internal strife.

"The United States having first interfered in the interest of those founding the government of 1893 upon the basis of revolution, concluded to leave to the Hawaiian people the selection of their own form of government.

"This selection was anticipated and prevented by the Provisional Government, who, being possessed of the military and police power of the kingdom, so cramped the electoral privileges that no free expression of their will was permitted to the people who were opposed to them.

"By my command and advice the native people and those in sympathy with them were restrained from rising against the government in power.

"The movement undertaken by the Hawaiians last month was absolutely commenced without my knowledge, sanction, consent, or assistance, directly or indirectly; and this fact is in truth well known to those who took part in it.

"I received no information from anyone in regard to arms which were, or which were to be, procured, nor of any men who were induced, or to be induced, to join in any such uprising.

"I do not know why this information should have been withheld from me, unless it was with a view to my personal safety, or as a precautionary measure. It would not have received my sanction; and I can assure the gentlemen of this commission that, had I known of any such intention, I would have dissuaded the promoters from such a venture. But I will add that, had I known, their secrets would have been mine, and inviolately preserved.

"That I intended to change my cabinet, and to appoint certain officers of the kingdom, in the event of my restoration, I will admit; but that I, or anyone known to me, had, in part or in whole, established a new government, is not true. Before the 24th of January, 1895, the day upon which I formally abdicated, and called upon my people to recognize the Republic of Hawaii as the only lawful government of these Islands, and to support that government, I claim that I had the right to select a cabinet in anticipation of a possibility; and history of other governments supports this right. I was not intimidated into abdicating, but followed the counsel of able and generous friends and well-wishers, who advised me that such an act would restore peace and good-will among my people, vitalize the progress and prosperity of the Islands, and induce the actual government to deal leniently, mercifully, charitably, and impassionately with those who resorted to arms for the purpose of displacing a government in the formation of which they had no voice or control, and which they themselves had seen established by force of arms.

"I acted of my own free will, and wish the world to know that I have asked no immunity or favor myself, nor plead my abdication as a petition for mercy. My actions were dictated by the sole aim of doing good to my beloved country, and of alleviating the positions and pains of those who unhappily and unwisely resorted to arms to regain an independence which they thought had been unjustly wrested from them.

"As you deal with them, so I pray that the Almighty God may deal with you in your hours of trial.

"To my regret much has been said about the danger which threatened foreign women and children, and about the bloodthirstiness of the Hawaiians, and the outrages which would have been perpetrated by them if they had succeeded in their attempt to overthrow the Republic government.

"They who know the Hawaiian temper and disposition understand that there was no foundation for any such fears. The behavior of the rebels to those foreigners whom they captured and held shows that there was no malignancy in the hearts of the Hawaiians at all. It would have been sad indeed if the doctrine of the Christian missionary fathers, taught to my people by them and those who succeeded them, should have fallen like the seed in the parable, upon barren ground.

"I must deny your right to try me in the manner and by the court which you have called together for this purpose. In your actions you violate your own constitution and laws, which are now the constitution and laws of the land.

"There may be in your consciences a warrant for your action, in what you may deem a necessity of the times; but you cannot find any such warrant for any such action in any settled, civilized, or Christian land. All who uphold you in this unlawful proceeding may scorn and despise my word; but the offence of breaking and setting aside for a specific purpose the laws of your own nation, and disregarding all justice and fairness, may be to them and to you the source of an unhappy and much to be regretted legacy.

"I would ask you to consider that your government is on trial before the whole civilized world, and that in accordance with your actions and decisions will you yourselves be judged. The happiness and prosperity of Hawaii are henceforth in your hands as its rulers. You are commencing a new era in its history. May the divine Providence grant you the wisdom to lead the nation into the paths of forbearance, forgiveness, and peace, and to create and consolidate a united people ever anxious to advance in the way of civilization outlined by the American fathers of liberty and religion.

"In concluding my statement I thank you for the courtesy you have shown to me, not as your former queen, but as an humble citizen of this land and as a woman. I assure you, who believe you are faithfully fulfilling a public duty, that I shall never harbor any resentment or cherish any ill feeling towards you, whatever may be your decision."

What follows is a partial report of the court's proceedings regarding my statement.

"After deliberation the court requested that the following portions of the statement be withdrawn:

"A minority of the foreign population made my action the pretext for overthrowing the monarchy, and, aided by the United States naval forces and representative, established a new government."

"I owed no allegiance to the Provisional Government so established, nor to any power or to anyone save the will of my people and the welfare of my country."

"The wishes of my people were not consulted as to this change of government, and only those who were in practical rebellion against the Government were allowed to vote upon the question whether the Monarchy should exist or not."

"This selection was anticipated and prevented by the Provisional Government, who, being possessed of the military and police power of the kingdom, so cramped the electoral privileges that no free expression of their will was permitted to the people who were opposed to them."

"All who uphold you in this unlawful proceeding may scorn and despise my word, but the offence of breaking or setting aside for a specific purpose the laws of your own nation, and disregarding all justice, may be to them and to you the source of an unhappy and much to be regretted legacy."

"Mr. Neumann replied, that the paragraph relating to the establishment of the Provisional Government was made as a statement from the accused, was claimed as an actual fact, reflected upon no one. It set forth her views, and he must decline to ask his client to withdraw it. The words, 'and only those who were in practical rebellion against the constitution of the state,' etc., Mr. Neumann agreed should be stricken out. As to the passage setting forth that the accused owed no allegiance to the Provisional Government, counsel made the same answer as to the first item.

"The court retired, and returned with the decision that the objectionable passages should be stricken out. Colonel Whiting read them, and ordered that they be stricken from the record."

During the course of my trial, I noticed, in one of the seats behind those occupied by the foreign ministers a peculiar-looking man, who wore top-boots, and had long, flowing hair. I was afterwards told that this was Joaquin Miller, the "poet of the Sierras," and was shown specimens of his poetry, especially that which he had written on my deposition, and in which he had alluded to me in the most favorable terms. I have been told that he was sent out as a press correspondent, with the expectation that he would take the opposite view, and that when the "government" found out his real sentiments he was forced to leave Honolulu.

There was also one lady frequently present, who seemed to take a great interest in the proceedings of the court-martial. I recognized in her the wife of Lieutenant Werlich of the United States ship *Philadelphia*.

A few days after these events there was a parade of the men of the steamship on shore. After drilling out on the plains, they marched into the city, and made use of the walls of the Kawaiahao church, directly opposite my place of imprisonment, to show their agility and skill in scaling ramparts. In the yard about this great edifice lie buried the remains of many members of the old missionary families. But entirely without consideration for the sacredness of the spot, the troops were practised and cheered on at these walls; they clambered back and forth, came tumbling down one over the other, and showed their superior strength or quickness, while an officer was taking the time required for the drill. From thence they were called to order by the bugle, then marched in front of my windows with their guns pointing towards the building itself.

But while all this was going on, I saw a lady approach the palace until she stood beneath my window; there she stopped, and, looking up, kissed her hands to me. She remained, making no motion to leave, for perhaps ten minutes. Just as she was turning to depart, she raised her veil, and I at once recognized the countenance of the same lady who had been so faithful an attendant at my trial. As I stood watching her friendly attitude, kindly tears of sympathy rolled down her cheeks. I had known Mrs. Werlich as a welcome visitor at my own house in the days of my freedom, and it was a consolation for me to think that she had remembered me at the hour when I was a prisoner.

Chapter XLVI. Sentenced — My Prison Life

At two o'clock on the afternoon of the 27th of February I was again called into court, and sentence passed upon me. It was the extreme penalty for "misprision of treason," — a fine of $5,000, and imprisonment at hard labor for five years. I need not add that it was never executed, and that it was probably no part of the intention of the government to execute it, except, perhaps, in some future contingency. Its sole purpose was to terrorize the native people and to humiliate me. After Major Potter had read to me my sentence, and carefully pocketed the paper on which it was written, together with other papers in the case (I might have valued them, perhaps, as souvenirs), I was conducted back to my place of confinement.

No especial change was perceptible in my treatment or mode of life by reasons of my trial and sentence. Though I was still not allowed to have newspapers or general literature to read, writing-paper and lead-pencils were not denied; and I was thereby able to write music, after drawing for myself the lines of the staff. At first I had no instrument, and had to transcribe the notes by voice alone; but I found, notwithstanding disadvantages, great consolation in composing, and transcribed a number of songs. Three found their way from my prison to the city of Chicago, where they were printed, among them the "Aloha Oe" or "Farewell to Thee," which became a very popular song.

I was notified that I might be permitted to walk the veranda for my relaxation after the business hours of the day. My friends were allowed to send me tokens of sympathy, so bouquets of flowers and baskets of fruit of all varieties came in almost every day. I had also, at pleasure, the flowers of my own gardens at Uluhaimalama. In good things for my table I did not suffer. Rich cakes, clear jellies, and many other delicacies arrived every day of my imprisonment. Where so many were attentive, it seems hardly possible to mention individuals; yet the names of Mrs. S. C. Allen, Mrs. Mary Carter, Mrs. Samuel Parker, Mrs. Haalelea, Mrs. Coney, Mrs. James Campbell, Mrs. Minerva Fernandez, Mrs. Victoria Ward, and Mr. and Mrs. Mana recur to me at this moment, and besides, many other ladies, to whom I am sure I have never ceased to be grateful for their kind remembrance

It was the duty of the guards to search whatever was sent to me before it was delivered into my hands; so the baskets, whether of food, flowers, clothes, or papers, went to them first, and at least at the start were closely examined; yet there were some kindly disposed towards me and not over-critical. Every newspaper, however, had to come through the hands of Mr. Wilson; and if he detected in it anything whatever relating to the government, he would take it away, not permitting me to see it. I used to find great comfort in the bits of newspaper that were wrapped around my bouquets which were brought to me from my own garden at Uluhaimalama.

These were generally wrapped in the newspapers, foreign and local, obtained from Mr. Whiting's house, near my own; and I cannot resist adding that even in my imprisonment the humor of the thought occurred to me, that, if any person ever literally fulfilled the ancient proverb about "living in glass houses," it was this so-called judge who had been called to pass sentence upon me. Some of the very wealthy under the monarchy had retreats in the suburbs of the town, somewhat answering to what Americans call "summer residences;" and these were called "glass houses," because so open, or largely composed of glass. Under the oligarchy several in the government are not content with less than two such pleasure houses.

Flowers from home I unwrapped myself, so as to be sure to save these bits of news which I sought opportunity at intervals to read. There were times when I saw something of such interest that I could not resist the temptation to mention it to my companion, Mrs. Wilson. Then it seems she would faithfully report all that I said to her husband, whose custom it was to call every other day, sometimes at longer periods, for the purpose of ascertaining if there was anything required. At such times he would withdraw with his wife to the boudoir, where she would repeat to him what had been said by me, telling him also what had been received in the prison through her. By some things she occasional mentioned he thought that newspapers had been secretly sent in; but when finally he discovered that they had come as wrapping-paper, it made him very angry, and his poor little wife had to suffer for it, even bursting into tears at his sharp reproaches. For this reason I became quite guarded in what I said to her.

Our first duty in the morning after the regular devotions of the day was to arrange our flowers and decorate our apartments. At half-past seven the military companies would return from their parade; and at eight precisely Captain Good, attended by one of the officers, would knock at my door, which was always opened by Mrs. Wilson, unless Mrs. Milaina Ahia were with me. (Mrs. Wilson usually went out on Saturday evening and returned to me on Monday morning. During this absence her place was taken by Mrs. Ahia.) On opening the door Captain Good inquired what there was he could do for us, and if the prisoner was within and safe. On being answered in the affirmative, he would touch his cap, and return to report to his superior officer, Colonel McLean, and then rejoin his company. After their departure I occupied my time in crochet-work, in attending to my ferns or pots of flowers, or in reading the books allowed me. I also found much pleasure in the society of my canary-birds, and in practicing on my autoharp and guitar. These luxuries had, after the first severity, been permitted to me.

I received letters; but they were always opened, and, I presume, read, before being delivered. Rt. Rev. Alfred Willis, the Anglican Bishop of Honolulu, sent me a Book of Common Prayer. Sisters Beatrice and Alpertina offered little acts of tenderness and kindness which brought anew to my mind that passage in Scripture, "I was in prison and ye visited me." Although my Christian (?) jailers denied to me their sacred ministration and actual presence, yet none the less were these good and true Christians there in the loving tokens of kind remembrance, and in the spirit of the Divine Lord, during my bondage.

In June of 1895 there was a rumor that I was to be released; but day after day went by, July came and went, and I was still a prisoner. My health was not strong, and my regular medical attendant had gone to San Francisco. It was proposed by Dr. Cooper and Colonel McLean, that I should take a drive somewhere or somehow every day; but I did not feel inclined to go about town under guard of soldiers, and preferred to take long walks on the veranda by night, always, of course, under the inspection of the guard or sentry on duty there.

In August an epidemic broke out, to which Mrs. Wilson was one of the first to succumb. She had to leave me for a few days, but returned on her recovery. While she was away, I was stricken with the disorder; but I used such remedies as I happened to have with me, and recovered without serious consequences. After this we heard that the whole city was suffering. It was said to be a form of Asiatic cholera. Many deaths occurred, and it was some three months before normal conditions were restored. It was at this time that the ladies of Honolulu, both native and foreign, organized a society for the relief of the poor, who, under the circumstances, were unable to support themselves. There were relief stations in the outskirts all around the city, where ladies who had been assigned to each district assembled to supply necessary provision to those who were in need. It was a most praiseworthy mission; and although I could not be present personally, I provided a house and lot on my place at Waikiki for carrying on the benevolent enterprise under the care of Mrs. James Campbell and Mrs. Douglas, who had charge of that district.

Chapter XLVII. Released On Parole

On the 6th of September, about eight months after my arrest, I was notified by Colonel McLean that he was no longer responsible for my custody, and that at three o'clock that afternoon I might leave the palace. So a carriage was called, and I was driven from the doors of the beautiful edifice which they now style Executive Building, and was assured that I was under no further restraint. My pardon, as it was called, arrived at a later day. All the intervening time I was supposed to be under parole, and could have been arrested and recommitted at any moment.

As, in company with Mr. and Mrs. Wilson, I was driven from my prison—once my palace—to the gateway at Washington Place, my earlier home, it seemed as though Nature, our kind mother, smiled on my return. The flowers, the shrubs, the trees, had never to me looked so charming. How I enjoyed their welcome! Surely they could not have been so beautiful when I saw them daily in previous years! The orchids, the violets, the chrysanthemums, the geraniums, were still in bloom, and seemed to greet me with joy, expressive as silent. Bunches of red bananas hung from their stalks, clusters of yellow Loquot plums danced in the sunshine, and the bright red berries of the coffee-tree drooped down gracefully, waiting to be gathered. But my welcome was not altogether from the silent, waving leaves. Those of my people who had been released from imprisonment were here to greet me also with their fond Aloha.

On the morning following Mr. Wilson informed me that I had been released only on parole, and had been placed in his charge by President Dole. My custodian further notified me that but sixteen servants were allowed to me, and that my retainers (accustomed to maintain a system of watches for my protection ever since the death of my husband) were not to be permitted to come near me again. I was also prohibited from going where there was any concourse of the people, nor could I have any gathering at my own house. In consequence of these regulations I never went to church or to any public place. But I was not forgotten by his lordship, the bishop, who with Mrs. Willis was one of the first to call on me. Other friends expressed their sympathy in person; amongst these Mrs. J. S. Walker, who had lost her husband by the treatment he received from the hands of the revolutionists. He was one of many who from persecution had succumbed to death.

It was at this time that Bishop Willis invited me to be confirmed as a member of his church; to which proposal I very gladly assented, and I find much comfort in its fellowship.

The duties of Mr. Charles B. Wilson could not have been very irksome. I do not remember requiring him to do anything, or asking a favor at his hands. He took good care to keep my gates under lock and key, that no visitors might enter without his knowledge, because he was obliged — he said — to give to Mr. Dole a faithful report of all my visitors and doings each day. Some of my friends who prayed to be allowed to visit me were denied. I was very conveniently spared, however, the calls of strangers, who would have encroached upon my retired life simply from motives of curiosity.

Two events of some interest to me should be mentioned as related to these days. While the *Philadelphia* was the flag-ship of the squadron of the Pacific, the time of Admiral Irwin expired, and he was daily expecting his successor. Before he left, he very courteously called on me at Washington Place. He was accompanied by a member of his personal staff. I appreciated this mark of his attention, and it has never been forgotten by me; for it showed a kindly spirit on his part towards one who had received many officers of the navy in other days and under different circumstances.

On another occasion Admiral Walker visited the Islands. Exactly on what mission I have never been informed. If, as I have sometimes heard, and if one is to judge from the long report he made to the Department of the Navy on his return, it was for investigating the political situation, he certainly did not adopt the method of fairness and equal treatment to both sides pursued by Hon. James H. Blount. He was scarcely in position to have any but the most prejudiced ideas; for he was an old friend and guest of one of my enemies, and immediately on his arrival the missionary party took possession of him, and scarcely allowed him to move unless some one of their number was at his elbow.

On the 6th of February, 1896, while at dinner with Mrs. Wilson and Mr. Kamakau, we were informed that a messenger from the office of Mr. Dole was waiting to enter my presence in order to deliver a document; but Mrs. Wilson went for the paper, and took it from the young man, Mr. Alexander St. Maur McIntosh. I did not see him; but the document proved to be my release from parole as a prisoner, although I was still forbidden to leave the island of Oahu. Mrs. Wilson said that this could not possibly be genuine; because her husband had not been made aware of it, and that everything like this had to come to me through him. I re-read the document to be assured there was no mistake. Mrs. Wilson immediately started to notify her husband, who sent her back for the paper, which I allowed her to take. It convinced, but much astonished, Mr. Wilson, for he made the comment that he ought to have been notified first; but it would appear that the president thought otherwise, and, without advising the custodian, had released the prisoner from his unwelcome custody.

Some days later, in company with Mr. and Mrs. Joseph Heleluhe, I took a drive out to my residence at Waialua, where we spent two very delightful weeks with the Rev. Mr. Timoteo and his agreeable wife. We had a quiet little celebration all to ourselves, fishing and riding, and the time sped by so pleasantly that we forgot to count the hours. While there we received a visit from Hon. Samuel Parker; Mr. Boyd, Secretary of American Legation; Mr. Lanse (who has since married Miss Widemann); Mr. J. S. Walker, the younger; and others—who spent a pleasant day with us on the beach. We caught fish, and placed them immediately on hot coals, supplementing our picnic with bread and butter, and our native poi. Then, a week or so later, I went to my residence at Waikiki; and in this, my ocean retreat, I lived until my recent visit to the United States, only now and then, for a change, making a trip to my estates at Kahala. My life at the seashore was a tranquil and uneventful one, although while I was there a circumstance transpired of grave importance to my people.

Chapter XLVIII. Mr. Joseph Kahooluhi Nawahi

One morning, in the month of October, 1896, I heard of the death of Mr. Joseph Kahooluhi Nawahi o Kalaniopuu; and I shared the common sorrow, for this was a great blow to the people. He had always been a man who fearlessly advocated the independence of Hawaii Nei. He was for twenty years a legislator, and was one of the most active members of the legislative session of 1892-1893; with Mr. William White he had maintained a strict fidelity to the wishes of the people by whom he had been elected. The behavior of these two patriots during the trying scenes of this session, in such marked contrast to that of many others, won them profound respect. They could never be induced to compromise principles, nor did they for one moment falter or hesitate in advocating boldly a new constitution which should accord equal rights to the Hawaiians, as well as protect the interests of the foreigners. The true patriotism and love of country of these men had been recognized by me, and I had decorated them with the order of Knight Commander of Kalakaua.

When the vessel drew near on which were the remains of the dead patriot, the people turned out en masse to draw the carriage, on which the casket was placed, to his late home. No private individual in our land had ever received such a demonstration of love and respect as was now shown to the lamented member of the House. High honors were accorded to him. The services were read by the Rev. E. S. Timoteo, after which there was a long procession in line. The casket was accompanied by all the members of the Hui Kalaaina, and also of the Hui Aloha Aina, which last society was of his own establishment. Then followed the chief mourners and the ladies of the Patriotic League. The long, sorrowful escort conducted the body on board the steamer *Keauhou*; and after some last impressive services, the crowd watched the little steamer bearing off all that was mortal of the Hon. J. K. Nawahi towards Hilo, where on arrival another grand demonstration was made. He was laid in state at the Haili church in obedience to the expressed wish of the people.

    He was a member of the legislature when I appointed him as a cabinet minister, and was voted out with the ministry on the motion of "lack of confidence." He then consulted me as to his future, and stated that if he should run for the district of Hilo he felt confident of his election. Acting upon my advice, he left at the first opportunity for Hilo, arriving just in time to appear as a candidate in opposition to the candidate of the missionary party. He was returned by a large majority. Then it became necessary for him to leave on this same evening for the port of Honolulu, and the only vessel or means of reaching there was at Hamakua; but he was falsely informed by those in sympathy with his enemies that there was no way by which he could go.

    Nevertheless he fitted out two whaleboats with sails, compass, provisions, and water, and sailed immediately for the island of Mauai. At two o'clock next morning, as they were passing off Hamakaua, they saw the red light of the steamer *Iwalani*, and recognized that they had been purposely deceived so as to prevent the people's delegate from taking part in the deliberations at the legislature. All next day they were crossing the channel of Alenuihaha, but by evening the two boats reached Hana in safety. They awaited at the hospitable home of

Judge Kaai the first vessel for Oahu, which landed them duly at Honolulu. Thus, by the One who rules the wind and the waves, Mr. Nawahi had been favored with a most prosperous voyage; and much to the surprise of his enemies, arrived in time to take his seat in the legislature amongst those of his party and his personal friends, by whom he was warmly congratulated on his election and his prompt appearance.

At his death the Provisional Government, whose agents control all the despatches sent to the United States, caused it there to be promulgated that the liberal party had, since the loss of Mr. Nawahi, become discouraged, and were ready to vote for annexation. This was expressly to deceive the people of the United States. The cause of Hawaiian independence is larger and dearer than the life of any man connected with it. Love of country is deep-seated in the breast of every Hawaiian, whatever his station. Yet the above fact is worthy of notice as the testimony of our enemies to the sturdy patriotism of Mr. Joseph Kahooluhi Nawahi.

After the obsequies were over, and the remains of the deceased legislator were borne to Hilo, notice was given by the members for a new election of president to the two patriotic societies at whose head he had stood. This action was a great astonishment to the Provisional Government and all the friends of the missionary party, for it was hoped that the loss of such a leader would cause these organizations to dissolve. The Hui Aloha Aina and the Hui Kalaaina, with the sister organization of the Women's Patriotic League, are societies much dreaded by the oligarchy now ruling Hawaii. Sufficient time was given to reach the members in the most distant parts of the Islands, who were notified to meet in convention, which they did. Perfect harmony prevailed; and James Keauiluna Kaulia was elected president of the Hui Aloha Aina, while David Kalauokalani was chosen as the head of the Hui Kalaaina; and both these societies are still intent on their patriotic work.

One day in the month of October, 1896, while with trowel in hand I was separating and transplanting my ferns at my Waikiki residence, Major George C. Potter entered, bearing a document, which on examination I found purported to be an entire release of all restrictions, an absolute pardon, and a restoration of my civil rights. This, to be sure, places me in the same position as before my arrest and trial; but let me ask, if I was deprived of my civil rights at the moment of my imprisonment, of what value was the signature procured to my supposed or alleged act of abdication? Was it legal, of binding force, or effective? This question I will leave for decision to all those learned in the law; they can draw their own conclusions as to the probable worth of an acknowledgment of that document as my free act and deed, or of the proper value of the form of signature not my own which at the request of others was attached thereto.

Chapter XLIX. A Change Of Scene To Forget Sorrow

On receiving my full release I felt greatly inclined to go abroad, it made no difference where, as long as it would be a change. Calling to mind my many acquaintances in San Francisco, and remembering the relatives of my husband living there, and across the bay in Oakland, I decided to sail for that city, and at once quietly began my preparations.

On the fifth day of December, 1896, shortly after breakfast, with my companion, Mrs. Kia Nahaolelua, I drove up to the residence of President Dole. As I entered, he rose from his seat, approached me at once, and extended his hand, which I took. Asking us to be seated, he inquired of me to what he was indebted for the honor of this early visit. I informed him of my intention to take a trip to San Francisco. He inquired if I intended to go farther on, to which I replied I would probably visit my relations in the city of Boston, and perhaps might cross the Atlantic to call on my niece, the Princess Kaiulani, in England. At this Mr. Dole rose and called his wife, who entered immediately, and greeted me with a pleasant smile. In the course of an agreeable conversation they expressed their great anxiety and solicitude for me, in that I was undertaking such a journey in the depth of winter.

The climate of Boston, they said, was one of great severity; especially was this true in its effect upon strangers, and they warned me to prepare myself most carefully against the dangers of a winter there. Thanking them for their kind interest, I bade them good-by; but the president very gallantly escorted me to my carriage, and of his own accord proposed to send from the foreign office passports for myself and for those of my party. He then politely bowed an adieu as the carriage was driven out of his yard, and thus we parted.

Taking leave of my cousin, the Prince Kalanianaole, on the way, I returned to my own residence. Intending to make but a hasty stop there, I found awaiting me Mr. D. Kalauokalani, the president of the Hui Kalaaina, and Mr. William White, also Mrs. Joseph Nawahi, the chairman of the central committee of the Women's Patriotic League. They expressed much surprise at learning that I was about to leave so soon; but my trunks and other baggage awaiting transportation spoke silently in support of my intentions. A few words of explanation and direction were exchanged, the farewells to all of my household were said, and my party started for the wharf.

There I found Hon. J. O. Carter, with Mrs. Carter and their family, waiting to see me off. There were a few other friends, and only a few, for I had purposely kept my intention to depart to myself. I shook hands with Mr. F. J. Testa, the proprietor of the *Independent*, who seemed very much surprised to see me, and then mounted the gangway that led up the side of the vessel, accompanied by Mr. Carter. Having taken a glance at the rooms which were assigned to me, I returned to the deck, where Major George C. Potter, aid to Mr. Dole, had already arrived, and presented to me my passport.

It was signed by Mr. W. O. Smith as Minister of Foreign Affairs, granting to Liliuokalani of Hawaii permission to come and go in distant parts under the protection of the Hawaiian government, and charging all representatives of that government to afford me protection.

But I could not help noticing that in making out this document the name of the family of my husband, Governor Dominis—the name they had compelled me to affix to the document, and which, as there combined, had never been mine, or my legal signature—was not mentioned, and perhaps they had failed to think of it. What had become of that signature they had required to my act of alleged abdication? Passports were also given for my suite, Mr. Joseph Heleluhe and Mrs. Kia Nahaolelua.

Hon. Samuel Parker came on board the steamship, and asked in astonishment where I was going. I gave him a like answer to that given to President and Mrs. Dole, and then the steamer proceeded on her way out of the harbor. The usual farewells of waving handkerchiefs and hats signalized our departure, and then for the first time in years I drew a long breath of freedom. (For what was there worthy of that sacred name under the circumstance in which I had lived on shore?) Not knowing but what every word, every look, every act, of mine was being noted down by spies to be reported somewhere to my hurt.

The captain of the *China* was very kind, the officers and everyone on board most attentive, and a short and pleasant run of five days brought us to the coast of California. When the steamer was fast to the wharf at San Francisco, we were met by Colonel George W. Macfarlane, who awaited us; and, conducting us to our carriage, we were driven at once to the California Hotel, where apartments had been engaged for me and my suite. I telegraphed at once to my friends in Boston, notifying them of my arrival on American soil, and in reply received a despatch kindly inviting me to join them in the celebration of their Christmas holidays. I remained in San Francisco ten days, and had every reason to be content with my welcome.

Many friends had hastened to call upon me; amongst these were Mr. and Mrs. Claus Spreckels, Mrs. J. D. Spreckels and her lovely daughter, Miss Emma Spreckels, Mr. and Mrs. C. A. Spreckels, Mr. Charles R. Bishop, Mr. and Mrs. Shrader of San

Rafael, Mrs. Annie Barton of Berkeley, Mrs. Toler of Oakland, Mrs. Hitchings, and many other persons of prominence whose names have escaped my memory. Colonel and Mrs. Macfarlane, with their niece, Miss Gardie Macfarlane, had their apartments at the hotel where I stopped; and this made me feel at home at once, for they were most kind and attentive throughout my stay.

And it seems, too, that I was not to be without a delightful traveling companion, for Mrs. Kaikilani Graham, formerly of Honolulu, was in California, and was on the point of directing her course eastward with her children. So preparations were made for crossing the continent, and we took the Sunset Limited via New Orleans. Colonel Macfarlane had decided that to be our best route, so that I and my suite might get accustomed gradually to the change of climate, and pass by degrees into the cold weather of the East. It was a kind thought on his part, and one to which perhaps I owe more than can now be estimated. Taking this beautiful curve to the southward, we passed through the charming open country in and about Los Angeles, where we saw miles of orange-groves, the trees all laden with their golden fruit.

Miles after miles of rich country went by as we gazed from the windows of the moving train, and all this vast extent of territory which we traversed belonged to the United States; and there were many other routes from the Pacific to the Atlantic with an equally boundless panorama. Here were thousands of acres of uncultivated, uninhabited, but rich and fertile lands, soil capable of producing anything which grows, plenty of water, floods of it running to waste, everything needed for pleasant towns and quiet homesteads, except population. The view and the thoughts awakened brought forcibly to my mind that humanity was the one element needed to open to usefulness and enjoyment these rich tracts of land. Colonies and colonies could be established here, and never interfere with each other in the least, the vast extent of unoccupied land is so enormous. I thought what splendid sugar plantations might here be established, how easily and profitably rice might be grown, and in some other spots with what good returns coffee could be planted. There was nothing lacking in this great, rich country save the people to settle upon it, and develop its wealth.

And yet this great and powerful nation must go across two thousand miles of sea, and take from the poor Hawaiians their little spots in the broad Pacific, must covet our islands of Hawaii Nei, and extinguish the nationality of my poor people, many of whom have now not a foot of land which can be called their own. And for what? In order that another race-problem shall be injected into the social and political perplexities with which the United States in the great experiment of popular government is already struggling? In order that a novel and inconsistent foreign and colonial policy shall be grafted upon its hitherto impregnable diplomacy? Or in order that a friendly and generous, yet proud-spirited and sensitive race, a race admittedly capable and worthy of receiving the best opportunities for material and moral progress, shall be crushed under the weight of a social order and prejudice with which even another century of preparation would hardly fit it to cope?

As we passed eastward on our journey, the people crowded to the railway stations, eager, no matter how brief our stop, to get a glimpse of the Queen of Hawaii. At times this curiosity became so troublesome that the train officials were obliged to lock the car-doors, or close up our section, to prevent intrusion. At such times as these Mrs. Graham proved herself not only a pleasant companion, but of great service; she was always a skillful and ready defence against importunities. She was tall, handsome, very commanding in her presence, and very ladylike and polite in her manner. She was always courteous to the news-gatherers; and they retired quite pleased with such statements as she was able to give concerning me and my journey, and not a little charmed with the strategist who had communicated the information. At Washington we parted, she going to New York, and I to Boston.

We reached the national capital in six days, and were much interested in observing the snow, which lay on the ground, covered the tops of the houses and the roofs of our cars. It was a new sight to my suite, because in our country it only appears as a white mantle resting on the summits of our highest mountains. We made no stay in the city of Washington, for my friends in the Puritan city were expecting me. Having telegraphed my approach, in response to my wish Captain Julius A. Palmer met me on the arrival of the train at the Park-square Station at about nine o'clock on the evening of Christmas Day. The train, having been detained a few hours, was behind its schedule time of arrival. Captain Palmer conducted me to the Parker House, where my cousin, Mr. William Lee, with his wife, Mrs. Sara White Lee, and their daughter, Miss Alice Lee, were awaiting me.

I was at once amongst my friends, or rather, with my own family; for kisses, embraces, and congratulations followed each other very rapidly. I was received also with greetings of leis, made after the pattern of those in my own land; and thus my husband's relatives had made me feel I was not a stranger in a strange land, and contrived almost to make us forget the distance from our own beautiful Hawaii. It is indeed pleasant to receive such greetings from faithful hearts and loving hands in a foreign land. In order to be near my cousins, after a few days' rest at the Parker House, I moved to the Stirlingworth Cottage, just off Beacon Street, in Brookline.

Chapter L. A New England Winter

At Stirlingworth Cottage I passed a most delightful month, although the frost often covered the window panes, the snow whirled around the house, and the icicles formed on the trees; the kindly greetings of my Boston friends and the warmth of their hearts deprived a Northern winter of all its gloom. The health of my party was excellent, and it seemed to be a matter of surprise to those who met us that we suffered so little by the change from the mild air of our beautiful islands to the rigors of a New England winter.

    The first Sunday of my stay in Boston I accepted the kind invitation of Mr. and Mrs. George W. Armstrong to test the pleasures of a sleighride with them in their carriage-sleigh. In an open sleigh were seated Miss Alice Lee and the members of my suite, Mrs. Kia Nahaolelua, Mr. Joseph Heleluhe, and Captain Julius A. Palmer. The last-named gentleman visited me every day during my residence in his native city, attending to my correspondence or other business simply from motives of love to my people and of interest in me; and as long as I remained in Boston he declined other compensation than the approval of his own conscience.

It was a bright and beautiful day when the jingling bells and prancing horses acquainted me with the much-praised experience of sleigh-riding; and my kind host had determined that I at least should suffer no inconvenience from the cold, for our sleigh was abundantly provided with robes, and was warmed by a recently invented apparatus. My two Hawaiian attendants, however, in the open sleigh, felt the cold most severely. In truth, I must say that I failed to see the delight and exhilaration of the sport, although I enjoyed the afternoon very much indeed; but if I had had the same charming companions on a good road with an easy-riding carriage, it seems to me the pleasure of the ride would have been greater. It reminded me of the play of the Hawaiian children, where they draw each other along with smooth logs for runners. But it was extremely thoughtful in Mr. and Mrs. Armstrong to suggest this for my entertainment, and was only one of the many ways in which these friends showed their goodness of heart towards me. When I returned from a little trip to Niagara, Mr. Armstrong met me at the station, and cordially placed his private carriage and driver at my disposal to convey me to my Brookline apartments, which were not far from his elegant residence on Beacon Street.

During my sojourn in Brookline I attended All Saints' Church. The rector was the Rev. Mr. Addison, and I was pleased to notice the close attention given to his sermons by the congregation. He seemed to be a very popular man with his parishioners; and well they might appreciate such a pastor, for he showed himself to be a man whose heart and soul were in the great and glorious work of teaching the truths of Christianity, and leading others in the worship of God.

One morning Cousin Sara (Mrs. Lee) brought a letter from a lady who was collecting dolls for an International Doll-Show, to be exhibited at fairs for the benefit of charities for children. Having always been interested in the welfare of the young, I was happy to grant the request to have a Hawaiian doll for the charitable object. It much amused my cousin to see me sewing; and it was a pastime for me to make the clothing for the very pretty doll, that resembled somewhat some of my people who had intermarried with the foreigners.

The doll, for some reason, did not make its public début until quite recently; and I take the opportunity to insert here a clipping from the *Boston Globe*, Dec. 4, 1897, of the occasion, which is noteworthy, as that paper, I am informed, has been strongly for annexation, and heretofore has had but few kindly comments for the other side.

"Mrs. William Lee of Brookline gave an interesting talk last evening to a goodly gathering of women, and a slight sprinkling of men, at the doll-show opened in Hotel Thorndike, for two days, yesterday, for the benefit of the New England Home for Crippled Children.

"This doll-show, which for variety and size exceeds any previous one in Boston, is notable for one thing—in having among the exhibits three genuine royal dolls, that is to say, three dolls contributed by royalty. Two of them, miniature representations of Eskimo babies, made by the Eskimos themselves, and dressed in full Arctic costume of sealskin, were sent here by Queen Victoria from her own private collection, which is said to be the largest and finest in the world.

"The third one was given by ex-Queen Liliuokalani of Hawaii, who dressed it and decorated it herself in the mother-hubbard-like gown characteristic of Hawaiian women, and the head wreath and neck garland of flowers to which they are so partial on gala occasions. The ex-queen named the doll Kaiulani, for her niece and heir.

"Mrs. Lee talked about her friend Liliuokalani, whose name, she said, signifies the preservation of the heavens, and gave an interesting description of Hawaii's history and the peculiar customs of the people.

"She asserted that the native Hawaiians are more intelligent and better educated than they are generally credited with being; most of them being able to read and write their own language, and many of them being equally accomplished in English.

The End of Hawaii's Independence 293

"Their constancy and their trustful nature, she claimed, have been their misfortune. At one period, she said, Hawaii was governed by no laws save the Ten Commandments.

"Mrs. Lee expressed the opinion that in view of the power wielded by the whites, and the little influence possessed by the natives at the time of the late revolution, it was no wonder the queen wished to promulgate a new constitution to restore to her people some of the rights of which they had been deprived.

"She said further, 'I tell you from the bottom of my heart, I have never found a more devout and perfect Christian under all circumstances than Liliuokalani. I have never yet heard her utter an unkind word against those who persecute her.

"I am American by ancestry from the earliest days of the Massachusetts Bay Colony, and I love the American flag, and would be the last to see it hauled down if rightly raised; but (here Mrs. Lee spoke with visible emotion) if a Captain Kidd or any other pirate should raise the American flag simply as a decoy in order to destroy, we should be the first to resent it.

"I do not oppose annexation as such, but it grieves me to see the way our countrymen have gone to work to bring it about.

"I believe the Hawaiians should have their independent government, and that the natives should have something to say as to what that government shall be.'"

On New Year's Day, 1897, a brilliant reception was given by Mrs. William Lee at her residence, where I found myself the guest of honor. It might be noticed here that, in regard to such occasions as this, the feelings of one who has been imprisoned, politically or otherwise, can only be understood by a person who has passed through the ordeal. With Mrs. Lee's numerous friends and high social position, she would most gladly have given to me an opportunity to receive attentions from the clubs and societies of which she is a distinguished member, and I would thereby have met many very delightful people. But although, since my earliest remembrance, I have been accustomed to ceremonies and receptions, yet, even after a winter's experience in Washington, it is not easy for me to get over that shrinking from the gaze of strangers acquired by recent years of retirement, eight months of experience as a prisoner, and the humiliations of the time when I was under the supervision of government spies or custodians.

Therefore, while I was grateful to Mrs. Lee for the wish, I told her that save in her own house and to meet her personal friends, I would be obliged to decline public receptions. But the number of gallant gentlemen, beautiful ladies, and fair young girls (two of whom served as ushers) that honored this occasion, caused me to be happy that I had made an exception. Music was furnished by some of the younger visitors, one of whom, Miss Sara MacDonald, a sister of the two charming ushers, played most sweetly and skillfully on the harp; and Mrs. Frank M. Goss, Mrs. Farwell, and the Misses Morse and Foster, assisted at the beautifully decorated refreshment table. Although the invitations had only been received on the morning of the reception, the attendance was very large. It comprised many of the most prominent people of Boston and Brookline, as well as those of surrounding towns.

The lovely January day was terminated by a light fall of snow, through which we found our way back to our home, with much gratitude in our hearts towards the kind entertainers and their many pleasant friends who had wished the Hawaiian party a happy New Year.

Mr. J. T. Trowbridge and Mr. W. T. Adams, the latter better known as Oliver Optic, two very interesting literary gentlemen, I met by the introduction of Mr. and Mrs. Lee. Although of advanced years, Mr. Adams was a bright and genial man, and his conversation was adorned with flashes of quiet wit and abounded in good humor, just as he shows himself in his fascinating books. He has since died; and these, his life-long friends, will long mourn his loss to them and to literature.

While at Stirlingworth Cottage Mr. and Mrs. Yeaton, whom I met at Mrs. Lee's reception, very kindly presented me with a token which I shall always prize—a paper-cutter, made by the gentleman himself from the original wood of the old ship-of-war, the *Constitution*. I have an indistinct recollection that the frigate visited the Islands years ago, when I was quite young, and that I was then told that she was one of the most famous of American vessels.

During my stay in Boston, I made a winter excursion to Niagara Falls. The trip was accomplished in three or four days, without the least inconvenience, although we were all strangers to the route, and to the hotel where rooms had been engaged by wire for myself and suite. All the tales I had ever heard of the grandeur of the great cataract fell far short of the truth; and I was impressed with an awe quite impossible to express in words when I came to look upon that everlasting volume of waters. As I stood at the edge of the precipice on Goat Island, my most constant thought and vivid impression was that of the insignificance of man when brought face to face with nature. While standing by this, one of the great wonders of the world, I felt as in the very presence of the Creator.

And yet man knows no fear, and his ingenuity has mastered here, as elsewhere, the strength of the elements; and by his inventive genius and skill he is now turning this fierce Kühleborn into an obedient servant. A company has been created, and its efforts to build a flume supplied from the cataract have been successful. The water-power is carried into a large shed, and there made to generate the electricity which furnishes the whole district about the Falls with light and power. The current for these and various other purposes, I am informed, is carried over more than twenty miles to the city of Buffalo.

We had a fine view from the American side of the Falls; there were wreaths of mist curling upward in the air, blown into fantastic shapes by the breezes which came forth from the Cave of the Winds. Showers also passed over the river, or followed its rapid flow. After lunch we took carriages and drove along the brink, then crossed the great Suspension Bridge to the Canadian side. The bridge itself is a wonder, showing to rare advantage the ingenuity of the brains which contrived and the hands which built it. At the Horseshoe Fall, as well as while approaching it, we found abundant evidences of the wintry season; there were icicles on the fences and houses, the trees were covered with shining crystal, and the trellis-work of wire on the banks at the edge of the precipice was marvelously garnished with pendent icicles of every size and shape. We also visited the boiling lake, had our photographs taken out-of-doors on the snow, and, after a most instructive and delightful visit, returned to our Brookline quarters with a picture to be treasured in memory for life.

Before leaving Boston, as it was my intention to do some time during the month of January, my cousin, Mr. N. G. Snelling, gave a family party at his house, to which my suite was invited, and I had the pleasure of meeting as many of the family as could be brought together. More than thirty relatives and a few of the most intimate friends of the kind host were present. An elegant table laden with refreshments and adorned with flowers occupied the centre of one of the rooms, and the event was made in all respects as delightful as possible to us.

To meet these relatives, and receive from the lips of each some cordial expression of welcome, was unusually grateful after my long, sad experiences; and it vividly recalled to me the previous family gathering, when my dear husband greeted his family kin, and we, with Queen Kapiolani, were Boston's honored guests.

Chapter LI. Washington—Pseudo-Hawaiians

On Friday, Jan. 22, 1897, I bade adieu to my cousins, Mr. and Mrs. William Lee, and the other friends who had rendered my four weeks' stay at Boston so interesting and agreeable that I had scarcely noticed the flight of time, and took the evening train for Washington. By my request, Captain Julius A. Palmer accompanied me as my private secretary, and remained as one of my suite from that date to the 7th of August, when he asked and most cheerfully received permission to take a vacation, for he had been most constant and devoted in every official duty. Captain Palmer had been presented to me at Honolulu just as I have met other visitors and correspondents; we had no personal acquaintance until my visit to Boston, but I knew those in my native city who were connected with his family by marriage. Besides which, his interest in the Hawaiian people, and his reputation as a man of unblemished honor and integrity, recommended him to me; and I needed the services of some person more familiar with matters and manners in the United States than could be expected of my Hawaiian secretary, Mr. Joseph Heleluhe, who was now on his first trip abroad.

I have found Captain Palmer to be well informed on all matters relating to Hawaii, whether in those earlier days when he visited the Islands under the monarch, or since 1893 under the rule of the Provisional Government. Like many others I might mention, he went there soon after the overthrow, and was petted and flattered by the party in power. But all the time he was quietly investigating the situation for himself. The result of his observations was a conclusion that the right of the Hawaiian people to choose their own form of government should be affirmed, and that they should be protected in this choice by the power of the United States, in which event he was fully assured that their queen would be overwhelmingly restored to her constitutional rights.

While in Boston I was constantly asked if there was any political significance in my visit to America, and if I expected to see the President. It seemed wise to say nothing about my purpose at that time, but frankness would now indicate an opposite course. By the first vessel that arrived from Honolulu after I reached San Francisco, documents were sent to me by the patriotic leagues of the native Hawaiian people, those associations of which I have already spoken in full; and these representative bodies of my own nation prayed me to undertake certain measures for the general good of Hawaii. Further messages of similar purport reached me while I was visiting my Boston friends.

All the communications received, whether personally or in form, from individuals or from the above-mentioned organizations, were in advocacy of one desired end. This was to ask President Cleveland that the former form of government unjustly taken from us by the persons who in 1892 and 1893 represented the United States should be restored, and that this restoration should undo the wrong which had been done to the Hawaiian people, and return to them the queen, to whom constitutionally, and also by their own choice, they had a perfect right.

This was further in the line of the only instructions which to this day have ever been given by the United States to the so-called Republic of Hawaii, and those were that the President acknowledges the right of the Hawaiian people to choose their own form of government. Were that one sentence literally carried out in fact today, and the Hawaiians sustained in the carrying out of the same, it would be all that either my people or myself could ask.

The second package of documents received by me in Boston was addressed to President McKinley, and was similar to the others I already had, only they were addressed to Hon. Grover Cleveland while he was president. Accompanying these papers were other documents, showing that full power was accorded to me, not only as their queen, but individually, to represent the real people of Hawaii, and in so doing to act in any way my judgment should dictate for the good of the Hawaiians, to whom the Creator gave those beautiful islands in the Pacific. Commissions were also issued to Mr. Joseph Heleluhe, empowering him to act with me; he having been chosen by the Hawaiians as the special envoy of those deprived by the Provisional Government, not only of the franchise, but also of any representation at the capital of that American nation to which they have never ceased to look for the redress of national wrongs, brought upon them by the hasty action of the United States officers.

When I speak at this time of the Hawaiian people, I refer to the children of the soil — the native inhabitants of the Hawaiian Islands and their descendants. Two delegations claiming to represent Hawaii have visited Washington at intervals during the past four years in the cause of annexation, besides which other individuals have been sent on to assist in this attempt to defraud an aboriginal people of their birthrights — rights dear to the patriotic hearts of even the weakest nation. Lately these aliens have called themselves Hawaiians.

They are not and never were Hawaiians. Although some have had positions under the monarchy which they solemnly swore by oath of office to uphold and sustain, they retained their American birthrights. When they overthrew my government, and placed themselves under the protectorate established by John L. Stevens—as he so states in writing—they designated themselves as Americans; as such they called on him to raise their flag on the building of the Hawaiian Government. When it pleased the Provisional Government to give their control another name, they called it the Republic of Hawaii. To gain the sympathy of the American people, they made the national day of the Independence of the United States their own, and made speeches claiming to be American citizens. Such has been their custom at Honolulu, although in Washington they represent themselves as Hawaiians.

At Honolulu these annexationists made speeches abusing the Senate of the United States for the delay in annexing Hawaii; they further said the most grossly insulting things of President Cleveland because he frustrated their plans, and included Secretary Gresham in their condemnation because he failed to recognize them as Americans. Of these pseudo-Hawaiians, Mr. Hatch is a lawyer from New Hampshire. His first exploit in the ring of adventures was not a diplomatic success. He met some of his annexation associates at Canton, Ohio. Mr. McKinley sent word that the state of his health obliged him to decline to receive visitors, so the embassy returned to the national capital. "Minister" Cooper, another alien (less than a year in Hawaii in 1893, when he stood on the steps of Iolani Palace, and read the proclamation against me), has been given office, probably as a reward for the risk he ran. Mr. William A. Kinney has been better acquainted with life at Salt Lake City, as it was in the past, than with simple, amiable—but, alas, no longer happy—Hawaii. Without military experience, he was commissioned a captain, and afterward charged with the duty of Judge Advocate in attacking me, and those of my people who sought liberty from the foreign oppressor. So I could go on multiplying indefinitely recollections of these and other so-called Hawaiians. Those who are not recent arrivals are sons of the missionaries, or allied to the families connected with the American Mission, and claim foreign citizenship to this day. When a political question was under discussion, they would be very active in soliciting the native Hawaiian vote for the side of the missionary party. The true Hawaiian, you see, has no representation in these several commissions.

The number of articles written or inspired by the Commissioners or their allies is enormous; articles skillfully calculated to deceive the American people on most important topics; also articles intended to place me in an awkward or utterly false position in the great and good land where I have been four times a visitor. I can see the inspiration of it all, because I know the character of several of the men so engaged. Allusion to episodes in the career as a monarchial official of one of these men has already been made. Mr. Thurston's political methods need no mention. His measures with the press are well known, but unfortunately for him, he rewarded newspaper enterprise once too often. His position as at least a nominal member of the diplomatic corps gave him certain advantages, which he treacherously used to give official correspondence to the press. For this he was promptly rebuked by Secretary Gresham, and recalled to Honolulu as persona non grata. The Dole government was too weak to defend its agent, and Mr. Thurston went home in disgrace. He is again attempting to negotiate a treaty, bartering away his adopted country.

Another without gratitude, and false to the country to which he owes his life, whose letters to the press have frequently appeared, is Sereno E. Bishop of Honolulu, a man who owes his seventy years or more to the vigor given to his infancy from the breasts of Hawaiian women. Broadcast have been his letters reviling my people, and repeating the vilest of falsehoods as to myself, since he failed to have Hawaii annexed by praising the country, its people, and his queen. One has but to peruse Mr. Bishop's paper in the *Review of Reviews* for September, 1891, to see how false must be his later statements. I trust those who read these pages will obtain that number of the *Review*, and read the article.

I cannot impress too strongly upon those who truly desire to know about my country and to do it justice, the importance of reading that "article" of September, 1891. Although it was written not to serve Hawaii, but in the interest of the annexationists, the plea used was that the Hawaiians had shown themselves so capable of self-government, and were so proud of their autonomy in the Pacific, that they would be well qualified to be United States citizens. How vastly opposite and false is the plea that is made by them now for annexation!

Early in their present mission the Annexationists secured the services of Mr. John W. Foster, who succeeded Mr. Blaine as Secretary of State under Mr. Harrison, and employed him to deliver in Washington a lecture on Hawaii. Before this, I had received a letter from an American residing in that city, advising me to lose no time in retaining the services of Mr. Foster in presenting my case to the National government. To this, as to several other offers of legal aid, I returned the reply that I thanked the friendly counselors, but that I had already in my letters and protest placed my case before the Chief Executive (since my first communication more than one president has occupied that position), and that I would trust in their honor for redress. But if I had not believed in the integrity of the American nation, and its treaty-making representatives, it would have been well to have awaited the delivery of this lecture, before retaining the services of Mr. Foster; because had he shown such a lamentable ignorance of my affairs as he did of those of Hawaii when he tried to speak of that country, her rulers, her people, even her situation geographically and socially, my case as a client would have suffered from his ignorance. Notwithstanding the historical truths, that although the gospel has been preached in Polynesia for a century or more, and that there is no other nation which has made such rapid progress in civilization and Christianity, yet Mr. Foster had the assurance to stand up in Washington, and revile all the native Hawaiian sovereigns. Not content with the using bad language about my brother, King Kalakaua, and myself, he had to take up each one of the Kamehamehas, and refuse to them successively even one good quality, or to the Island people one redeeming characteristic.

This is only one of Mr. Foster's blunders—truly a serious one. Another blunder savors of the ridiculous; I did not see it, but it was described to me by those who did. It seems that his remarks were to be illustrated by lantern slides; and on opening this series of illustrations, there first appeared on the screen a dark form, which no one in the audience could recognize, yet the lecturer nothing daunted, with pole in hand, began to describe the situation of the Islands; then it suddenly occurred to him that the dots on the Pacific as shown by the slides were placed near enough over to annex, if not to the United States, then to Mexico; so he paused in his remarks while the artist made a second attempt; but he had only fled from one extreme to another, for now the unfortunate group, so far as location was concerned, had every appearance of annexation to Japan. This was going from Scylla to Charybdis. It was not until the third trial, when poor little Hawaii regained that position in the Pacific Ocean in which the hand of the Creator had left her, that the lecturer, after some hesitation in order to be sure that this time he was right, dared to proceed with his discourse. There was not one original idea in his lengthy misrepresentation of my native land, its people, and its sovereigns.

Mr. Foster made one brief trip to Honolulu, in the interest, it is said, of the cable company projected by Mr. Z. S. Spaulding. Whether this was a mere pretence or an original motive ending in failure, cannot be decided now. But the present rulers took charge of him at once, as they do of all new-comers; and he was greeted, feasted, and generally entertained by the members of the government and by their friends. A meeting was held where the cable scheme was discussed, annexation also receiving some notice. A feeble opposition was developed under the leadership of Mr. W. G. Irwin. Mr. Foster immediately replied that unless there was perfect agreement on the part of the planters, nothing could be done, there was no further use for his services; and if the cable scheme was so unpopular he might as well leave, which he did without even warning those friends who had been so attentive to him. Soon after his arrival in Washington, he delivered his lecture, and then had it printed at the public expense, and sent to the Senate by the money of the people, all upon a subject about which he knew nothing save the absurd stories and intentional misrepresentations repeated to him by those who were writing them out continually for the American newspapers.

Time would not admit of a particular criticism of each of the individuals who have been working so hard at Washington from the close of the last Republican administration to the present date, with the sole object of bettering a small minority of American ancestry at the cost of forty thousand Hawaiians (not to count those of other nationalities to the number of over sixty thousand), who have no voice in public affairs, either in Hawaii or in the representation of the present government at Washington. And to oppose this project, and represent this down-trodden people, there was in Washington simply the presence of one woman, without legal adviser, without a dollar to spend in subsidies, supported and encouraged in her mission only by three faithful adherents, and such friends as from time to time expressed to her their sympathy.

Amongst the last-named, even in the city of my husband's family, I could not count the representative of the Hawaiian Republic. Somewhere about the year 1848, possibly earlier, a young man from Boston landed on the shores of our Islands; he was about eighteen years of age, an entire stranger, coming out to those distant fields of labor to seek his fortune. My adopted father, the chief Paki, befriended him, gave him the first helping hand which welcomed him to his new country, and rendered him such assistance as was in fact the means of showing to him the opportunity of making his way in the world; as years passed by he established himself in business, and soon became one of the leading merchants of Lahaina, at that time the port of call in the Islands for the whaleships, ranking second only to Honolulu.

It was then the base of supplies to this fleet of vessels, was a thoroughly thrifty place, and a business city of growing commercial importance. But the oil-wells of the land have thrown into neglect the oil-ships of the sea, and since this decline and decay Lahaina is little more than a city of ruins. Mr. Gilman probably saw the approaching decline of the industry by which the place was supported; for he broke up his business connections there, sundered certain personal ties, and returned to the East with a very handsome fortune, it is said, the result of the accumulation of years of mercantile life on Hawaiian soil and under Hawaiian laws. From Honolulu he returned to Boston, where he has resided ever since, save that once, since the overthrow of the monarchy, he made a brief visit to his Honolulu friends.

In 1887, during my journey with Queen Kapiolani, we met Mr. Gilman, who was at that time very kind and attentive to me. To be sure, he had a point to gain; he wanted a decoration from the king, and did not hesitate to say so. On the return of the queen's party to the Islands, letters were received from Mr. Gilman, directly applying for the honor to my brother. Chiefly by means of my personal influence his petition was granted, and he was made a Knight Companion of the Order of Kalakaua, and the decoration forwarded to him.

The next thing I heard from Mr. Gilman was that he had espoused with alacrity and fidelity the cause of the revolutionists of the month of January, 1893, and that he avowed his implicit belief in all the absurd and wicked statements circulated by the missionary party against my own character and that of my people. Papers were sent to me where Mr. Gilman had repeated and vouched for the truth of these abominable political slanders; and at first I could scarcely credit it, for this man was often at the house of my adoption, and showed great partiality for my society when I was a young girl and he a young man. He knew Paki and Konia, a couple of the strictest morality, whose household was organized on the basis of the most regular family habits and the most pious Christian customs; and these had taken me from my very birth under their parental care.

He further knew me as the foster-sister and daily companion of Mrs. Bernice Pauahi Bishop, where I was ever under the kind care of her husband, Hon. Charles R. Bishop, a couple whose principles of exalted piety, whose love for all that is good, honorable, and pure, are too well known to need at this moment the least praise from me, and whose protection was ever and always surrounding my earlier life. From their house, when married, I went directly to that of my husband's mother, with whom I lived to the day of her death, not so very long ago.

Such were the lives of those with whom my own life has been passed; such were the families with whom Mr. Gilman knew I had been in daily association, and where he met me. At the time when he hastened to avow his allegiance to my enemies, and to ask them for the decoration of a consular station, in the year 1893, I was fifty-six years of age. Yet the past was reckoned by him as naught; he permitted himself to be instantly prejudiced against his early friend, and to be led away by the base slanders and political falsehoods of her adversaries. He proceeded to vilify me in such articles as those sent to me from his pen, and has been a zealous servant of the men who placed him in the office; he has rushed into print not only his own misstatements, but has endeavored to nullify the influence of any article written in my favor, or in defence of the rights of the Hawaiian people.

Such has been the animosity, openly and secretly expressed, toward me, not only as a queen, but as a woman, by those whom all the claims of gratitude should bind to me as friends, and who should rally to my assistance, that, since leaving home and arriving in America, I have constantly received communications from Hawaii, often by special message, begging me to be careful of my life, still regarded as "infinitely precious to the people of the Islands," reminding me that I was surrounded by enemies, some of whom from home were entirely unscrupulous, and assuring me that great anxiety was felt by all classes, as it was a persistent rumor that evil was intended me.

Chapter LII. President And Mrs. Cleveland

Arriving in Washington on Saturday, my party took rooms at the Shoreham; and amongst the very first callers to greet me was the Hon. Daniel Nash Morgan, the Treasurer of the United States. A Mason of the highest degree himself, Mr. Morgan noticed at once the jewel of the Mystic Shrine which I wore upon my breast, and asked for its history.

I told him that General Powell, a grand commander of the Mystic Shrine in the Western jurisdiction, visited the Hawaiian Islands about the time of my return from the Queen's Jubilee. When he met me he took the decoration of the order from the lapel of his own coat, and pinned it on the front of my dress. As he fastened it on my breast, wishing me God-speed, he said that, should I travel and find myself in need of any aid or protection, it would be of great assistance to me; and I have worn it ever since. Mr. Morgan was much interested in this narration, and, with his charming wife and lovely daughter, as well as with others of his family, did much to render my stay in Washington pleasant to me.

My first call, after arriving at the Shoreham, was at the White House. The day of my departure from Boston, President Cleveland had gone on one of his hunting excursions. This was immediately telegraphed over the land, and his going made out to be a consequence of my coming. As no person, excepting the three members of my suite, knew of my intention to visit Washington, of course this was impossible. However, it was as true as the long list of falsehoods written during my residence at Washington and elsewhere.

On Monday morning, Jan. 25, Mr. Cleveland set the gossips at rest by appearing at the executive office; and at eleven o'clock my secretaries delivered to Hon. Henry T. Thurber, the President's secretary, a brief note from me, advising him of my presence in the city, and offering to express to him my friendly feeling by a personal call, if it would be convenient to receive me. I had suggested no day nor hour; but they had scarcely reached the hotel on their return when a most courteous note was received from the President, conveying to me his sympathy, and welcoming me to call upon him at three o'clock that very afternoon, which I did with the three members of my suite.

The President received me in the little Red Reception-room. Every door opened as we passed in; and the crowd of reporters on the piazza were forced to be content with a mere glimpse of my party, and to draw on imagination for any account of the interview. Not a hint was given by me as to any intention to visit Mrs. Cleveland. The President very naturally spoke of his wife, who had shown me such consideration the last time I was in the executive mansion; and I expressed the hope that she continued in good health after so many trying duties and social responsibilities had been laid upon her.

To this Mr. Cleveland immediately said that he would like to have me see for myself, and that he hoped she was at home, but that he had come directly from his business office, and had had no opportunity to speak with her since hearing from me. He then added that he would ascertain, and went to the corridor to inquire of the usher, who told him that Mrs. Cleveland had gone out for her afternoon walk; so we resumed our conversation, during which I handed him the documents prepared for his inspection by the patriotic leagues of which I have already spoken.

These he took impressively, thanking me for them. It was a great pleasure to me to tell him personally how dear his name was to the Hawaiian people, and how grateful a place he held in my own heart because of his effort to do that which was right and just in restoring to us our lost independence. We always thought him to be sincere in his attempt to right the wrong; and since I have fully acquainted myself with the obstructions placed in his way by the supporters of Minister John L. Stevens, I understand far better than formerly that he failed through no fault of his own. It was a very pleasant interview; and when it was over, I returned with my party to my hotel.

Mrs. Cleveland's accidental absence was made use of by the press to cast a slur upon me. No one seemed to notice that had the first lady in the land been rude as reported — well, it would not have been Mrs. Cleveland, that is all. Two or three days later, a note arrived unexpectedly from the executive mansion, which stated that Mrs. Cleveland would be happy to see me, and that as she was to give a private reception at five o'clock in the afternoon, she thought that if I would call a quarter of an hour or so previous to that hour, we could have a pleasant chat together in her parlor.

The delicacy of thus arranging in advance that I might have the opportunity for social enjoyment apart from the visitors is indeed worthy of a lady whose grace and beauty are in accord with the kindness and goodness of her heart. At the hour appointed, accompanied by the three members of my suite, I again visited the White House parlors, and was received by the lovely mistress of those halls.

It is not my purpose to detail private conversation with those who have made me their guest; but it must be testified here that I never have had the least cause to retract my early assurance that in Grover Cleveland I had met a statesman of splendid ability, rare judgment, and lofty standards of right.

And equally do I believe that to few among the nations has it ever been granted to have at the head a woman more worthy the name of queen than that one who presided with so much grace and dignity for eight years at the White House.

One day in February, the proprietor of the Shoreham notified me, that, as I had failed to engage my apartments for inauguration week, he had rented them to others, and that every room in the hotel would then be occupied because of the crowd of visitors that occasion would summon to the city. Rather than await the arrival of the future occupants of those rooms, and then have to look out for my party when the throng should be doing likewise, it seemed best to me to move at once. So I sent my secretaries to consult Mrs. Mary Longfellow Milmore, widow of Joseph Milmore, the celebrated sculptor, and sister-in-law of Martin Milmore.

Knowing me simply from history, and sympathizing with me by reason of the kindness of her own heart, Mrs. Milmore had written to me while I was in Boston, and then had followed her cordial letters by calling on me when I arrived in Washington. To any lady traveling or residing in a strange city, there are many little attentions which cannot be so perfectly rendered as by a person of her own sex, one who understands the customs of the community, and is familiar with the places and people. Mrs. Milmore not only came when I needed advice as a recent arrival, but she continued her kind and sympathetic visits to the latest days of my stay, at about which time she herself went abroad for a European trip.

There rarely passed a day when her cheerful face and friendly voice did not appear at my door. Flowers, fruits, cakes, and other tokens of her loving care, came almost daily; and to her hospitable dwelling I often went to luncheon, meeting, besides herself, Sister Angelica, or other friends who seemed to be of the same kindly spirit as the generous hostess. Wherever I may be in the future, her many attentions during that winter cannot be forgotten, and she will always have a warm remembrance in my heart.

By her advice and selection, on or about the 14th of February, I moved with my party to the large thirteen-story building on Q Street, N. W., known as "The Cairo." Its newness and immaculate cleanliness impressed me favorably at once. My rooms were in the southwest corner, from which I had a glorious view over the country and down the Potomac; and although unused to being on the tenth story of any building, yet, when I became accustomed to the height, it ceased to worry me. Everything was done by the owner, Mr. Schneider, and his lovely wife, as well as by the manager, Mr. Sherman, and his amiable wife, to render the stay of our whole party agreeable to us. There we remained until about the 9th of July, at which time I removed to New York City, with no further intention of visiting Washington, although I did subsequently return, for reasons which will be stated in the proper place.

Chapter LIII. Inauguration Of President Mckinley

Time would fail me to speak of the countless new friends who vied in making my visit to Washington one of the most delightful seasons I ever passed. It was my custom to give a reception about every fortnight; to receive callers at eight to nine any evening, and often at other times. Both houses of Congress were well represented at my receptions, if not always by the gentlemen themselves, by their wives or daughters. Although all were presented through Captain Palmer by name and by card, yet it will be seen that, when there were seldom less than two hundred callers, and my largest reception numbered nearly five hundred persons, it was not possible for me to return all calls.

I therefore made it a rule to pay return visits only to those connected with the government, and even then it was scarcely possible to keep up with the number of my visitors. But there are two persons at least of whom I must make mention by name. These are Senator George C. Perkins, formerly governor of the State of California, and Representative Samuel G.

Hilborn, also of that State. Both of these gentlemen have visited Honolulu.

I had had the pleasure of entertaining Governor Perkins when he was there, but was in retirement at the time Mr. Hilborn went there accompanied by his wife and daughter. Like many other visitor, Mr. Hilborn landed in Hawaii supposing that my government had been a failure, and that the present rulers were the choice of the people, and annexation desirable for both nations. And like any person who goes there and examines the situation frankly and fairly, Mr. Hilborn returned with his mind made up to the contrary.

While I was at the Shoreham, Mr. Hilborn called, and introduced his wife and daughter; and the beautiful voice of Miss Grace Hilborn, as she sang some of my own Hawaiian songs, to our instrument, the ukulele, gave to me that joy, so sadly sweet, of listening to the sounds of home in foreign lands. This charming family never relaxed their attentions to me while I resided in Washington, and I am indebted to each of them in more ways than I can speak of in these recollections. Mr. Hilborn is a hard-working man in his public life, yet he always found the time for any friendly chat with me if I wished to speak with some gentleman on whose good judgment I could rely.

Governor Perkins received me on my first visit to the Senate Chamber, where I went with my party simply to watch the deliberations; he provided us at once with seats in the gallery reserved for the personal friends of the senators, but subsequently he did a greater and more conspicuous kindness than this. On Friday noon, the 26th of February, I informed Captain Palmer that I had great curiosity to see the inauguration of the President of the United States, if it were possible to get seats. He said that it was rather late to make the proper arrangements. I requested him to communicate my wish to Governor Perkins. So, at two o'clock of that day he went to the Capitol, was welcomed by Senator Perkins, introduced to the members of the committee, and leaving the matter in their hands, he returned to the hotel.

Almost immediately on his arrival there, Captain Palmer received a despatch saying that it had been agreed between Senator Sherman and Secretary Olney that two seats in the gallery reserved for the diplomatic corps should be assigned to me, and that it was much regretted that I had not applied earlier, when I could have had seats for three, in the place of one attendant. We said nothing about our intentions; and leaving Captain Palmer and Mrs. Nahaolelua in the carriage, I, attended by Mr. Joseph Heleluhe, witnessed the interesting ceremonies.

The storm which burst from the reporters' gallery when they saw me there will be remembered by those who read any of the newspapers on the day following. As it had been a very gallant act on the part of quite a number of gentlemen, and especially of Secretary Sherman and Secretary Olney, I permitted nothing to be said by my secretaries in answer to the misrepresentations made in the press. But they were not to go unrebuked; for Mr. Sherman's letter, bearing the date of the very afternoon when my secretary called at the Senate chamber, was given by Mr. Olney to the press without comment, and there was immediate silence on the subject, for with which administration were the critics to find fault?

After the inaugural ceremonies were over we visited the building of the Central National Bank, where I was most courteously received by the president of the board of directors; and after resting with my suite in his office, we were conducted to a room in the building from which I saw and intensely enjoyed the grand procession. The day was all that could be desired; my friends accused me of having imported it from our own perfect climate expressly for the new administration. Although too weary to attend the ball in the evening, I felt that I would not have missed for anything that which I had seen during the day.

But there was another pleasure in store for me that very night; for in the carriage with the President, and representing the United States Navy, was Admiral George Brown, who, with his wife, had already visited me at the Shoreham. In meeting with me under the changed circumstances which had befallen since he knew me as the Princess Royal at the date of his attentions to my brother, the gallant sailor could not restrain his emotions, and the tears flowed from his eyes. On the last days of the sessions of the Senate, a bill had passed by unanimous consent permitting sundry officers of the United States service to receive decorations which had been conferred by King Kalakaua, and also by myself while reigning sovereign; and amongst these was one bestowed upon Admiral Brown.

"There, I have waited over four years for the privilege of wearing that," he exclaimed, as he entered my parlor that night; "and now that it is mine, I am determined that you shall be the very first one to see it." I thanked him warmly, as I handed him back his coveted decoration, for, indeed, I fully appreciated his loyalty in bringing it to show me. Since that meeting he has been retired from active service, but it is to be hoped that so gallant a gentleman and efficient an officer may long be spared to his friends and his country. I can never forget his kindness to my brother during the king's last days on earth.

One object of my visit to Washington was to ask a favor of the Masonic fraternity; so, while at the Shoreham, I sent a letter to Mr. Frederic Webber, Secretary of the Supreme Council, thirty-third degree, asking him to call at my apartments, a request with which he very promptly complied. He remembered me perfectly from our meeting in 1887, when he had been one of the thirteen Masons of high degree to call on the party of Queen Kapiolani; of that committee of the Supreme Council, General Albert Pike, now gone to the great majority, was the head. Besides this, Mr. Webber was, during the lifetime of Governor Dominis, in correspondence with my husband on matters connected with the order.

I showed Mr. Webber my jewel of the Mystic Shrine, which I prize very highly, and asked if I might be permitted to wear my husband's Masonic jewels; to which he replied in the affirmative, and then added he would like also to present me with a medal which was ornamented on one side with certain emblems of the thirty-third degree of Masonry, and on the other with a bas-relief likeness of General Pike. To thus receive permission to use the decorations or insignia of Masonry belonging to my husband, and further to be presented with a likeness of the head of the fraternity, and a valued correspondent of Governor Dominis, was certainly a happy welcome from the brotherhood my husband loved.

Secretary Webber also sent me books containing the accounts of the meetings of the council, and of proceedings in many of their branches, thus informing me in regard to the extent of their works of charity and benevolence. On one afternoon, by his invitation, I visited the chambers of the council, attended by my suite; and quite a number of the brethren were presented to me, much to my pleasure, which I sincerely trust was reciprocated. I was shown a photograph of my husband, which, with his correspondence, is preserved there in the archives of the order. In more ways than I can mention, Mr. Webber and his daughter showed themselves to be true friends during my visit.

From several benevolent and literary associations of Washington requests were received to set apart a day to receive their members as a body; but to all such suggestions I instructed my secretary to reply that a committee of the ladies or gentlemen might call upon me at their own convenience, but that I must decline any large public receptions. The only exception I made to this rule was in favor of the National Park School for young ladies at Forest Glen, Md., who sent one of the faculty to ask the favor of a general reception. I have so long been interested in the education of the young, especially of young girls, that I could not refuse myself the pleasure.

The affair took place at the Shoreham; and it was indeed refreshing to look into the pure, good, beautiful faces before me. Including the teachers who came with them, the company numbered over a hundred. Their music interested me very much; they sang with great taste and sweetness. They presented me with their college colors; and I gave them a copy, made with my own hands, of my most popular song, the "Aloha Oe," or "Farewell to Thee," with which they seemed to be much pleased. But they were not quite satisfied, I was told, because I had made no address.

I have already spoken of the shrinking from publicity felt by me ever since my imprisonment, and I had prepared nothing; however, I decided to tell them of one thought which impressed me, so, by the published report in the newspapers, this is what I said: "I wish to extend to you my thanks for the honor you have shown me by this visit. It shall always be remembered as a bright spot in my memory of this stay in America. I am glad to see you all, and to know that each of you is desirous of attaining intellectual advancement. It shows the progress of the world. The world cannot stand still. We must either advance or recede. Since my arrival in this country I have been impressed with its grandeur, but nothing more favorably impresses me than the advantages you have for learning. Again I desire to thank you, and I wish you all a prosperous and happy future."

There were many delegations of patriotic or literary societies amongst my visitors at the Cairo, such as Daughters of the Revolution, and Veterans of the Southern Confederacy. At Arlington, on Decoration Day, I was overwhelmed with pleasant attentions by the Grand Army of the Republic. Then the delegates to the International Postal Congress; the Chinese Embassy; a large political delegation from Missouri; Governor Clough, with some twenty members of his staff in full uniform, from Minnesota; many associations of teachers from distant States; frequent calls from the young ladies of colleges — one after the other seemed to find pleasure in visiting me to pay their respects.

From all denominations of the Christian church I have received representative visitors, and from the Sisters of the Holy Cross and from the Methodist Society of Rev. Lucien G. Clark accepted invitations to be present at their receptions. At the former I twice had the pleasure of meeting Monseigneur Martinelli, the papal delegate to the capital. Rev. J. H. Perry, the rector of St. Andrews, was very kind and attentive; and as I am a communicant in the Episcopal Church, I generally attended the church of his parish in Fourteenth Street.

Chapter LIV. My Literary Occupation

In the early part of May it became necessary for my companion, Mrs. Kia Nahaolelua, to return to Honolulu. Three months was the length of time I had expected to be absent when I asked her to accompany me; but five months had passed away, and her husband and large family of children needed her. So I sent her to San Francisco under the charge of Captain Palmer, where he was to meet Mrs. Joseph Heleluhe, and conduct her to Washington.

During their absence I invited my cousin, Mrs. William Lee, whom, after leaving Boston, I had met in New York on the occasion of the dedication of the Grant mausoleum, to visit me at the Cairo. In her honor I issued cards for a special reception given in the elegant ballroom of that hotel. Manager Sherman spared neither pains nor money to make the occasion worthy of the guest; choice flowers and music, some of it from Hawaiian sources, made the celebration a charming one. Mrs. Lee is a very handsome woman, of commanding presence, brilliant in conversation, cultivated in mind, and of a high order of intellect. During her short stay, for the days sped quickly by, she attracted much attention by her social qualities, and won the hearts of many of those with whom she came in contact.

The synopsis of my social pleasures for the six months or so I was in Washington is necessarily incomplete, and to render it perfect would be to extend these leaves into too much of a volume. With such numberless callers as I have daily received from all parts of the United States, the frequent courtesies from the families of congressional members, and the occasionally accepted invitations to the theatre, the opera, or other public entertainments (many of which invitations, while appreciating the kindly spirit, I was obliged to decline), my leisure moments were much occupied. It was singular, and at times amusing, to notice the question in the public journals, asking, "What is the queen doing in Washington?" and in reply, to read the ingenuity shown in inventing all sorts of political falsehoods, and publishing these as facts.

Besides what has been stated, my time was much engrossed with correspondence and literary labors, in which latter might be included my music. For I have been engaged on two other works besides "Hawaii's Story." During my imprisonment I had nearly translated an ancient poem which has been handed down exclusively in our family from the earliest days. This I completed during my visit to the national capital; and it is now issued from the press of Lee & Shepard, Boston. It is the chant which was sung to Captain Cook in one of the ancient temples of Hawaii, and chronicles the creation of the world and of living creatures, from the shell-fish to the human race, according to Hawaiian traditions. It is not designed for general circulation, but for my friends, and will be placed in the libraries of some scientific societies.

For years my name has been at the head of a list of members of the Polynesian Society, as patron. This organization, with headquarters in New Zealand, is devoted to the study of languages, literature, folk-lore, history, in short, all things connected with the inhabitants of that vast extent of archipelago in the Pacific Ocean known as Oceanica. When I accepted the position as patron, Mr. Alexander assured me that it was tendered to me, not only because of the fact that the Hawaiians were the most highly civilized of any of the ancient people of those seas, but further, because I had been known so long as the friend of education, of art, and of all those refining influences which exalt the nation, and elevate the character of the individual. Therefore it seemed fitting for me to send to this society some account of our earliest days.

I have had more calls for my music than I could possibly supply. An edition of "Aloha Oe," published by me in Washington this winter, simply for gifts to my friends, is nearly exhausted. No copies have ever been offered for sale; but in response to the very general wish, I have collected a number of my songs, chants, and pieces written or translated by me during the past twenty years or more, and hope soon to put them into the hands of the publisher, so that any stranger desiring to possess samples of Hawaiian music may have that opportunity. Two specially prepared volumes of such compositions were appropriately bound and inscribed in Washington the past winter. One of these was placed in the new Congressional Library; the other was sent abroad as my contribution to the souvenirs of this Jubilee year of Her Majesty, the great and good Queen Victoria.

From this brief sketch of my life at the capital, it would appear that my mind was fully employed, had there been no political questions to interest me. Yet was it natural that I should forget my own people and their misfortunes? Let me, therefore, return to the annexationists and their plots. While I had been no more than an interested observer, quietly awaiting the course of justice, and conscious of the strength derived from truth and right on my side, their commissioners, with such influences as their indomitable assurance could command, had been working very had to get the present rule in Hawaii out of its political and financial difficulties, by passing over to the United States a country whose hospitality they have betrayed, a land which they do not and never can own.

My friends in Honolulu had never forgotten me, and the arrival of every mail kept me informed of all that transpired throughout Hawaii. With the advantages which were mine of learning the attitude of men and parties in Washington, there was little that took place with which I was not thoroughly acquainted before it reached the columns of the newspapers. Thus, understanding perfectly the kind of men sent one after another by the so-called Republic of Hawaii to Washington, I was easily able to separate truth from falsehood in the accounts inspired by the missionary party, published by them or their agents in Honolulu, written from thence to the press in America, or invented by enterprising scribblers for the purpose of deceiving the American public.

Having tried in vain to excite the American people against Great Britain, and having willfully violated treaty obligations with the friendly power of Japan, they then got the Senate into a hopeless quarrel over the reciprocity treaty and the sugar schedule; so that to allay all these disturbances, and yet do nothing decisive, on June 16, 1897, President McKinley sent their annexation treaty to the Senate. Congress had been in session ever since December, and had shown no interest whatever in the troubles of a few adventurers two thousand miles from California, claiming to be both Americans and Hawaiians.

Nothing was done by me in the matter until the treaty was officially made public in the Senate. These commissioners had often said that there would soon be a treaty signed, and had so often deceived the people that it was well to await knowledge from the proper authority. But just as quickly as I learned that action had been taken upon the proposed cession of Hawaii to the United States, I sent my secretaries, Mr. Joseph Heleluhe and Captain Julius A. Palmer, to the Department of State with the following protest.

Chapter LV. My Official Protest To The Treaty

"I, Liliuokalani of Hawaii, by the will of God named heir apparent on the tenth day of April, A. D. 1877, and by the grace of God Queen of the Hawaiian Islands on the seventeenth day of January, A. D. 1893, do hereby protest against the ratification of a certain treaty, which, so I am informed, has been signed at Washington by Messrs. Hatch, Thurston, and Kinney, purporting to cede those Islands to the territory and dominion of the United States. I declare such a treaty to be an act of wrong toward the native and part-native people of Hawaii, an invasion of the rights of the ruling chiefs, in violation of international rights both toward my people and toward friendly nations with whom they have made treaties, the perpetuation of the fraud whereby the constitutional government was overthrown and, finally, an act of gross injustice to me.

"Because the official protests made by me on the seventeenth day of January, 1893, to the so-called Provisional Government was signed by me, and received by said government with the assurance that the case was referred to the United States of America for arbitration.

Yielded To Avoid Bloodshed.

"Because that protest and my communications to the United States Government immediately thereafter expressly declare that I yielded my authority to the forces of the United States in order to avoid bloodshed, and because I recognized the futility of a conflict with so formidable a power.

"Because the President of the United States, the Secretary of State, and an envoy commissioned by them reported in official documents that my government was unlawfully coerced by the forces, diplomatic and naval, of the United States; that I was at the date of their investigations the constitutional ruler of my people.

"Because such decision of the recognized magistrates of the United States was officially communicated to me and to Sanford B. Dole, and said Dole's resignation requested by Albert S. Willis, the recognized agent and minister of the Government of the United States.

"Because neither the above-named commission nor the government which sends it has ever received any such authority from the registered voters of Hawaii, but derives its assumed powers from the so-called committee of public safety, organized on or about the seventeenth day of January, 1893, said committee being composed largely of persons claiming American citizenship, and not one single Hawaiian was a member thereof, or in any way participated in the demonstration leading to its existence.

"Because my people, about forty thousand in number, have in no way been consulted by those, three thousand in number, who claim the right to destroy the independence of Hawaii. My people constitute four-fifths of the legally qualified voters of Hawaii, and excluding those imported for the demands of labor, about the same proportion of the inhabitants.

Civic And Hereditary Rights.

"Because said treaty ignores, not only the civic rights of my people, but, further, the hereditary property of their chiefs. Of the 4,000,000 acres composing the territory said treaty offers to annex, 1,000,000 or 915,000 acres has in no way been heretofore recognized as other than the private property of the constitutional monarch, subject to a control in no way differing from other items of a private estate.

"Because it is proposed by said treaty to confiscate said property, technically called the crown lands, those legally entitled thereto, either now or in succession, receiving no consideration whatever for estates, their title to which has been always undisputed, and which is legitimately in my name at this date.

"Because said treaty ignores, not only all professions of perpetual amity and good faith made by the United States in former treaties with the sovereigns representing the Hawaiian people, but all treaties made by those sovereigns with other and friendly powers, and it is thereby in violation of international law.

"Because, by treating with the parties claiming at this time the right to cede said territory of Hawaii, the Government of the United States receives such territory from the hands of those whom its own magistrates (legally elected by the people of the United States, and in office in 1893) pronounced fraudulently in power and unconstitutionally ruling Hawaii.

Appeals To President And Senate.

"Therefore I, Liliuokalani of Hawaii, do hereby call upon the President of that nation, to whom alone I yielded my property and my authority, to withdraw said treaty (ceding said Islands) from further consideration. I ask the honorable Senate of the United States to decline to ratify said treaty, and I implore the people of this great and good nation, from whom my ancestors learned the Christian religion, to sustain their representatives in such acts of justice and equity as may be in accord with the principles of their fathers, and to the Almighty Ruler of the universe, to him who judgeth righteously, I commit my cause.

"Done at Washington, District of Columbia, United States of America, this seventeenth day of June, in the year eighteen hundred and ninety-seven.

"Liliuokalani.

"Joseph Heleluhe.

"Wokeki Heleluhe"
Witnesses to Signature."
"Julius A. Palmer.

In the matter of providing me with seats in the diplomatic gallery at the ceremonies of the inauguration, I have already expressed my gratitude to Secretary John Sherman. It is but just that I should repeat here my appreciation of the kind, gallant, and courteous treatment again received at his official hands. For although it was my directions that this document should be delivered to any person authorized to receive it, yet as soon as Secretary Sherman saw the cards of my commissioners, he at once accorded them a private audience.

My protest, and a like remonstrance made on behalf of the patriotic leagues of the Hawaiian people by Hon. Joseph Heleluhe as their authorized commissioner, were both placed in the secretary's hands by that gentleman; and Mr. Sherman read them both through. He then turned to Captain Palmer, and had an agreeable conversation on the points at issue, after which my commissioners retired. The accustomed tissue of falsehoods was woven about this interview; some stating that Secretary Sherman had refused to see my messengers, others again giving the names of some one or other of his subordinates with whom my commissioners had had an interview, and finally asserting that the protests went into the archives of the department without examination, and were pigeon-holed; all of which statements, it is needless to say, were untrue. Secretary Sherman by his action showed that, a skilled diplomatist, he had not forgotten to remain a gallant gentleman.

Chapter LVI. The Treaty Analyzed

Anything like an extended criticism of the proposed treaty will not be attempted here. The first articles convey nothing, and do not even profess to convey anything; would not any capitalist, anticipating an investment of four millions, and a contingent liability of as much more, demand an exact schedule of the property for which he is paying, and a warrant of the legitimacy of the title?

Suppose that the claims of foreign governments for indemnification for acts of outrage and imprisonment committed under the rule of the Republic, the Japanese indemnity, and the value of the crown lands, should raise the debt limit to eight millions, do the parties ceding this territory come under personal obligations to pay the over plus indebtedness?

In regard to the crown lands, even the best-informed citizens of the United States do not understand the difference between these and the lands of the Hawaiian government. Originally all territory belonged to the king, by whom it was apportioned for use only, not for sale, to the chiefs, who in turn assigned tracts, small or large, to their people; an excellent system for us, by which the poorest native had all the land he needed, and yet it could not be taken from him by any designing foreigner.

But about fifty years ago there came, in place of our own method, the land system delivered to us by the missionaries. In effect this divided the territory of the Islands into three parts, not necessarily equal, although nearly so. One-third was devoted to the use or expenses of government; one-third was apportioned to the people; and the remainder continued, as from all ages, the private property of the chief highest in rank, in other words, the reigning sovereign.

That part of Hawaii given by the king to the people has almost entirely left them, and now belongs to the missionaries and their friends or successors. Of the portion reserved to the government nothing need be said. If the present rule may be called a government, it probably has the right to the income of these lands. But one of their commissioners, Mr. Kinney, made a public statement through the press that it would be as well for an ex-president to claim the White House as for me to claim my income in the crown lands.

Mr. Kinney could scarcely have chosen a more effective method to prove his ignorance; and in response I have had the following brief statement prepared by one who thoroughly understands the matter:

BY MR. KINNEY.—"The fealty of the native Hawaiian to his chief knows no limit. Such loyalty exacts corresponding devotion; it was to meet this necessity that the chief highest in rank was never divested of the crown lands or private purse."

REPLY.—"The White House and other official estate form an investment made with the money of the American people for the use of their chosen executive. The crown lands were never the property of the people, no, not even of any monarchical government. Not citing the testimony of ages, when all the lands belonged to the chiefs, in 1848 the ruling king reserved these very lands as 'his private estate,' and the legislature confirmed this act 'as the private lands of His Majesty, his heirs and assigns forever.' In 1864 the Supreme Court decided that 'each successor' could regulate and dispose of the same according to his will and pleasure as private property.

In 1865 payment was made to Queen Emma in lieu of dower in these lands, although she had not been on the throne, but was the widow of a monarch deceased two years previously. In 1880 Mr. Spreckels paid the Princess Ruth $10,000 to release her claim to a small tract of these lands, although she had never ascended the throne. The act of the legislature by which these lands were made 'inalienable, to descend to the heirs and successors of the Hawaiian crown (N. B., not of any Kamehameha) forever,' has never been reversed, the constitution expressly confirming this by the words, the 'successor elected shall become a new stirps for a royal family, regulated by the same law as the present royal family.'

"Were Kalakaua, Liliuokalani, or Kaiulani, of another race (instead of having, as they most certainly have, the blood of Kamehamehas), it would still be true that no intelligent lawyer would invest the money of his client in a tract of hereditary crown land unless the living representatives were to join in the deed. It is just possible that the lawyers who have visited Washington know these facts, as the first two articles of their conveyance to us by treaty are only quit claim deeds; they expressly limit the grantors' warrant to that which at this date belongs to them. Any person could execute such a conveyance to the White House estate, and it would not convey anything, nor even pretend to put the grantee in possession of anything. Will American capitalists invest at their own risk in land which constitutes one-fourth of the whole proposed territory of Hawaii?"

But it is in the sixth article that the missionary party show their determination to keep the same position under the flag of the United States that they have held at the Islands ever since the revolution of 1887. By this, which is made part of the treaty, and so, if it should be ratified as it stands, it can never be changed, not even by Act of Congress, the President is to appoint five commissioners, two of whom shall be residents of the Hawaiian Islands; by these all legislation in regard to that territory is to be recommended to Congress.

Which means that the missionary party shall continue to control all measures enacted in regard to Hawaii and the Hawaiians; that there shall be no essential change in their greedy and deceitful policy, that they shall still coin money through the manipulation of the sugar interest and the management of the plantations and the labor question. And what advantage or return will the United States Government ever receive from such a territorial administration as that? The President and Secretary of State having agreed to such enactment, it only remains for the needed two-thirds of the Senate to ratify it to make it the law of the land.

The voters of this great and good nation are too free from suspicion. They have no idea how they have been deceived, how much more they can be deceived. The poor Hawaiians, strangers on their native soil, excluded from their own halls of legislation, have had their experience; alas, a bitter one. The Japanese, urged and inveigled and bought to come to Hawaii while they were needed to increase the foreigners' gold, have had theirs; but the American people have theirs yet to get. The Hawaiian sugar planters are having theirs from the drain on their pockets to support Thurston and those he employs in this country.

Here I may state that seldom or never had the Hawaiian government, during the days of monarchy, been known to place itself in such a position as it has fallen into since in the hands of this missionary oligarchy. It has had to borrow money several times from the two banks in Honolulu, and to ask funds from the planters. When in prison in 1895, Mr. Wilson told me, in the presence of his wife, that that year's taxes had been mortgaged to the amount of $800,000 to Mr. C. B. Bishop. Under the monarchy there was always enough from its own revenues to pay all expenses until the time came when such enterprising people as wanted to make money for themselves came into office, and prevailed on the government to make new improvements; from that time the government became indebted.

There is one more bit of political history of which I will speak, and I shall then have said all that it is my intention to give to the public for the present. Soon after the inauguration of President McKinley, it was my hope to assure him in person of my kindest wishes for a happy and successful term of office, but more especially to present to him, as the representative of my people, certain documents and petitions which had been sent to me for the purpose; then my duty in the case would have been done.

No attempts of any kind or nature were ever made in my behalf by any person whomsoever, to arrange an interview between the President and myself. No public man in Washington, whoever he may be, has ever declined to see me or any one of my party. The despatches which the press have published on that point have not a basis of truth. Events transpiring at the capital made it inexpedient for me to carry out the wishes and requests of my people.

The President was so overwhelmed with pressing business, so beset by office-seekers, his time so filled with matters requiring his direct attention, that he could not be expected to give consideration to any subject outside of the administration of the affairs of the United States government; which, there being no annexation movement above board at that time (the first week in March), was certainly the case with the matter intrusted to me by my people.

On the 10th of July I bade adieu to the beautiful city of Washington, where I had spent such a delightful half-year. I had called at the Capitol two or three times, not with any petition or request, but simply to thank those gentlemen who had kindly taken an interest in me and in the Hawaiian people. I had also left my card for those Senators whose families had been represented among my callers, and made a few parting visits to my friends in the city.

On Saturday afternoon I arrived in New York, and remained at the Albemarle two weeks, visiting the places of interest, attending the opera, and receiving the visits of a few of my friends who lived in that city or its immediate vicinity.

But while there, I received further information from the patriotic leagues, the members of which organizations expressed much regret that I had not presented the documents in my hands to President McKinley, and urging me to do this at once. Accordingly on Saturday, the 24th of July, with my whole party, I returned to Washington, this time taking rooms at the Ebbitt House. On Monday morning I sent the papers to President McKinley, by the hands of Mr. Joseph Heleluhe, and Captain Palmer, who accompanied him.

Then, learning that it was the regular reception-day of the President, and also the last one prior to his vacation, without consultation with any person, I told the members of my suite that, before leaving Washington again, we would call socially on the President. Arriving at the door of the White House, I requested Captain Palmer to send up our cards, which he did before we entered the East Room; and in response an officer, who had received his instructions, came to us, conducted us to the farther end of the room, and provided us with seats, which we were requested to retain when the President should enter to meet the hundred or so strangers who were standing at the opposite end of the large reception-room.

While we were waiting, one of the President's secretaries came down from his office with a special message from President McKinley to like effect. After the President had finished his official handshaking, he approached the place where I sat. Observing him, I arose and advanced to meet him. We had a most delightful conversation; and I found him to be a most agreeable gentleman, both in manner and in words. He spoke very prettily of his wife's delicate health, alluding to the matter of his own accord, and voluntarily expressing his regret that he could not at once invite me in to visit her. I have been thus particular to describe the facts of my social relations to the White House, because upon no subject has the desire been more frequently shown to prejudice me and my cause in the eyes of the American people.

Strangers have remarked that in no part of the world visited by them have they found the rules of etiquette so exactly laid down and so persistently observed as in Honolulu, when the Islands were under the monarchy. It is to be expected, therefore, that I know what is due to me; that further, as the wife of the governor of Oahu, as the princess royal, and as the reigning sovereign, it was not necessary for me to take lessons in the departments of social or diplomatic etiquette before residing in the national capital of the United States, or making and receiving visits of any nature.

Chapter LVII. Hawaiian Autonomy

It has been suggested to me that the American general reader is not well informed regarding the social and political conditions which have come about in the Sandwich Islands, and that it would be well here to give some expression to my own observation of them. Space will only permit, however, a mere outline.

It has been said that the Hawaiian people under the rule of the chiefs were most degraded, that under the monarchy their condition greatly improved, but that the native government in any form had at last become intolerable to the more enlightened part of the community. This statement has been substantially repeated recently by certain New England and Hawaiian "statesmen" in speeches made at the Home Market Club in Boston. I shall not examine it in detail; but it may serve as a text for the few remarks I feel called upon to make from my own — and that is to say, the native Hawaiian — standpoint.

I shall not claim that in the days of Captain Cook our people were civilized. I shall not claim anything more for their progress in civilization and Christian morality than has been already attested by missionary writers. Perhaps I may safely claim even less, admitting the criticism of some intelligent visitors who were not missionaries—that the habits and prejudices of New England Puritanism were not well adapted to the genius of a tropical people, nor capable of being thoroughly ingrafted upon them.

But Christianity in substance they have accepted; and I know of no people who have developed a tenderer Christian conscience, or who have shown themselves more ready to obey its behests. Nor has any people known to history shown a greater reverence and love for their Christian teachers, or filled the measure of a grateful return more overflowingly. And where else in the world's history is it written that a savage people, pagan for ages, with fixed hereditary customs and beliefs, have made equal progress in civilization and Christianity in the same space of time? And what people has ever been subjected during such an evolution to such a flood of external demoralizing influences?

Does it make nothing for us that we have always recognized our Christian teachers as worthy of authority in our councils, and repudiated those whose influence or character was vicious or irreligious? That while four-fifths of the population of our Islands was swept out of existence by the vices introduced by foreigners, the ruling class clung to Christian morality, and gave its unvarying support and service to the work of saving and civilizing the masses? Has not this class loyally clung to the brotherly alliance made with the better element of foreign settlers, giving freely of its authority and its substance, its sons and its daughters, to cement and to prosper it?

But will it also be thought strange that education and knowledge of the world have enabled us to perceive that as a race we have some special mental and physical requirements not shared by the other races which have come among us? That certain habits and modes of living are better for our health and happiness than others? And that a separate nationality, and a particular form of government, as well as special laws, are, at least for the present, best for us? And these things remained to us, until the pitiless and tireless "annexation policy" was effectively backed by the naval power of the United States.

To other usurpations of authority on the part of those whose love for the institutions of their native land we could understand and forgive we had submitted. We had allowed them virtually to give us a constitution, and control the offices of state. Not without protest, indeed; for the usurpation was unrighteous, and cost us much humiliation and distress. But we did not resist it by force. It had not entered into our hearts to believe that these friends and allies from the United States, even with all their foreign affinities, would ever go so far as to absolutely overthrow our form of government, seize our nation by the throat, and pass it over to an alien power.

And while we sought by peaceful political means to maintain the dignity of the throne, and to advance national feeling among the native people, we never sought to rob any citizen, wherever born, of either property, franchise, or social standing.

Perhaps there is a kind of right, depending upon the precedents of all ages, and known as the "Right of Conquest," under which robbers and marauders may establish themselves in possession of whatsoever they are strong enough to ravish from their fellows. I will not pretend to decide how far civilization and Christian enlightenment have outlawed it. But we have known for many years that our Island monarchy has relied upon the protection always extended to us by the policy and the assured friendship of the great American republic. If we have nourished in our bosom those who have sought our ruin, it has been because they were of the people whom we believed to be our dearest friends and allies. If we did not by force resist their final outrage, it was because we could not do so without striking at the military force of the United States. Whatever constraint the executive of this great country may be under to recognize the present government at Honolulu has been forced upon it by no act of ours, but by the unlawful acts of its own agents. Attempts to repudiate those acts are vain.

The conspirators, having actually gained possession of the machinery of government, and the recognition of foreign ministers, refused to surrender their conquest. So it happens that, overawed by the power of the United States to the extent that they can neither themselves throw off the usurpers, nor obtain assistance from other friendly states, the people of the Islands have no voice in determining their future, but are virtually relegated to the condition of the aborigines of the American continent.

It is not for me to consider this matter from the American point of view; although the pending question of annexation involves nothing less than a departure from the established policy of that country, and an ominous change in its foreign relations. It is enough that I am able to say, and with absolute authority, that the native people of Hawaii are entirely faithful to their own chiefs, and are deeply attached to their own customs and mode of government; that they either do not understand, or bitterly oppose, the scheme of annexation. As a native Hawaiian, reared and educated in close intimacy with the present rulers of the Islands and their families, with exceptional opportunities for studying both native and foreign character, it is easy for me to detect the purpose of each line and word in the annexation treaty, and even to distinguish the man originating each portion of it.

I had prepared biographical sketches and observations upon the mental structure and character of the most interested advocates of this measure. They have not refrained from circulating most vile and baseless slanders against me; and, as public men, they seemed to me open to public discussion. But my publishers have flatly declined to print this matter, as possibly it might be construed as libelous.

And just here let me say that I have felt much perplexity over the attitude of the American press, that great vehicle of information for the people, in respect of Hawaiian affairs. Shakespeare has said it is excellent to have a giant's strength, but it is tyrannous to use it like a giant. It is not merely that, with few exceptions, the press has seemed to favor the extinction of Hawaiian sovereignty, but that it has often treated me with coarse allusions and flippancy, and almost uniformly has commented upon me adversely, or has declined to publish letters from myself and friends conveying correct information upon matters which other correspondents had, either willfully or through being deceived, misrepresented. Perhaps in many cases libelous matter was involved. Possibly the press was not conscious of how cruelly it was exerting its strength, and will try, I now trust, to repair the injury.

It has been shown that in Hawaii there is an alien element composed of men of energy and determination, well able to carry through what they undertake, but not scrupulous respecting their methods. They doubtless control all the resources and influence of the present ruling power in Honolulu, and will employ them tirelessly in the future, as they have in the past, to secure their ends. This annexationist party might prove to be a dangerous accession even to American politics, both on account of natural abilities, and because of the training of an autocratic life from earliest youth.

Many of these men are anything but ideal citizens for a democracy. That custom of freely serving each other without stipulation or reward which exists as a very nature among our people has been even exaggerated in our hospitality to our teachers and advisers. Their children, and the associates they have drawn to themselves, are accustomed to it. They have always been treated with distinction. They would hardly know how to submit to the contradictions, disappointments, and discourtesies of a purely emulative society.

It would remain necessary for them to rule in Hawaii, even if the American flag floated over them. And if they found they could be successfully opposed, would they seek no remedy? Where would men, already proved capable of outwitting the conservatism of the United States and defeating its strongest traditions, capable of changing its colonial and foreign policy at a single coup, stop in their schemes?

Perhaps I may even venture here upon a final word respecting the American advocates of this annexation of Hawaii.

I observe that they have pretty successfully striven to make it a party matter. It is chiefly Republican statesmen and politicians who favor it. But is it really a matter of party interest? Is the American Republic of States to degenerate, and become a colonizer and a land-grabber?

And is this prospect satisfactory to a people who rely upon self-government for their liberties, and whose guaranty of liberty and autonomy to the whole western hemisphere, the grand Monroe doctrine, appealing to the respect and the sense of justice of the masses of every nation on earth, has made any attack upon it practically impossible to the statesmen and rulers of armed empires? There is little question but that the United States could become a successful rival of the European nations in the race for conquest, and could create a vast military and naval power, if such is its ambition. But is such an ambition laudable? Is such a departure from its established principles patriotic or politic?

Here, at least for the present, I rest my pen. During my stay in the capital, I suppose I must have met, by name and by card, at least five thousand callers. From most of these, by word, by grasp of hand, or at least by expression of countenance, I have received a sympathy and encouragement of which I cannot write fully. Let it be understood that I have not failed to notice it, and to be not only flattered by its universality, but further very grateful that I have had the opportunity to know the real American people, quite distinct from those who have assumed this honored name when it suited their selfish ends.

But for the Hawaiian people, for the forty thousand of my own race and blood, descendants of those who welcomed the devoted and pious missionaries of seventy years ago—for them has this mission of mine accomplished anything?

Oh, honest Americans, as Christians hear me for my downtrodden people! Their form of government is as dear to them as yours is precious to you. Quite as warmly as you love your country, so they love theirs. With all your goodly possessions, covering a territory so immense that there yet remain parts unexplored, possessing islands that, although near at hand, had to be neutral ground in time of war, do not covet the little vineyard of Naboth's, so far from your shores, lest the punishment of Ahab fall upon you, if not in your day, in that of your children, for "be not deceived, God is not mocked." The people to whom your fathers told of the living God, and taught to call "Father," and whom the sons now seek to despoil and destroy, are crying aloud to Him in their time of trouble; and He will keep His promise, and will listen to the voices of His Hawaiian children lamenting for their homes.

It is for them that I would give the last drop of my blood; it is for them that I would spend, nay, am spending, everything belonging to me. Will it be in vain? It is for the American people and their representatives in Congress to answer these questions. As they deal with me and my people, kindly, generously, and justly, so may the Great Ruler of all nations deal with the grand and glorious nation of the United States of America.